LATIN AMERICAN THOUGHT: PHILOSOPHICAL PROBLEMS AND ARGUMENTS

LATIN AMERICAN THOUGHT: PHILOSOPHICAL PROBLEMS AND ARGUMENTS

Susana Nuccetelli

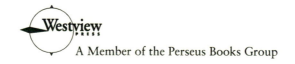

A Member of the Perseus Books Group

Westview Press books are available at special discounts for bulk purchases in the United States by corporations, institutions, and other organizations. For more information, please contact the Special Markets Department at The Perseus Books Group, 11 Cambridge Center, Cambridge MA 02142, or call (617) 252-5298.

Published in 2002 in the United States of America by Westview Press, 5500 Central Avenue, Boulder, Colorado 80301-2877, and in the United Kingdom by Westview Press, 12 Hid's Copse Road, Cumnor Hill, Oxford OX2 9JJ

Find us on the World Wide Web at www.westviewpress.com

A CIP catalog record for this book is available from the Library of Congress.

ISBN: 0-8133-3967-7; 0-8133-6553-8 (pbk.)

The paper used in this publication meets the requirements of the American National Standard for Permanence of Paper for Printed Library Materials Z39.48-1984.

10   9   8   7   6   5   4   3   2   1

To my husband,
whom I love so much

CONTENTS

PREFACE

A plausible conception of genuine philosophical issues is that they are the sort of questions that can engage philosophical thinking in a search for solutions that, in some cases, may continue for centuries. Since I believe that the philosophical issues that have arisen in Latin American thought are precisely of this sort, I have set out to examine some such issues here. This book is an attempt to offer an overview of the historical contexts in which they have originated, together with thematic discussions where the available solutions are evaluated according to their philosophical merits. In addition, some new solutions are proposed.

That a philosophical study offering a historical perspective on Latin American thought is long overdue is clear from pragmatic considerations. Outside Latin America, little attention has been paid to the history of ideas there. And since persons of Latino heritage are the fastest growing minority group in the United States, there is greater need than ever for all North Americans to become acquainted with Latin American thought. Clearly, the moment is favorable for broadening cultural horizons and including points of view that have been overlooked, for multiculturalism has now become an accepted value, and a certain dogmatic indifference to new philosophical perspectives is in retreat. All of these considerations point also to the need for offering a *thematic* discussion of major philosophical issues in Latin American thought.

It is also beyond doubt that the philosophical problems and arguments of Latin American thought are well worth studying for their own sake. Although some similar questions have arisen in other cultures, it is also true that some of the issues discussed in this book are uniquely related to the reality of the Latin American subcontinent. And Latin Americans often sought to resolve philosophical problems by proposing novel arguments that suggest new conceptual frameworks and provocative, alternative ways of thinking about familiar ideas.

Yet students, teachers, and other scholars who seek to learn about Latin American thought currently find an obstacle in the lack of adequate materials. Original sources, if not completely unknown, are often difficult to obtain. Furthermore, there has been no readily available survey that could provide a guide to the subject as a whole. In Argentina, where I began my education, expertise in Latin American philosophy is widely available, but the situation in North America is quite different. The dearth of adequate materials of this sort became apparent to me when I taught philosophy at Lehman College of the City University of New York and began preparing a new course in Latin American thought, motivated in part by the interest of Dominican students at the college. It took me several years of research and some trips to South America to gather adequate materials. My perseverance, however, was rewarded, for the Latin American philosophy course I developed and taught at Washington and Lee University and at Carleton College consistently proved popular with students of many different cultural and educational backgrounds. Among those who enrolled were majors in philosophy and Latin American studies but also majors in economics, English, and other disciplines. "Why have you registered for this class?" I often asked. "To learn about something different" or "to know about Latin Americans" were the most common responses.

I believe that such expectations could be met, in part, by providing an introduction to the history of ideas in Latin America, and this book accomplishes that. But to satisfy these expectations fully, historical questions must lead to substantive philosophical discussions, where each position is assessed on its philosophical merits. At the same time, by broaching a variety of issues that have concerned Latin American thinkers (e.g., human rights, feminism, relativism, collective identity), the book will be a useful tool for undergraduate teaching. My experience with undergraduate courses has led me to favor those textbooks that blend historical perspectives with thematic ones while raising philosophical questions of current interest.

It might be asked, how could a book on Latin American thought truly satisfy a student's desire to learn something *different*, when many of the philosophical questions raised by Latin American thinkers are among the perennial problems that have concerned philosophers at different times and in different places throughout the Western tradition? My answer to this is that, in fact, the problems are not altogether the same—for they have been adapted by Latin American thinkers to capture problems presented by new circumstances, and these thinkers have sought resolutions with arguments that are indeed novel. This book explains how well-established philosophical traditions gave rise in the New World to a characteristic form of thought not to be found in other cultures. There was no clean sweep of the past and an attempt to start over. Rather, Latin American thinkers gradually adapted European ideas to their needs, sometimes borrowing on a larger scale, sometimes smaller. It is then no surprise that, under Iberian rule, Scholasticism became the accepted view and began to lose its grip only when the rulers did. But what does seem surprising is the radical way in which those traditions were on occasions challenged, as illustrated by the cases of José de Acosta, a Jesuit priest in Peru, and the Mexican nun Juana Inés de la Cruz—each of whom spoke out against certain aspects of the official philosophy in colonial society. And when theories familiar elsewhere arrived in Latin America, as in the cases of positivism and Marxism, they were often seen differently in the light of new circumstances.

Above all, then, my aim in this book is to show that there is a body of interesting philosophical arguments offered by Latin Americans concerning problems that have arisen in Spanish- and Portuguese-speaking parts of the New World. In connection with this purpose, I examine how Latin Americans have thought about general philosophical issues belonging to metaphysics, philosophy of science, cross-cultural psychology, feminist epistemology, ethics, and social and political philosophy. These I take up in due course here, paying special attention to questions of rationality, gender discrimination, justice, human rights, reparation for historically dispossessed peoples, and relativism versus universalism—all matters of continuing concern in Latin American thought, from its earliest stirrings to the present day. And among some specific issues that have generated heated controversies from the early twentieth century to the present, I explore how Latin Americans and their descendants abroad think of their own cultural identity, I examine their critique of U.S. mass culture and moral philosophy, and I consider at some length the vexing problem of which name, if any, is the correct one to use to refer to all of this exceedingly diverse ethnic group.

The first two chapters consider the question of whether the Mayans, one of the major traditional cultures of Latin America, could be said to have developed intellectual skills, such as critical thinking and a rational understanding of the natural world, comparable to those of Western culture. Most books written on Latin American thought have completely ignored this issue, and I believe that such neglect is regrettable for several reasons. For one thing, although questions about the nature of rationality seem to matter now more than ever, due in part to new findings in cross-cultural psychology, philosophers have been largely indifferent to related questions about rationality that arise when we consider the written evidence left by ancient non-Western peoples, such as the Mayans. Furthermore, it is important for a book on Latin American thought to look at philosophical issues concerning the native peoples—since, after all, those peoples' ways of life have always been crucial to the cultural and social profiles of Latin America and have been a distinctive component of its collective identity.

Chapter 3 opens the debate on whether there is a characteristically Latin American philosophy by looking closely at its possible origins. Had the indigenous peoples reached an understanding of the natural world that could stand comparison with Western conceptions grounded in philosophy and science? To the extent that some elements of non-Western worldviews persist among indigenous societies

of the Americas today, we too must ask about these radically different ways of understanding the world; thus the possibility of making
such comparisons remains of significant interest to us. It is argued
here that, to avoid having double standards, the same reasons that
are often provided to exclude the Indians' cosmologies from philosophy and science must equally be taken to disqualify the theories of
the pre-Socratic philosophers of ancient Greece. After all, the latter
seem likewise to have focused on questions that, at the time, made
little sense to ask and never really got close to the truth about the origins of the universe.

Chapter 4 examines some aspects of the classic dichotomy—relativism versus universalism—as it arises in discussions of the conflict
between the Old World and the New when they met in the late fifteenth century. Ever since that world-changing encounter—disastrous for the Indians and fateful beyond all comprehension for the
Europeans—the cultures of the indigenous peoples of the Americas
have been disparaged by a long and varied tradition of ethnocentrism. This chapter looks more closely at certain arguments that have
been used in attempts to justify European domination, urging ultimately that the ancient native peoples of Latin America had cultures
that were rich and insightful in ways that deserve respect. Their
achievements are documented in many written texts, such as the
books of *Chilam Balam* and *Popol Vuh*, and in the historical records
of, among others, Bernardino de Sahagún and José León-Portilla. I
argue that these significant contributions could be acknowledged
without falling into the quicksand of cultural relativism.

Chapter 5 considers the question of whether natural law theory is
able to solve some moral dilemmas, as many believed at the time of
the Iberian Conquest—and as some still believe today. Prominent
among these are dilemmas concerning human rights. Was war
against the Indians justified? And what of the coercive measures that
deprived them of their freedom and property? Arguably, natural law
theory was of no help in solving such dilemmas since it provided
only inconclusive, and sometimes contradictory, moral assessments.
Francisco Vitoria, for example, argued persuasively against the
abuses of the Conquest by invoking principles based on natural law

theory, yet the theory seems also to have been appealed to by the opposite side in a famous public debate on the subject in the mid-sixteenth century held in Spain, at Valladolid, with Juan Ginés de Sepúlveda defending the abuses and Bartolomé de Las Casas condemning them.

Of course, in the case of the Conquest, as in any other morally problematic episode in history, there would seem to be no basis for moral accountability and blame unless some universalist assumptions, such as those of natural law theory, are invoked. What, for instance, could cultural relativists say about it? Would it make sense for them to make judgments of moral culpability? To do so, they would have to assume that some right claims are objectively justified over and above cultural differences so that they could judge that something wrong had occurred. Yet they cannot do this since the universality of human rights is incompatible with relativist assumptions. It seems then that neither natural law theory nor cultural relativism can fully accommodate our moral intuitions in cases where human rights are violated. Perhaps some combination of these doctrines could do so, as today's liberation theologians seem to think. But are those doctrines really compatible?

Chapter 6 focuses on some philosophical issues that concerned Latin Americans during the colonial period and immediately afterward, when they were in the process of national organization that followed the wars of independence. Because of restrictions imposed on the colonies by Spain and Portugal, colonists experienced severe limitations on what they were permitted to read (and equally on what they were permitted to believe). As a result, challenges to Scholasticism, the official philosophy, were rare. A few thinkers, however, managed to call into question some major assumptions of Scholasticism. In the 1590s, Acosta launched a forceful attack against Aristotelian science in a book with the odd title *The Natural & Moral History of the Indies*, where he appealed to his own experience in South America and the results of geographic explorations conducted by Spain and Portugal to show that some tenets of Scholastic science were in fact nothing more than prejudices. I argue that Acosta thus offered a pioneering modernist view on cosmography that had far-reaching consequences. Chief among these was that Acosta made available for the first time a way of thinking about geography grounded on an understanding of the discoveries of explorers sailing abroad in the names of Spain and Portugal. That in turn helped reorient the sciences to a modern view of our planet crucial to the articulation of the paradigm that would replace ancient and medieval conceptions.

Equally significant was the work of Juana Inés de la Cruz, who in the seventeenth century challenged intellectual practices in Mexico by asserting a woman's right to knowledge. Although feminism in epistemology is a twentieth-century phenomenon, the feminist demands made by de la Cruz in her "Reply to Sor Philotea" lead me to ask which (if any) contemporary feminist approach might be more compatible with her views. At her time, her position was indeed radical, though it differs considerably from that of contemporary radical feminists. I also argue that, since she championed the primacy of empirical knowledge, together with her feminist demands, her tragic life and writings are historically important as well as significantly progressive in the context of her culture.

Chapter 6 also explores some issues of social and political philosophy that rose to prominence after most Latin American nations (with the exception of Cuba) won their independence from Spain shortly after 1824. Special attention is devoted to the works of Simón Bolívar and Domingo F. Sarmiento, whose ideas on the cultural identity of Latin America played a prominent role in the process of national organization. The central question on the agendas of Latin American thinkers was then how to go about achieving that organization. More than three centuries of colonial rule had made these nations eager for liberation, and the revolutions of the nineteenth century had generated optimistic expectations among them that they could finally live as politically independent peoples and choose their own forms of government. Yet achieving that goal proved to be difficult, as was famously illustrated in Sarmiento's book *Facundo*. I evaluate his arguments and ultimately reject them. On the other hand, Bolívar's view on national organization rests on the thesis that different peoples in different places with different cultural traditions may require different kinds of political systems—an idea whose time had not come in Bolívar's day, and apparently has not come yet. I call this view "Bolívarism" and take it to amount to a pioneering challenge to the *Norteamericano* assumption of the universal validity of liberal democracy.

Chapter 7 explores questions of cultural and political sovereignty that became important with the final defeat of Spain as a colonial ruler in 1898 and the emergence of a new foreign threat, the United States. But Latin Americans at the time also wondered how their own worldviews and practical achievements compared with those of Western powers. The chapter opens by examining answers to such questions offered by positivists, whose ideology eventually came to affect the academic life in the subcontinent in ways comparable only to that of colonial Scholasticism. Since the movement comprised various doctrines absorbed differently in different parts of Latin America, generalizations must be avoided, and so I focus on the experiences of two nations. A close look at the cases of Brazil and Mexico shows that, among the practical consequences of positivism, some are laudable, others disastrous. I then turn to the work of José Enrique Rodó, who contributed greatly to the fall of positivism. Although his *Ariel* is shown to offer a perspective on Latin American identity that was basically wrongheaded, I argue that when charitably reconstrued, its arguments do after all amount to a provocative critique of U.S. mass culture and philosophy.

I also consider here the views of José Martí, who, though not strictly a philosopher, was an original thinker in the Latin Americanist tradition of Bolívar. I argue that Martí developed that tradition further, incorporating his own concerns about economic and social justice and thus preparing the ground for his ideological successors in Latin America, the Marxists and the socialists. I then turn to José Carlos Mariátegui's "indigenous question," showing how the actual social behavior of the Indians in Peru worked to undermine Mariátegui's Marxist resolution of that question since it appears that they have remained loyal to a social system clearly unjust and unfavorable to them. In light of such cases, Mariátegui's confidence in the Indians' prompt conversion to socialism seems to have rested less on reality than on a praiseworthy but ultimately romanticized view of the psychology of the oppressed.

In Chapter 8, I look more closely at the defining elements of Latin American identity. What characteristic features, if any, distinguish them from other peoples of the world? Is there a characteristically Latin American form of thought? And what name, if any, can be used to refer to Latin Americans and their descendants abroad? These are familiar questions that are often conflated. I treat them separately, favoring a historically based account of Latin American identity. The existence of a characteristically Latin American philosophy can be shown—though not by appealing to some reasons already well known in the literature. And to resolve the question concerning a correct ethnic-group name, I propose a direct reference approach. In my view, both "Latinos" and "Hispanics" count as correct names to designate Latin Americans and their descendants in other parts of the world, simply because these names have caught on in our linguistic community, and there is no current practice of using them as epithets of contempt.

Research for this book was funded in part by a generous grant from the National Endowment for the Humanities. I wish to thank the Endowment for their support. In addition, there are many people I wish to thank who have contributed to this book in various ways. Comments on my views on ethnic group names from Jorge Gracia, Michael Root, John Greenwood, Jordan Curnutt, and Gary Ostertag have been beneficial. Discussions with Matthias Steup, Kate Gill, and Carla Johnson have helped me to think about some of the issues addressed here. Stephen Schiffer and Bernard Baumrin encouraged me to pursue this work, and I am grateful for their support. Stephen Stich's ideas on rationality have been influential in my thinking since I first became acquainted with them as a graduate student at the City University of New York. And I have profited enormously from discussions of Professor Stich's writings on this topic at a senior seminar I offered at St. Cloud State University, which featured him as a guest lecturer. I am also grateful to Westview Press's reviewers for their comments and to their editor, Sarah Warner, who offered me helpful advice. Gary Seay deserves a special mention for having read the entire manuscript, making numerous comments that helped me to improve it greatly.

Note to Instructors

Chapters 1 and 2 are focused on the question of how to evaluate the rationality of the Mayans and should be read together. Each of the other chapters is more or less self-contained, so, although they are arranged in historical order, one could assign chapters to be read independently, depending on which philosophical topics one might choose to discuss.

I

THE EPISTEMIC PRACTICES OF
LATIN AMERICAN INDIANS:
A PUZZLE FOR PHILOSOPHERS

During the time of Aquarius, bleeding is good only for him who needs it, and medicines should not be given; but it is a time that is good for bathing and swimming, and an appetite for eating is evident. Men born on the days ruled by this sign are small, always sad, very fond of women, and noted for using great quantities of small chiles with their meals. . . . Women will live fifty-six years and will have two illnesses: the first at the age of thirty-four years, the second perhaps at thirty-seven.

The Codex Pérez and
The Book of Chilam Balam of Maní, "Almanac"

When European explorers and *conquistadores* first established contact with the indigenous peoples of the Americas at the end of the fifteenth century, they found cultures with habits of thinking utterly alien to their own. This raised a philosophical problem for both groups: Who were these strange beings? And did they think as we did? This chapter explores whether one of the major traditional cultures of Latin America, the Mayans, developed intellectual skills, such as critical thinking and rational understanding of the natural world. We shall examine some original sources, but our interest will be predominantly philosophical rather than historical. In consequence, our answers to those questions could also apply *mutatis mutandis* to some other groups of indigenous peoples in Latin America, especially those whose thought, even today, bears relevant similarities to that of the Mayans.

It is of course well known that before and after the arrival of the Spaniards, the Mayans, Aztecs, and Incas produced important documents revealing how they reasoned about a variety of matters, including their own welfare and history, the natural, and the supernatural. There is some evidence, available not only in buildings and stone monuments but also in several collections of alphabetic texts, that the Mayans set about their intellectual tasks in ways very different from what would be acceptable to us. If such differences were indeed radical, our whole philosophical enterprise would face a considerable obstacle, for it might then make little sense for us to attempt to determine whether any such radically different ways of thinking could count as rational according to our own criteria. Yet we shall show that this obstacle can be overcome, for a closer look at some practices common among the Mayans suggests that, when it comes to ways of thinking, cultural differences are less radical than they appear at the outset.

Why Should We Care About Native Cultures?

Before we even begin to examine those differences, we must first consider why we should care at all about whether any of the major indigenous cultures of Latin America have had "intellectual skills," such as critical thinking and rational understanding of the natural world. Most books on Latin American thought have completely ignored this issue, but I believe that such neglect is regrettable for several reasons. First, in many Latin American countries, the ways of life of indigenous peoples have always been crucial to the cultural and social profiles of those countries. Furthermore, they are a distinctive component of the collective identity of the region as a whole. Yet Latin American thinkers have often neglected important philosophical problems related to these peoples, probably because they have also commonly ignored most questions about the realities of Latin American life that lie close at hand. There is a notorious tendency among many of these thinkers to emulate the methods of Western philosophy and to focus entirely on its subject matters (particularly that of the so-called continental tradition, although certain topics from analytic philosophy have attracted attention, too).

It is difficult, however, to fit into a borrowed dress. Not surprisingly, Latin American professional philosophers have mostly failed to make substantial contributions to the philosophical discussion of their favored topics. The attitude of such thinkers is open to criticism not because of their interest in general philosophical questions that have preoccupied philosophers at different times and places throughout history, but because an interest in those questions can be made compatible with concern for how such general issues may bear upon everyday reality. Even a cursory look at the development of philosophy in the last part of the twentieth century suggests that this objection is well supported. The increasing growth of applied areas in the discipline clearly shows that paying attention to issues arising in the thinker's own physical and cultural context can introduce novel perspectives in many of the most traditional problems of philosophy and also be intellectually stimulating in its own right. The issue that we are about to explore is a case in point, for the attempt to determine whether any group of indigenous peoples of Latin America have had certain intellectual skills will lead us to reconsider some general philosophical questions about critical thinking and rational evaluation.

Rational Prediction in the West

At different times and places, people of many cultures have made rational efforts to know about the course of future events in the natural world. Westerners, for instance, have attempted to gain such knowledge from antiquity to the present, as shown by the system-

atic study of the required means carried out by scholars in philosophy of science, logic, and methodology. Attempting to know, however, falls short of actually knowing: Western philosophers often
emphasize that it is still a matter of dispute how accurate assertions
about the future could be. Given that they rest on induction, which
is a form of reasoning that cannot guarantee the truth of conclusions drawn from true premises, such assertions could amount only
to hypotheses. Nonetheless, the general consensus among philosophers now is that predictions based on sound inductions (i.e., those
whose conclusions are the most likely to be true among other com-
peting hypotheses) are conducive to valuable epistemic goals (such
as knowledge)—but that predictions resting on, for example, magical cause/effect connections are not.

   Imagine a hypothesis about some future event that is grounded on
a statistical generalization from a premise supported by what has
been observed to hold in 99 percent of the relevant cases, and compare that prediction with one reached by either gazing at a crystal
ball, reading tea leaves, or interpreting an astrological chart. Would
it be capricious if we trust only the former? Certainly not, given
that, when properly applied, the inductive method (of which the
former may be considered just one variety) has a good track record
of producing reliable conclusions. Even in everyday life, when we
wonder which predictions can be taken seriously, our reasoning, if
inductively sound, will follow certain rules that guarantee the rationality of any conclusion reached in this way. There is nothing
magical about our confidence in inductive predictions because we
have learned through our own personal experience and the testimony of experts that inductively based predictions are generally
conducive to the achievement of valuable epistemic ends, such as
satisfying our intellectual curiosity about the future, testing our empirical theories, and solving some puzzles about future events.[1]

Prediction Among the Mayans

Of course, predicting is not an exclusively Western practice. The ancient Mayans developed great subtlety in prediction, as their books

of *Chilam Balam* conclusively show. The name here is taken to mean literally "jaguar priest" because in the Mayan language, Yucatec, a *Chilam* is a prophet or priest, and *Balam* stands for jaguar. Most of these books were destroyed by Spanish conquerors and priests, but among those preserved, the manuscripts from the towns of Chumayel, Tizimín, and Maní are especially important. These consist of various alphabetic texts, written in the vernacular with Spanish scripts during the seventeenth and eighteenth centuries and typically used by Mayan priests during local ceremonies. Scholars have noticed spurious European materials in these books, probably accidentally incorporated because they seem to have been the result of transcriptions from memory of older hieroglyphic manuscripts. In spite of such exogenous elements, however, the books of *Chilam Balam* are still an important source for the study of Mayan thought and culture.

Presumably, each Mayan town had its own group of books of this sort. But could most of the predictions in these books be considered the outcome of a rational attempt to predict future events? To answer this, we will now have a closer look at those from the town of Maní and Chumayel.[2] With astronomical phenomena, the Mayans did well. They accurately predicted certain eclipses and the position of some planets. Here, there is no doubt that these people not only made an effort to find out as best they could what was going to happen but actually implemented rational means. Historians of science have often praised the Mayans' ingenuity in constructing various systems of measurement, including their famous calendar that allowed them to predict some astronomical events about which they appear to have felt great intellectual curiosity.

The Case of Mayan Astrology

Clear evidence that the Mayans did attempt to know the course of future events in the natural world by rational means can indeed be found in the books of *Chilam Balam*. But at the same time, these collections also contain other materials that seem to show these people as quite irrational when it came to understanding future events that affected their own lives. They also made a considerable number of astrological and prophetic predictions entirely on the basis of some easily testable, though false, cause/effect claims. So obviously false were such claims that they could hardly have escaped inspection by even a minimally rational human mind.

Mayan documents such as those from the books of Chumayel and Maní contain unquestionable evidence pointing to both the rationality and the irrationality in the ways these peoples went about predicting future events. Furthermore, such books are not alone in displaying highly rational calculations of future events together with astrological and prophetic predictions, for these disparate features are also frequently found in similar texts that have been preserved in other Mayan towns. This contradictory evidence, then, generates a puzzle about Mayan thought. From our perspective, these books are puzzling because we simply do not know what to make of the evidence that they provide about the Mayans' methods of understanding nature.

The possibility that they never reached a fully rational (or even logical) understanding of future events seems supported by evidence offered in a salient part of their major documents. Consider, for example, the astrological predictions presented in the "Almanac" of the Books of Maní. This is a self-contained text organized according to the usual European conception of the zodiac except each sign is supposed to govern a certain month of the year. Months have individual entries that contain lengthy descriptions of some effects allegedly caused by the zodiac sign reigning during that period. The style of the narrative also resembles Western astrology because each zodiac sign determines particular events in the lives of individuals and their practical affairs. Some advice on health, cultivation of crops, and other ordinary affairs generally follows these predictions.

The reader familiar with Western astrology would find the "Almanac" original in other respects. First, this text focuses on specific subjects of great importance to the Mayans. Some involve questions about health, such as when blood should be drawn from a man's or a woman's body, given that the person was born under a certain zodiac sign. There are also directives concerning the Mayans' own welfare, often about which particular crops would allegedly grow better under the reign of such and such sign. Needless to say, at the time these books were written, the Mayan people depended upon the success of their crops in order to survive and to pay the heavy burden of tribute in goods required by the Spaniards. Nonetheless, as in the much-discussed case of the Azande,[3] the Mayans seem to have neglected the use of rational tools in their attempts to make accurate predictions about questions that ought to have been of crucial importance to them. Surely, from the Western perspective, that appears quite irrational.

Yet what is the evidence for our contention that many Mayan astrological and prophetic predictions were made entirely on the basis of some easily testable, albeit false, cause/effect claims? And if they were indeed false, why think that the falsity of such claims could not escape the inspection of even a minimally rational human being? To answer the first question, let us examine one of the numerous astrological predictions made in the Books of Maní. Solely on the basis of some alleged cause/effect connections between month of birth and sign of the zodiac reigning during it, the writers of the "Almanac" claim that men born in March would live for exactly seventy-five years, but then add the qualification, "unless they shorten their lives with carnal pleasures during the conjunction of the moon. . . ."[4]

Let us assume that this qualification refers to some identifiable astronomical phenomenon involving the moon (e.g., an eclipse). The prediction now is clearly testable, for it involves only empirical claims about phenomena of the natural world, such as the actual length of some human lives, an individual's engagement in certain pleasures, and the occurrence of eclipses. Predictions of that sort in principle are open to falsification or test by refutation. Then what, if anything, did prevent people as clever as the Mayans from carrying out those tests? Surely, they ought to have been able to realize that, in order to falsify the prediction, they simply needed to find some representative counterexamples. Of course there must have been many men among the Mayans who were born in March, never engaged in any of the relevant pleasures (at least, during the specified celestial event), and nonetheless failed to live for seventy-five years.

The Case of Mayan Prophecies

The Mayans, then, seem to have believed that celestial bodies have causal powers to affect the natural world in specific ways. But at the same time, these people ought to have realized that, in most cases, the putative effects of such causal powers were not in fact obtained. Positive instances confirming the astrological doctrines of the Books of Maní must have proved extremely rare, while readily available counterexamples to that doctrine surely could not have gone unnoticed by people as intellectually curious as the Mayans. They must have observed that very often men born in March did not in fact live the seventy-five years predicted by that doctrine. Yet it is also clear that, in spite of the evidence, the Mayans continued to use the books of *Chilam Balam* in their ceremonies for several centuries and behaved as if they truly believed in their predictive and prophetic powers. This suggests that they held on to their belief that the position of the planets, at certain periods of the year, had causal powers to affect the natural world precisely as described by the astrological doctrine of the *Chilam Balam*.

It is important to note here that the example discussed is typical and not an anomalous case. Each month of the year is listed in the "Almanac" of the Books of Maní together with similar predictions, many of which have no qualifying clauses to interfere with their empirical testability, and so would be easier to falsify than the claim concerning the life span of men born in March discussed above. Moreover, the *Chilam Balam* of Maní is not the only group of texts illustrating some malfunction in the ways the Mayans went about predicting future events. The books of Chumayel,[5] for instance, contain numerous prophecies allegedly revealing the designs of the gods to the Mayans through their jaguar priests.

To consider one last example: According to an often-mentioned prophecy, it was decided by supernatural forces that at some future time, the autochthonous religion of the Mayans would come to an end.[6] The Books of Chumayel foretell of such an apocalypse on the arrival of some white men from the East, who would eventually succeed in imposing their own god and ways of life on the Mayans. Of course, the Mayans took the Spaniards, who actually arrived from the East, to be the very men prophesied by that narrative, thereby giving the prophecy the status of confirmed. No doubt the arrival of the Spaniards likewise must have reinforced the Mayans' credence in other prophecies contained in their sacred books.

What Sort of Rationality Is Mayan Rationality?

Again, something seems to have gone wrong with the ways the Mayans thought about future events in the natural world. Clearly, their response to the *Chilam Balam*'s prophecies amount to some rational malfunction, for it suggests that these people took utterly coincidental events (such as the arrival of the Spaniards) to confirm the truth of predictions made by jaguar priests, who were believed to "transmit" supernatural plans. Of course, even when predictions actually come out as expected according to a certain doctrine, that does not mean that the latter has been fully confirmed. In the case under consideration, although the prophecy of the jaguar priest may appear to have been confirmed with the arrival of the Spaniards, people as intelligent as the Mayans were certainly in a position to realize that there was always room for mere coincidence. What reason, if any, did the Mayans have to overlook that possibility? And what, then, are we to make of the rationality of such people, given that they could have easily checked the truth-status of the propositions they accepted but seem not to have carried out the required tests, undoubtedly assuming that those propositions were in fact true?

To see how puzzling the *Chilam Balam*'s astrological and prophetic predictions are, consider what is entailed in ascribing belief in a prediction. Standardly construed, "belief" is a mental attitude that a person has with respect to a certain proposition (or description of a state of affairs). More precisely,

> If a person believes that some proposition *p* is the case, then under normal circumstances, she would have the psychological attitude of accepting that *p*.

Note that beliefs in astrology and prophecies seem relevantly similar to empirical ones because in holding a belief of any of these kinds, an agent accepts that a certain state of affairs in the natural world is (or would be) the case. Ultimately, whether or not the proposition accepted is in fact the case amounts to something that, of course, cannot be known a priori (or just by thinking) but only empirically—that is, by hypothesis and investigation of the environment. Furthermore, since (at least in principle) in all these cases the accepted propositions are testable by either confirmation or refutation, which amount to procedures likewise empirical, beliefs of these kinds seem to have in common the epistemic property of being knowable only empirically.

That similarity is exactly what makes a solution to our puzzle about the rationality of the Mayans so elusive. Presumably, these people accepted many empirical propositions on the basis of astrology and revelation, yet had they performed the proper tests, they would have realized that such propositions were predominantly false. According to available documents, not only did the Mayans take the astrological and prophetic claims of the books of *Chilam Balam* quite seriously, but those claims seem to capture a representative sample of the very sort of propositions about the natural world that they accepted most firmly.[7] If these beliefs amounted to empirical ones, then since they regularly failed to correspond with any facts in the natural world, it appears that those who held them—a whole group of people—were irrational after all. Indeed, the Mayans seem vulnerable to the charge of irrationality, given that they held a mostly false picture of the world when there was abundant evidence available to them suggesting its falsity.

An Argument for Strong Rationalism

If an entire group of human beings were in fact irrational, there would be room for doubting whether they could count as people at all. This is because, arguably, to qualify for personhood, a creature must either have an actual full-fledged rationality or a potential for developing it. But mature adults who regularly hold false pictures of the natural world, even when all the available evidence points to the contrary, would indeed fail to be eligible for either full-fledged rationality or the potential to develop such rationality. The validity of reasoning along these lines is clear:

1. To count as *people*, beings must either have an actual, full-fledged rationality or a potential for developing it.
2. Beings who regularly hold false pictures of the natural world, even when all the available evidence points to their falsity, fail to have either full-fledged rationality or the potential to develop such rationality.

Therefore,

3. Beings who regularly hold false pictures of the natural world, even when all the available evidence points to their falsity, do not count as *people*.

Something is wrong with the strong version of rationalism presupposed by premise (2) of this argument. For were we to take the Mayans' beliefs in the predictions and prophecies of the *Chilam Balam* to be empirical (i.e., to be about the natural world), then we appear committed to the absurd consequence that these and other peoples of some so-called traditional societies are irrational—or at least less rational than, for instance, Westerners. Consider the commonsensical and scientific procedures accepted in the West. They appear to have delivered not only progress but also beliefs about the natural world that, unlike those of primitive people, have actually been confirmed by empirical tests. And that has often been considered a good indication that those beliefs and theories are true or approximately true. Of course, this suggests that the ways Westerners think about the natural world are better—compared, for instance, with those implemented by the natives of traditional societies—in securing the correspondence of their beliefs and theories to facts in that world.

Such a view of rationality, however, now seems implausible. Though favored by some nineteenth-century theorists who attempted to apply positivist and evolutionist ideas popular at that time to social science, we have reason to be skeptical of the uncritical confidence in the scientific method presupposed by that view. In *The Golden Bough*, for example, Sir James George Frazer took the magical beliefs of the natives of traditional societies to amount to mistaken explanations of natural phenomena, so that when compared with Western empirical beliefs, those of the natives came out as providing only quasi-rational and prescientific explanations of events in the natural world. It is not difficult to perceive Western chauvinism in this version of rationalism, and we shall see that there are other reasons to reject that view.

The Principle of Charity Versus Strong Rationalism

What strong rationalism overlooks is that when we interpret the words and describe the intentional states (beliefs, thoughts, desires, and so forth) of people from a radically different culture, some principle of *interpretative charity* is required. To see this, consider what is involved in *radical translation,* or the attempt to interpret expressions in a native language never encountered before. The contemporary American philosopher W. V. O. Quine recommends that in any such attempt, we follow the principle of interpretative charity, which holds that, in interpreting the utterances of a native, we must choose the translation that makes "his message less absurd."[8] Otherwise, his utterances would turn out to be uninterpretable, and we could neither translate them nor describe his intentional states at all. We could have no idea what his words mean or which intentional states (beliefs and desires) are in his mind. Quine urges that in interpretation, whether radical or domestic, we must construe our interlocutor's expressions in a way that minimizes nonsense, logical failure, and even silliness. He writes,

> To take an extreme case, let us suppose that certain natives are said to accept as true certain sentences translatable in the form "*p* and *not p.*" Now this claim is absurd under our criteria. And, not to be dogmatic about them, what criteria might one prefer? Wanton translation can make natives sound as queer as one pleases. Better translation imposes our logic upon them, and would beg the question of prelogicality if there were a question to beg. . . . The maxim of translation underlying all of this is that assertions startlingly

false on the face of them are likely to turn on hidden differences of language. . . . The common sense behind the maxim is that *one's interlocutor's silliness, beyond a certain point, is less likely than bad translation*—or, in the domestic case, linguistic divergence.[9]

A Further Objection to Strong Rationalism

The principle of interpretative charity could be understood in more than one way. On the one hand, it may require that, in translating the utterances of a native, we should aim at maximizing truth—in other words, we must interpret them so that we can ascribe to him as many true beliefs as possible on the basis of what we believe to be true.[10] But when read as requiring a presumption of humanity instead of truth, the principle prescribes that in order to understand another, we ought to "bear in mind that the speaker is a person and has certain basic similarities to ourselves when we are choosing between translations."[11] *Presumed humanity*, then, amounts to the prescription that in order either to understand or to translate someone's utterances, we must use ourselves as models and thus ascribe to him beliefs, desires, and other intentional states on the basis of what we would believe and desire, if we were in his shoes.

Note, however, that according to each of these principles, the values to maximize in translation (viz., either true beliefs or intentional states similar to ours) are quite different. Therefore, they may well come into conflict, so that ascribing to some interlocutor intentional states analogous to those we would have could actually compete with optimizing the truth of his beliefs. But there are persuasive reasons for thinking that in such situations, humanity overrides interpretative charity.[12]

In any case, if the objections invoking either of these principles are plausible, the strong view of rationality would be in trouble since that view regards beliefs held by primitive people as irrational—or as less rational than those of Westerners—without even considering the possibility of a failure at the level of the interpreter's understanding of such beliefs. And this clearly conflicts, for instance, with interpretative charity. Furthermore, there is now a paradox facing the strong rationalist, for to think that these people have false beliefs and defective logical reasoning, he must first understand them. If their beliefs are mostly false and lack common logical connections, then, given charity and humanity, it would follow that they do *not* amount to beliefs or any other intentional states similar to those we are able to entertain. How then could the strong rationalist understand them at all?

However, one could avoid this problem by giving up strong rationalism altogether. Those who wish to defend universal rules of rationality may argue instead that there are conceptual grounds for taking primitive people's utterances to be mostly true, to make sense, and to mirror logical reasoning. According to this strategy, in order to understand the words or thoughts of these peoples at all, we must agree on some shared conceptual grounds from the very beginning. Let us now consider this version of rationalism.

The Bridgehead View

We have taken Quine's principle of charity to recommend that, in interpreting the meaning of an individual's utterances and describing his intentional states, we should avoid ascribing complete falsehood, nonsense, and silliness. We must assume at the outset that people of different cultures possess some ordinary logical abilities and true beliefs about the world, especially if we wish to understand them. "[U]nderstanding is only possible," writes Martin Hollis, "if it advances from a bridgehead of true and rational empirical statements."[13]

In Hollis's view, three things figure prominently among the assumptions of the bridgehead required for interpretation: that primitive people have certain perceptions, ways of referring to things perceived, and a notion of empirical truth similar to ours. Without these, we could not even begin to identify the propositions about the natural world that they accept and distinguish them from those that are the contents of their ritual beliefs. If the view is correct, then since the latter propositions would typically fail to correspond to any empirical reality (and even lack coherence), they could not constitute *all* the beliefs entertained by the natives. This is because, as Hollis explains,

> that would give us sufficient reason to reject the identification on the grounds that, given this degree of laxity, we no longer have any way of deciding between rival translations. A man may believe a contradiction but, if he were also to believe that it was a contradiction, he might believe anything and neither we nor he could identify what he did believe.[14]

According to Hollis, then, the principle of charity, as it applies to translation of languages never encountered before, turns out to be an aprioristic or conceptual constraint. Without it, we could not attempt to interpret the natives' words and thoughts at all. Although Quine himself would probably disavow an interpretation of his intuition about the constraints on radical translation along these a priori lines, Hollis is not alone in recasting the principle this way. For example, Steven Lukes argues that, where S is a traditional society,

> if S has a language, it must, minimally, possess criteria of truth (as correspondence with reality) and logic, which we share with it and which simply *are* criteria of rationality. . . . But *if members of S did not have our criteria of truth and logic, we would have no grounds for attributing to them language, thought or beliefs and would a fortiori be unable to make any statements about these.*[15]

This we may call the Bridgehead Argument:

1. If members of S did not have our criteria of truth and logic, there would be no grounds for either interpreting the contents of their words, describing their intentional states, or passing judgment on the rationality of their beliefs at all.
2. Yet there are grounds for such interpretation, description, and evaluation.

Therefore,

3. Members of S do have our criteria of truth and logic.

In a valid argument, if its premises are true, the conclusion must be true. Since the Bridgehead Argument's conclusion amounts to the very claim proposed by the Bridgehead theorist, and the argument is valid, therefore if its premises were true, we must accept that claim. But are the premises true?

First Objection to the Bridgehead View

If the natives of some radically different culture really did fail to reason in ways similar to ours, then it seems plausible that we could neither understand them nor be in a position to describe their intentional states (beliefs, desires, and the like). In that case, we would have no choice but to be agnostic (or suspend judgment) about both linguistic interpretation and intentional description. And agnosticism about these would entail that we abstain as well from attempting to evaluate the rationality of these people. Thus the first premise of the Bridgehead Argument appears well supported. Since the argument is valid and the first premise plausible, we shall have to say that it is sound if there is also strong support for the general claim made in the second premise. (An argument is deductively sound if and only if it is valid and its premises are true.)

According to premise (2), there are indeed grounds not only for interpreting the utterances of primitive people but also for describing their intentional states and evaluating the way they reason, so that agnosticism about any of these is unjustified. Yet this premise seems open to challenge. Suppose that we repeatedly try to translate the language of certain natives so that we can describe their intentional states and assess their rationality. But imagine also that we regularly end up with what appears to be sufficient empirical evidence that these people do not follow our criteria of truth and logic. That would certainly count as a reason for being agnostic about the possibility of justifiably choosing among alternative translation manuals. Moreover, in scenarios of that sort, we would have grounds for neither intentional description nor rational evaluation. The most that we could do, given our acceptance of Quine's principle, is to conclude that such recalcitrant empirical data turn into bad translations—thus we should remain agnostic, not only about the meaning of the natives' words, but also as to whether they have any intentional states at all. Yet our agnosticism clearly amounts to granting that, at least sometimes, there are no grounds for linguistic interpretation, description of intentional states, and rational assessment. If this is correct, then the Bridgehead Argument's second premise, as it stands, must be rejected. And were the Bridgehead theorist to insist, contrary to the empirical evidence, on the truth of that premise, he would be begging the question.[16]

Second Objection to the Bridgehead View

In addition, because the Bridgehead theorist's criteria of rationality are, as we shall see, quite demanding, many agnostic scenarios may turn out to be actual. According to his criteria, there are at least three types of malfunctions that must be avoided if our beliefs are to count as rational:[17]

1. *Logical malfunction:* holding a belief that is either (1) inconsistent with other beliefs one entertains, or (2) based on an invalid inference;
2. *Failure of truth:* accepting a set of propositions that is either (1) partially or (2) wholly false; and
3. *Failure of sense:* holding a belief about a proposition that is either (1) conceptually or (2) logically impossible.

Overwhelming evidence suggests that the Mayans did in fact hold beliefs that, according to these criteria, fail to count as rational. The following propositions and inferences illustrate some of the malfunctions listed above:

1. It is the case both that the jaguar priest (or Chilam Balam) has predicted that all men born in March would live for seventy-five years and that some men born in March did not in fact live for seventy-five years. Yet the jaguar priest's prediction is true.

2a. Some white men arrived from the East; *therefore,* one of the prophecies of the jaguar priest has been confirmed.
2b. The Spanish conquerors were sent to the New World by the gods.
 3. Some Mayan priests are jaguars.

Of course, these are a small sample of beliefs held by the Mayans that would turn out to be irrational according to the above criteria. Moreover, the above criteria are not the only ones for rational failure in the Bridgehead theorist's list. According to him, the following may also count as failures of that sort:

 4. Accepting propositions that are situationally specific or ad hoc; and
 5. Holding a belief in any of the following epistemically defective ways:
     a. Based on either irrelevant or bad reasons;
     b. Based on insufficient evidence;
     c. Accepted uncritically; or
     d. Protected against disconfirming evidence.

But if the criteria of rational belief required avoiding all of these logical and epistemic malfunctions, then the empirical evidence suggests that very few beliefs entertained by primitive people pass such a demanding test. Given the Bridgehead Argument's first premise, the Bridgehead theorist would in that case be committed to agnosticism about primitive people's rationality. That is, he would have to acknowledge that he is unable either to interpret their words or to describe their intentional states. Worse, how could he ascribe to them any intentional states at all in such a scenario? The Bridgehead theorist then seems vulnerable to a counterargument:

 1. If members of *S* did not have our criteria of truth and logic, there would be no grounds for either interpreting their words, describing their intentional states, or passing judgment on the rationality of their beliefs at all.

2. Members of *S* do not have our criteria of truth and logic. *Therefore*,
3. There are no grounds for either interpreting their words, describing their intentional states, or passing judgment on their beliefs at all.

Again, the argument is valid. So if its premises are well supported, then we cannot reject the conclusion. Already we have examined some reasons supporting (1). And, given the Bridgehead theorist's list of irrational beliefs and the available empirical evidence about propositions commonly accepted by the Mayans and other primitive peoples, (2) seems also plausible. Yet it is absurd that we claim to be agnostic about whether these people have mental states such as thoughts, beliefs, and desires. What, then, has gone wrong with the argument?

Weak Rationality and Critical Thinking

The Bridgehead theorist maintains that either the empirical beliefs of primitive people predominantly satisfy our own standards of truth and logic, or we should be agnostic about whether they have any beliefs at all. But given his list of rational failures and malfunctions, those standards of truth and logic have turned out to be quite demanding indeed. On this account, we should be agnostic about the Mayans' rationality unless we were in a position to show that at least *some* of their empirical beliefs did satisfy such standards of truth and logic. And since according to this theorist's list, very few (if any) empirical beliefs held by these people meet those standards, we would then have no choice but to be agnostic about their rationality and that of other groups of primitive peoples. The account thus appears unable to reject the absurd, agnostic conclusion of the above counterargument to the Bridgehead Argument—for on which basis could the account help us to decide between an a priori assumption (the bridgehead of truth and logic) and the available empirical evidence so that such agnosticism could be avoided? In light of the evidence, the Bridgehead view can provide no compelling reason for either argument.

But in assessments of rationality, more than one notion may be at stake, so our verdict may be too hasty. The Bridgehead theorist has in fact maintained that two different concepts of rationality should be of concern in our attempts to understand primitive people. On the one hand, there is rationality of the kind susceptible to the failures and malfunctions listed above, which corresponds to a strong notion, sometimes called "perfect rationality,"[18] that is considered to hold universally, since its criteria amount to conditions for the possibility of any linguistic understanding, intentional description, and critical thinking at all. According to Lukes, for example, those criteria "specify the ultimate constraints to which thought is subject: that is, they are fundamental and universal in the sense that any society which possesses what we may justifiably call a language must apply them *in general*, though particular beliefs, or sets of beliefs, may violate them."[19] Moreover, it could be argued that universal standards of rationality of the sort Lukes has in mind are not only required for our being able to revise the beliefs we hold but also provide a rationale for our being critical thinkers. Without such standards, doubts may arise as to why we should engage in critical thinking at all.

If rationality could only mean perfect rationality, then the case of the Mayans would present a problem since their beliefs have been shown to fall short of what is required for rationality in that sense. But the Bridgehead theorist might meet this problem by suggesting that the Mayans' beliefs, provided they did have some reason to entertain them, could be considered rational in some other sense, to which we now turn.

Discussion Questions

1. Suppose that mature adults who fail to distinguish between reality and fantasy could be compared to children, in that they both have a prelogical mentality. On the basis of the books of *Chilam Balam*, may we infer that the Mayans failed to draw a distinction between reality and fantasy? If so, what would follow about their mentality?

2. Strong rationalism has been held to entail an implausible conclusion about the rationality of people living in traditional societies. What is this conclusion? Can you think of an objection to that form of rationalism?

3. The Mayans' rationality in this chapter generates a puzzle for philosophers. Which of their beliefs suggests that they were in fact rational? And which ones would undermine that claim? Why? Does the available evidence favor one conclusion over the other? If yes, which one? If not, explain why that would cause a puzzle.

4. State the principle of charity and explain why it may amount to an objection to strong rationalism.

5. State the principle of humanity and discuss how it is related to the principle of charity. Are they consistent? Could they come into conflict? If so, which one is more astringent?

6. In his *General History of the Things of New Spain* (Book 4), Bernardino de Sahagún argues that Western astrology may be compatible with individuals having free will. But if the events in the life of a person are determined by the position of the planets at the date and time she was born, could Sahagún be right? If so, explain how.

7. According to Sahagún, Western astrology can be tolerated because it is based on empirical evidence connecting time of birth, the position of the planets, and future events in the life of individuals. Yet he recommends that the astrology of the Aztecs be eliminated on the grounds that their practitioners took it to convey the will of a certain god. Do you agree with Sahagún on this matter? If so, explain why it is more acceptable to believe in Western astrology than in that of the Aztecs. If not, raise an objection against Sahagún's views.

8. What is the Bridgehead Argument? In what way is it vulnerable to criticism? How might it be defended?

9. Rationality, according to the Bridgehead Argument, rests on a priori grounds. What does this mean? And what follows from that view about the rationality of the Mayans?

10. Were the Mayans capable of thinking critically? Mention some conditions for being able to think critically, according to the Bridgehead view. Is there any evidence that the Mayans satisfied those conditions?

Suggestions for Further Reading

Craine, Eugene R., and Reginald C. Reindorp, eds. 1979. *The Codex Pérez and The Book of Chilam Balam of Maní*. Norman, Okla.: University of Oklahoma Press.

Edmonson, Munro S. 1986. *Heaven Born Merida and Its Destiny: The Book of Chilam Balam of Chumayel*. Austin, Tex.: University of Texas Press.

Hollis, Martin. 1970. "Reason and Ritual." In Bryan R. Wilson, ed., *Rationality*. Worcester: Basil Blackwell.

León-Portilla, Miguel. 1988. *Time and Reality in the Thought of the Maya*. Norman, Okla.: University of Oklahoma Press.

———. 1990. *Endangered Cultures*. Dallas: Southern Methodist University Press.

Lukes, Steven. 1970. "Some Problems About Rationality." In Bryan R. Wilson, ed., *Rationality*. Worcester: Basil Blackwell.

Stich, Stephen. 1991. *The Fragmentation of Reason: Preface to a Pragmatic Theory of Cognitive Evaluation*. Cambridge, Mass.: MIT Press.

Wilson, Bryan R., ed. 1970. *Rationality*. Worcester: Basil Blackwell.

Winch, Peter. 1970. "Understanding a Primitive Society." In Bryan R. Wilson, ed., *Rationality*. Worcester: Basil Blackwell.

Wong, David. 1984. *Moral Relativity*. Berkeley: University of California Press.

Notes

1. See, for instance, Wesley C. Salmon, "Rational Prediction," in A. Grünbaum and W. C. Salmon, eds., *The Limitation of Deductivism* (Berkeley: University of California Press, 1981).

2. See Eugene R. Craine and Reginald C. Reindorp, eds., *The Codex Pérez and The Book of Chilam Balam of Maní* (Norman, Okla.: University of Oklahoma Press, 1979) and Munro S. Edmonson, ed., *Heaven Born Merida and Its Destiny: The Book of Chilam Balam of Chumayel* (Austin, Tex.: University of Texas Press, 1986).

3. The case is discussed in Bryan R. Wilson's *Rationality* (Worcester: Basil Blackwell, 1970). Especially relevant to the debate about the rationality of the Azande are the papers by Alasdair MacIntyre ("Is Understanding Religion Compatible with Believing?") and Peter Winch ("Understanding a

Primitive Society"). A more recent contribution is in David Wong's *Moral Relativity* (Berkeley: University of California Press, 1984).

4. Craine and Reindorp, *Codex Pérez*, p. 24.

5. Edmonson, *Heaven Born Merida.*

6. Edmonson, "Christianity Reaches Merida," in *Heaven Born Merida,* pp. 107–111.

7. In *Endangered Cultures* (Dallas: Southern Methodist University Press, 1990), Miguel León-Portilla offers various testimonies to the effect that the Mayans secretly kept accepting the claims of their sacred books for many years after the Conquest. Numerous reports are available testifying the grief caused to these people by Spanish conquerors and priests when they managed to find and destroy those books. See, for instance, Bernal Díaz del Castillo, *The Discovery and Conquest of Mexico* (London: Percy Lund, Humphries & Co., 1928).

8. W. V. O. Quine, "Ontological Relativity," in *Ontological Relativity and Other Essays* (New York: Columbia University Press, 1969), p. 46.

9. W. V. O. Quine, *Word and Object* (Cambridge, Mass.: MIT Press, 1960), pp. 58–59.

10. This reading of the principle has been proposed by Donald Davidson in *Inquiries into Truth and Interpretation* (Oxford: Clarendon Press, 1984).

11. Richard Grandy, "Reference, Meaning, and Belief," in *The Journal of Philosophy* 70 (1973), p. 445.

12. See Grandy, "Reference, Meaning, and Belief."

13. Martin Hollis, "Reason and Ritual," in Wilson, *Rationality*, p. 237.

14. Hollis, "Reason and Ritual," p. 233.

15. Steven Lukes, "Some Problems About Rationality," in Wilson, *Rationality*, p. 210. Emphasis mine.

16. An argument begs the question when its premises amount to a restatement of the conclusion.

17. See Lukes, "Problems About Rationality."

18. In *The Fragmentation of Reason: Preface to a Pragmatic Theory of Cognitive Evaluation* (Cambridge, Mass.: MIT Press, 1991), Stephen Stich ascribes such a notion to Hollis. But the latter is in fact endorsing a conception of strong rationality first proposed by Lukes in his "Problems About Rationality."

19. Lukes, "Problems About Rationality," p. 212.

2

COULD THE MAYANS THINK?
AND WHAT ABOUT US?

These natives of all New Spain took and take great care to know the day and hour of birth of every person to foretell the attributes, the life and death of those who were born. Those who held this office were called tonalpouhque; to them went, as to prophets, anyone who had given birth to a boy, to a girl, to be informed of their attributes, life and death. These soothsayers were not governed by the signs nor the planets of heavens but by a formula which, as they say, Quetzalcoatl left to them. . . . This trick of reckoning is either a necromantic craft or a pact and invention of the devil which should be uprooted with all diligence.

Bernardino de Sahagún,
General History of the Things of New Spain, Book 4

Rationality might be within reach even when the requirements of perfect thinking discussed in the previous chapter fail to hold. If so, the Mayans' beliefs could be considered rational in a weaker sense, provided that the Mayans did have some reason to entertain them. In fact, the Bridgehead theorist has argued that, besides perfect rationality, there is also what we may call "weak rationality." Under this less demanding concept, some beliefs that fail to qualify for perfect rationality because they flout common standards of logic and truth may nonetheless be eligible for weak rationality if a reason for entertaining them could be offered by their holders. The specific ways of determining what counts as weak rationality cannot be universal since different contexts will suggest different criteria of "good reasons for holding a belief."[1] Weak rationality, then, is less a matter of meeting universal, logical standards than of the appropriateness of a belief in certain circumstances. Furthermore, to qualify for weak rationality, the content of beliefs must be true propositions, even though their truth would depend upon the coherence of those propositions among themselves and with others accepted by the same group of people. On this proposal, then, beliefs eligible for rationality of the weaker kind do have truth conditions, but their truth is not a matter of their correspondence with reality.

An attempt to understand the rationality of primitive peoples along these lines can be found in Martin Hollis's discussion of ritual beliefs. "A ritual belief p is rational," he contends, "if and only if there is a belief q such that q *supplies a reason for* holding p and p does not entail the falsity of q." As to the truth of beliefs of this sort, Hollis suggests that "since the Correspondence Theory of Truth is beside the point, we must make use of the Coherence Theory."[2] In this view, a set of ritual beliefs qualifies for weak rationality only if the following conditions hold true:

1. Some connections, which we would typically translate by using particles such as "because," "supplying a reason for," and the like, hold between the members of that set; and
2. Beliefs so related are logically consistent.

To the Bridgehead theorist, these criteria of weak rationality also boil down to a priori or conceptual assumptions needed for linguistic interpretation, intentional description, and rational evaluation.

The Weak Rationality Argument

The Bridgehead theorist then could defend his notion of weak rationality by reasoning as follows:[3]

1. Either we acknowledge that the natives connect their ritual beliefs through the relation "being a reason for," or we grant a metaphorical interpretation of such beliefs.
2. We cannot grant a metaphorical interpretation of such beliefs.

Therefore,

3. We must acknowledge that the natives connect their ritual beliefs through the relation "being a reason for."

Although (as we shall see) the second premise of this argument can be supported, the first amounts to a false dichotomy since aside from the metaphorical interpretation of those beliefs, there are other options—some of which may be competitors of the Bridgehead view. Before turning to such alternatives, however, let us first consider another question. Can the Bridgehead theorist's move of distinguishing perfect rationality from weak rationality save him from being stuck with the implausible conclusion that there are no grounds for evaluating the rationality of most beliefs held by primitive peoples?

Human Rationality and Animal Rationality

The distinction between perfect rationality and weak rationality was introduced in order to argue that ritual beliefs qualify only for the latter, whose minimal constraints are *connectedness* (through the relation "supplying a reason for") and *consistency* (among the beliefs thus related). Surely the Mayans' beliefs in astrological predictions and prophecies are rational in this sense, but so are many sets of beliefs held by infants and perhaps higher animals, such as chimpanzees and dolphins. No doubt small children, for instance, are capable of entertaining consistent sets of propositions that they connect in ways that we would translate by using particles such as "because" and "supplying a reason for." But were rationality to consist merely in requirements of this sort, the resulting view would be vulnerable to criticisms similar to those raised against strong rationalism. Here, too, the rationalist view would have the consequence that most propositions and theories accepted by primitive people would count as merely quasi-rational and prescientific beliefs about the natural world. This would be so because, according to the Bridgehead theorist, those beliefs qualify for no more than weak rationality, a kind that may equally apply to beliefs held by infants and, perhaps, by chimpanzees and dolphins. But the latter surely cannot be said to possess fully rational and scientific beliefs about the natural world.

Furthermore, it is also difficult to see how the Bridgehead view differs from that of the French anthropologist Lucien Lévy-Bruhl, who thought the beliefs of primitive people lay between prelogicality and mysticism on the one hand and logicality and correspondence with reality on the other.[4] In both theories, some questions arise as to whether the theorist is really acknowledging the rationality of primitive people—for if they have only weak rationality, these people neither reason in ways similar to ours nor have critical thinking skills. Recall that according to the Bridgehead theorist, the latter requires perfect rationality, and the available empirical evidence suggests that primitive people, by and large, fall short of having rationality of that kind. It appears then that the Bridgehead theorist is committed to holding that although some empirical beliefs held by primitive peoples are eligible for the kind of rationality required for critical thinking, most of them do not qualify for rationality in that sense.

On the other hand, many empirical beliefs and scientific theories accepted in the West could be said to qualify for perfect rationality since they seem connected in ways that mirror the laws of logic and have correspondence-with-reality truth conditions. But then the Bridgehead view entails that Westerners are capable of critical thinking whereas primitive people are not—being either minimally critical or even *non*critical in their reasoning.

Were the Bridgehead theorist to reply that that is precisely why traditional societies cannot compare to modern ones, the claim would be unsupported. Consider, for example, some societies in remote, developing areas of Asia, where people hold beliefs that are mostly of a religious, magical, or ritual sort—thus failing to qualify for the kind of rationality that, according to the Bridgehead theorist, is needed for critical thinking. When individuals from these traditional societies undertake studies in Western countries such as the United States, they often perform well, showing above-average critical thinking skills, according to psychological tests and academic reports.

This suggests that it makes little sense to regard people from traditional societies as, by and large, only weakly rational. Yet it would seem equally absurd to follow the Bridgehead view here and conclude that the Mayans failed to qualify for full-fledged rationality. Such a conclusion is belied by compelling written evidence that, in spite of their beliefs in astrological predictions and prophecies, these people carried out empirical and formal calculations requiring fully rational skills and critical thinking abilities. That was precisely the reason we were so puzzled about their acceptance of claims made in their sacred books. Perhaps some competitors of the Bridgehead view could show us how to solve that puzzle.

A Metaphorical Interpretation of Mayan Prediction

A promising alternative would be take the Mayans' beliefs in astrological and prophetic predictions to be expressive or symbolic—for it could then be argued that, like interpretations of works of art, such beliefs have their own rationale and result from emotional responses rather than intellectual judgment. In this "expressivist" view,[5] those beliefs should be understood metaphorically since they not only lack truth values but are also unanalyzable. But according to Hollis, expressivism cannot help explain anything, given that "claims to have identified the metaphorical uses of words and gestures must be rationally justified. This involves cashing the metaphors, and therefore the notion of 'metaphorical use' never has any explanatory force."[6] Expressivism also seems to ignore the obvious fact that native peoples, such as the Mayans, hold their beliefs in astrology and prophecies as true. And since the contents of such beliefs are surely propositions about the natural world, why should we follow the expressivist in thinking that they lack truth values?

If we agree, then, with some of the Bridgehead theorist's objections to expressivism, does this mean we concede his argument? Not at all, for as we will show, there are more plausible alternatives to his views. And if we are right on this, then the argument's first premise is false. Let us now consider some of these alternatives.

"True for the Mayans"

One of these views is cognitive relativism, which promises to solve our puzzle while avoiding the parochial viewpoints of the strong rationalist and the Bridgehead theorist. Relativism might afford a solution because it maintains that, if a certain proposition is accepted as true by some group of people or culture, then it *is* true for that group or culture. In fact, the cognitive relativist believes that there is no absolute concept of truth, valid independently of, for instance, when and where propositions thought as true are accepted. According to her, which propositions *are* true varies, depending on where and when those who accept them live.

A closer look at this thesis, however, suggests that some of its consequences may be highly implausible—for once the statement is embraced, nothing seems to stand in the way of arguing that, in the case of the *Chilam Balam*'s astrological and prophetic predictions, if they were true for the Mayans, then they were true, period. Although relativism about other matters may be plausible,[7] this view is very controversial since cognitive relativism is a claim about the truth of propositions concerning the natural world.

For one thing, it is a notorious fact that people have historically held the most outrageously absurd beliefs and theories about the natural world—involving, for instance, plainly false propositions about cause/effect relations and even about how things are. That witches cast spells and demons cause illnesses are examples of the former, while the sun orbits the earth and phlogiston is needed for fire illustrate the latter. A belief in anything of this sort amounts in fact to a counterexample to the cognitive relativist's attempt to draw a conclusion about the truth of empirical propositions and theories from premises concerning only peoples' acceptance of such propositions and theories. Clearly, given such counterexamples, there is no valid route from premises about belief to a thesis about truth such as that stated above.

The moral to be learned here is that believing a proposition to be true must be distinguished from that proposition's actually being true—a distinction sometimes expressed by saying that the former belongs to the epistemic domain, and the latter to the metaphysical. From an epistemic premise holding that a certain group of people believe a proposition to be true, nothing is deductively implied about a metaphysical claim concerning the truth of the proposition believed by them.

But the argument the cognitive relativist has in mind may involve a more modest relation between premises and conclusion than that of deductive implication (or entailment). She could instead simply maintain that what best explains the evidence conveyed by the following premise is her own thesis:

1. At different times and places, some people have believed different, and sometimes incompatible, propositions and theories to be true.

Therefore,

2. The best explanation of (1) is that which propositions and theories actually *are* true varies, depending on where and when those who accept them live.

Since the premise is supported by compelling empirical evidence, this cognitive relativist argument now seems inductively sound—that is, its conclusion appears to have a high probability of being true. However, note that by arguing along these lines the cognitive relativist has provided us with only *one* reason for accepting her thesis, and that that reason must of course be weighed together with counterreasons before making up our mind about her views.

Is Rationality Relative?

It has often been argued that, given a thesis such as the above one, the relativist is committed to holding that, at least in some cases, beliefs that appear to be about logically inconsistent propositions (e.g., p and not-p) could be equally true. Compare the sincere assertion of a heliocentric theorist, "The earth does move" with "The earth does not move" as sincerely stated by a geocentric rival. Clearly, we have the intuition that these statements contradict each other, and that therefore, no matter when and where they are made, they cannot possibly both be true. The first objection to the cognitive relativist's argument consists in simply pointing out that, in cases of that sort, he is committed to challenging this common intuition, holding that both statements—"The earth does move" and "The earth does not move"—could be true at once.

At this point we should recall that there is no valid argument from an epistemic premise about belief against the cognitive relativist's conclusion. But when his reasoning was recast as an argument against the best explanation of some empirical evidence, the relativist could indeed offer a reason for his thesis. That reason, however, must now be weighed with our objection—keeping in mind that failing to meet that objection would fall short of showing cognitive relativism to be false because we shall see that there is still some room for maneuvering here.

Since the first appearance of cognitive relativism in ancient Greek philosophy, in the teachings of Protagoras, supporters of the thesis have held that we should give up the ordinary notion of truth in favor of the more liberal concept "true *for*." The relativist may thus remind us of this and respond to our objection by noting that, on his account, statements about *the way things are* are in fact elliptical. They contain a hidden (or implicit) relativist qualifier suggesting that whatever is being held is always so only "for" those who take it to be the case. Therefore, when that qualifier is made explicit, it becomes clear that some statements apparently contradictory at the outset are nonetheless logically consistent. For example, the above assertions made by a heliocentric theorist and her geocentric rival must in fact be read as saying, respectively, "The earth does move *for me*," and "The earth does not move *for me*." There is no contradiction now because, although it appears that we have a statement and its negation, once the qualifier "for me" is added, each of these amounts to the assertion of a different proposition.

This defense of relativism is at odds with the historical fact that those who held geocentric and heliocentric theories perceived themselves as holding rival views that actually contradicted each other. Since this is compatible with our own intuition about such claims, why should we accept the hidden-qualifier theory of cognitive relativism? Recall that, in this view, any time someone asserts a proposition, her utterance should be understood as implicitly relativizing its truth to herself (or to a theory, conceptual scheme, culture, and so forth). Surely this amounts to ascribing to utterances in a public language hidden meanings that they do not seem to have.

Finally, we must ask what help, if any, the cognitive relativist could provide in the case of concern here. His view seems to lead to the conclusion that clearly false predictions and prophecies, such as those found in the books of *Chilam Balam,* may in fact have been true. But that will be no help at all in solving the puzzle about the rationality of the Mayans. Thus we must continue looking for other alternatives to the Bridgehead position.

"True in the Context of Mayan Culture"

In a much discussed case involving a traditional society, the Azande, Peter Winch proposes an approach that may be called "contextualist." According to this view, although the empirical beliefs held in that society may be said to have truth conditions and to be related by rules of rationality, each of these is contextually determined. If so, what counts as true empirical beliefs and accepted rules of rationality in the West may not coincide with what counts as such in the context of a radically different culture. For the contextualist, it is

entirely possible to regard astrology as a misguided step compared
to scientific psychology in the context of Western society and, at the
same time, to hold that astrological predictions could amount to an
adequate procedure among the members of a traditional society
such as the Mayans. In this account, people's practices differ greatly
from society to society and must be assessed according to their own
contextually determined rules and functions. Although the Mayans'
devotion to the deliverances of the *Chilam Balam* on matters concerning their own health and welfare appears to be nothing more
than the acceptance of false propositions about the course of future
events in the natural world, the contextualist would insist that this
is only because we are evaluating such beliefs according to rules and
concepts accepted in the technological societies of the West. Were
we to judge these beliefs in their proper context, the social and psychological roles they played in the lives of the Mayans would become apparent, so that they would cease to be seen as a misguided
step for those people.

According to this view, then, rationality is a matter of conformity
to contextually determined norms of reasoning. When people really
care about practical results in growing their crops, for instance, they
follow technical procedures considered acceptable in their societies
and try to avoid error. But in other contexts, for example a ritual
one, they may simply be concerned about expressing their attitude
toward a certain crop—for instance, by trying to convey how important it is for them. In that context, then, they need not care
about taking effective "precautions to safeguard that thing."[8] There
is nothing irrational about playing different social games, each of
which follows its own norms.

Thus contextualists such as Peter Winch would find nothing puzzling about the Mayans' beliefs in religious prophecies and astrology but would consider them to be perfectly rational. Moreover, if
some beliefs or practices of a certain society follow norms accepted
by its members, then it would appear that contextualists must always judge them to be rational. But what then should we say about
honor killing and female circumcision as practiced in some traditional societies of today? Generally, those who defend such practices

within their own societies appear to believe sincerely that they are the best for certain women and their families. Contextualists are stuck with the uncomfortable position of having to say that those practices, when understood in their proper contexts, cannot be regarded as misguided steps. Yet how plausible would that be? Surely those people are following norms established by their groups about what counts as true or right, and they may even be ready to provide an explanation concerning the psychological and social role of such beliefs and actions in the context of their societies. What would be lacking in those accounts is truth and rational justification—given that, for instance, the belief that circumcision is required for a girl to become a woman is not only false but fails to rest on any empirical evidence. Even when explanations of the psychological and social roles of such practices may be available, Westerners would still regard them as misguided steps.

It seems, then, that when it comes to truth and rationality, contextualists are too permissive, allowing that any belief or action well supported by norms internal to a certain society is rational. At this point, it is difficult to differentiate contextualists' position from that of cognitive relativists. In fact, since they are relativists in disguise, they fall prey to objections similar to those raised against cognitive relativists. For one thing, both views have unacceptable consequences. If no persuasive argument is offered, why should we take either the truth of a belief or its rational justification to be contextually determined when that conflicts not only with our intuitions but also with the intentions made explicit by the believers themselves?

Ordinary Thinkers Versus Super Thinkers

The Bridgehead theorist was on the right track in distinguishing different kinds of rationality, but he failed to reach a balance between perfect rationality (which was too demanding) on the one hand and weak rationality (which was too liberal) on the other. According to Hollis, the kind of rationality needed for critical thinking is one where beliefs must mirror at least the following laws of logic:[9]

Inference:
   The conjunction of P implies Q, and P entails Q.
   Identity:
   P implies P.
   Noncontradiction:
   It is not the case that P and not-P.

Since the laws of logic ordinarily include much more than this example (licensing a great variety of forms for valid deductions and
cogent inductions), the Bridgehead theorist is here constructing the
standards of rationality very narrowly, to a small set of basic laws.
Nonetheless, if the laws of inference, identity, and noncontradiction
were in fact the criteria of minimal rationality for critical thinking,
such thinking would be beyond the reach of ordinary human minds.
Consider, first, the law of inference. Under a charitable epistemic
construal, it may be taken to hold that if someone accepts both a
conditional proposition and its antecedent, then he is committed to
accepting its consequent. But only a "super thinker" could be constantly aware of *all* the propositions he accepts, so he would draw
the conclusions licensed by the law of inference. Clearly, a "common thinker" (i.e., someone with ordinary thinking abilities) may
well accept propositions of the form P implies Q and P, yet fail to
draw the entailed conclusion Q. If the Bridgehead theorist is right,
and the correct use of inference is a necessary capacity for a critical
thinker, he should be prepared to acknowledge that, by and large,
ordinary human beings fail to qualify. Were the rule of inference
thought to apply only to propositions a human agent holds currently and consciously, one could then object that very seldom do
ordinary people go about considering all the consequences of the
propositions accepted by them. Therefore, even when restricted to
the current, conscious beliefs of an agent, the law of inference falls
beyond the reach of ordinary minds.
   However, much the same can be said of identity and noncontradiction. Taken as universal criteria of rationality of the kind needed
for critical thinking, they are vulnerable to objections along similar
lines. First, it appears that identity and noncontradiction also must

be recast in order to apply only to propositions consciously and currently accepted by some agent. Furthermore, if the contents of those propositions were dependent on relations the agent bore to her environment (as some theories of reference maintain), then in many situations she could flout those criteria of rationality without realizing it. Suppose, for example, that the star she sees in the morning is, unknown to her, identical to that she observes in the evening. She may then sincerely deny the truth of propositions asserting the identity of such stars, thus violating the law of identity.

Finally, other universal criteria of rationality square no better. According to Steven Lukes's list, for example, another is the *avoidance of inconsistencies*—and Hollis seems to agree with this criterion since he takes the consistency of reasons to be a requirement for weak rationality. But again, an agent, in order to avoid inconsistency among the beliefs she holds, must be aware of all of them at once—which is humanly impossible, given that only a few of the propositions she accepts are currently and consciously entertained, and many are held only dispositionally, in the back of her mind. Even if the demand of consistency were limited to current, conscious beliefs, contradictions are sometimes too subtle for a thinker to notice, and factors external to her may interfere with her awareness of them.

Thus the Bridgehead theorist's universal criteria of rationality, when taken to apply only to beliefs consciously and currently held, turn out to be still too demanding. If such criteria were required for rationality, then a human agent would be expected to draw *all* the logical implications of the beliefs she currently and consciously holds, *and* be aware of any failure of identity and consistency that may arise among them. This seems within the reach of only a "super rational agent," not of an ordinary thinker. Moreover, it appears that Lukes's criterion of the avoidance of falsehood faces an "evil demon" problem since the victim of a perfect deception could hardly be considered irrational on the grounds that her beliefs were false, if their falsity were unknown to her. On the other hand, if all the evidence available to her suggested the falsity of the propositions she had accepted, and she were aware of this but failed to revise those propositions, then (but *only* then) would she have breached her responsibilities as a rational agent.

Cognitive Pluralism

When we consider broadly the problems of linguistic interpretation, intentional description, and rational evaluation, a weaker and perhaps more plausible casting of the Bridgehead view is that of what is now called "cognitive pluralism." Stephen Stich sees minimal rationality as an alternative to the Bridgehead demands of universal rationality. Although his minimalism concedes that linguistic interpretation and intentional description do require a conceptual constraint on rationality, he holds that the mastering of some logical procedures (even very simple ones) is sufficient to make one eligible for full-fledged rationality.[10] The view depends heavily on the fact that there is no way to tell which are the minimal requirements for rationality since different people's habits of thought may mirror the laws of logic differently, with some easily following certain laws, and others following completely different ones. According to cognitive pluralism, it is possible that there be very few, if any, rules of inference that all rational humans master equally.

"Minimal rationality" should be preferred here because it is a weaker view and therefore more plausible than "perfect rationality" as construed by the Bridgehead theorist. But note that the cognitive pluralist agrees with the latter in taking the criteria of rationality to be an aprioristic constraint on translation and intentional description. Thus those who argue for minimal rationality in that way (as Bridgehead theorists do) may similarly face the problem of how to reject an unwelcome conclusion based on recalcitrant empirical evidence, such as that of the counterargument to the Bridgehead Argument considered in Chapter 1.

Super Thinkers Versus Animal Thinkers

It should not be surprising that rationality, like knowledge and truth, may involve more than one concept. The Bridgehead theorist is right on this, but, as we have seen, his standards for the kind of rationality needed in critical thinking are too high. Yet, as will be shown here, his standards for weak rationality are too low. Recall that if we wanted to claim that the Mayans were weakly rational by the Bridgehead definition of rationality of that sort, we would then be committed to saying that they were rational only in a sense of what would apply equally to infants and chimpanzees. But now, weak rationality seems to amount to *animal* rationality, and since the evidence about these people suggests that they do not qualify for perfect rationality, it follows that the Bridgehead view must deny them *human* rationality. This is plainly a *reductio ad absurdum* (i.e., an argument proving that the consequences of that claim are absurd), so the view must be rejected.

Moreover, the criteria of weak rationality are such that, in order to be weakly rational, it is sufficient that one be able, if challenged, to show that the propositions one holds are connected in a way properly translatable by our "because." This, however, sets the standard of rationality too low since the criterion boils down to what is commonly described as having a rationale, which lacks the evaluative (and also the normative) force of ascriptions of rationality.

Consider what we do with our words when, for example, we say in an ordinary context that the beliefs of a certain person are rational. It appears that by this speech act we are both describing some facts concerning those beliefs and, in some sense, evaluating the performance of the individual who holds those beliefs. Suppose we sincerely state that

Jane's prediction that *x* will occur is rational.

In some sense, we are describing the ways Jane reasons about *x* since if her prediction has the property of being rational, then that *x* will occur follows from (or is strongly supported by) some premises available to her. Thus we are saying that her thinking in this case agrees with logical rules of inference. At the same time, we are indeed praising her reasoning and perhaps even suggesting that any critical thinker similarly situated (e.g., having the same evidence) ought to reason about future events as she does. Yet such evaluative and normative forces are absent in weak rationality since this notion boils down to that of having a rationale.

We may concede that the agent's having a rationale for the propositions he accepts constitutes a necessary condition of rationality. But it is not sufficient. Other criteria are needed as well since we have found that ascriptions of rationality also have certain evaluative and normative forces that must not be left out of account. We shall now see whether a more adequate notion could capture those forces.

Neither Super Thinkers nor Animal Thinkers

Although judgments about an agent's rationality may concern *both* his actions *and* his beliefs, it is only the latter that are important for the sort of rationality of concern here—which we may call "doxastic rationality." Note first that since the propositions an agent accepts describe states of affairs of many different kinds, doxastic rationality would vary according to the content of the belief, being mainly practical, moral, or cognitive. To make judgments about these different kinds of rationality, we must consider a variety of factors involving not only the beliefs we are assessing but also the agent who holds them. Among such factors are (1) how the agent reasons from a logical point of view; (2) what his aims are; and (3) whether he is doing his best to accept only propositions supported by the evidence and to revise them whenever rational malfunctions become evident. That is, in assessments of doxastic rationality, the logical relations among beliefs figure prominently, but so too does the perspective of the agent.

To illustrate assessments of doxastic rationality involving different kinds of beliefs, let us first consider a set of propositions about practical matters. Suppose an agent consciously and currently accepts the following propositions: (1) that she cannot afford paying any fines; (2) that people who disregard street signs while driving generally end up paying fines; but (3) that she could disregard signs of that sort while driving. To assess the rationality of holding such beliefs, we should ask ourselves, is that set consistent? And how does it square with her conscious, current belief that an individual must avoid getting into trouble with the law?

Imagine instead that we are interested in assessing the rationality of an agent's beliefs about ethical matters. At least at an initial level, we should ask similar questions but with an eye to determining whether, assuming certain moral desiderata, she is using proper reasoning in forming and sustaining her moral beliefs. For example, we must ask ourselves, given that the agent consciously and currently holds that she ought to be a good person (or have good intentions, maximize good, and the like), is this compatible with her conscious, current belief that she should profit from the labor of underpaid immigrants? How does the latter square with her belief that she should minimize suffering in the world?

Judgments about these cases belong to the evaluation of practical and moral doxastic rationality, respectively. Our concern here, however, falls within the domain of cognitive doxastic rationality since we are interested in assessing the Mayans' beliefs about the course of future events in the natural world. (Note that the word *cognition* is usually related to *learning* and to *knowledge* and that these are *success terms*—they entail, respectively, the acquisition of a certain competence and the truth of what is known. Could one have, for instance, learned a language without being competent in using it at all? And is it possible to know that something is the case without that thing actually being the case?)

Assessments of the cognitive doxastic rationality of a given set of beliefs must consider not only the logical connections among those beliefs and their evidential support but also the goals and epistemic character of the agent who holds them. These, then, are the relevant factors in cognitive doxastic rationality *(CDR)*:

A given set of beliefs is rational provided that
    1. Those beliefs:
    a. Rest, for their epistemic justification, on grounds that are either empirical or purely rational;
    b. Are consciously and currently held by an agent;

c. Cohere among themselves and with other propositions consciously and currently accepted by the agent; and

2. The agent:

a. Is either not aware of any of these beliefs' failings with respect to 1.c or otherwise would revise the set; and

b. Does her best toward securing not only the truth of such beliefs but also their epistemic justification as in 1.a.

Note that these conditions operate at the level of belief, so that the resulting view is in fact weaker than perfect rationality (which requires reasoning that mirrors laws of logic, whether or not the agent is aware of her beliefs' status with respect to those laws). In addition, *CDR*'s criteria of rationality include neither truth nor adequate evidence unless the agent becomes aware of a malfunction of her beliefs on either of those counts.

Mayan Rationality Reconsidered

Let us suppose that fulfillment of the above conditions of rationality is sufficient for cognitive doxastic rationality. Then, since the Mayans' beliefs in astrology and prophecies appear to flout those conditions, they would fall short of rationality of that kind. The Mayans seem to have accepted, consciously and currently, that both

1. A certain proposition q is false.
2. p logically implies q.

Although the acceptance of (1) and (2) must have led the Mayans to believe that p is likewise false, since they also clearly took p to be true, they seem to have flouted condition 1.c. To see this, let p be the proposition that men born in March live for seventy-five years (as predicted by the *Chilam Balam*'s astrology). Since the Mayans no doubt realized that many men born in March did not in fact live that long, and that some did live longer than predicted, had they been fully rational, they would have rejected the prediction. But despite the evidence, they accepted it, together with other easily falsifiable predictions of their sacred books.

Finally, recall that the arrival of white men from the East, an utterly coincidental event, appears to have been interpreted as confirmation of the prophecy of a certain jaguar priest. Given the criteria for rationality outlined above, it appears that the Mayans in that case flouted 2.b because they failed to do their best toward accepting only propositions that are both true and supported by the empirical evidence. Recall that a commonly granted principle of confirmation prescribes that

> An agent may consciously and currently accept that a certain proposition *p* implies another proposition *q*, and that *q* is true, but he cannot take such beliefs to entail the truth of *p*.

Because rational malfunctions of these sorts are quite common in the Mayans' beliefs in the books of *Chilam Balam*, one might be tempted to conclude that they were predominantly irrational. Yet something would surely be wrong with any account that portrayed a people as clever as these as unable to think rationally. It remains now to show how that puzzle can be solved.

Could the Natives of Latin America Think?

The books of *Chilam Balam* provide solid evidence that the Mayans were in error in their beliefs about some important future events involving their own well-being and their flourishing as a people. Yet the books also show their reasoning to be sound when they were concerned with other future events less crucial to the course of their lives, such as eclipses and the positions of distant planets. As suggested earlier, we are then driven to conclude that there is a puzzle about the rationality of the Mayans. To solve it, we must first follow the Bridgehead theorist in acknowledging that their astrological and prophetic predictions were meant to be true. Moreover, since these actually consisted of assertions about future events in the natural world, we should take them to be claims that are, in principle, either true or false—that is, that they have truth conditions. Thus we reject the metaphorical interpretation, which takes such predictions to lack truth values (much as musical compositions do). But we part company with the Bridgehead theorist in that we wish to treat those predictions as having correspondence-with-reality truth conditions. And, at the same time, we differ also from contextualists, for whom the actual truth values of such predictions may vary from context to context, depending on norms internal to each society. Our argument runs as follows:

1. The *Chilam Balam*'s astrological and prophetic predictions consisted in predominantly descriptive propositions about future events of the natural world.
2. Ordinarily, the Mayans took such propositions as corresponding to future events of the natural world and as based on solid evidence.
3. Often, those propositions corresponded to nothing in the natural world and lacked empirical support.

Therefore,

4. The Mayans were in massive error with respect to the truth and evidential support of their beliefs in the *Chilam Balam*'s astrological and prophetic predictions.
5. The criteria of cognitive doxastic rationality apply only to sets of beliefs based on either empirical (observational) evidence or a priori (purely rational) thinking.
6. *But,* the *Chilam Balam*'s astrological and prophetic predictions constitute a set of propositions whose acceptance rested on neither empirical nor a priori means.

Therefore,

7. The criteria of cognitive doxastic rationality fail to apply to the astrological and prophetic predictions accepted by the Mayans.

Therefore,

8. The Mayans' massive error with respect to the truth and evidential support of the *Chilam Balam*'s predictions does not entail the irrationality of their belief in those predictions.

Let us consider the premises of this argument. (1) and (2) hardly need support, for the *Chilam Balam*'s predictions clearly refer to future events of the natural world, and in the absence of evidence to the contrary, it would be uncharitable to conclude that the Mayans did not truly believe that the course of events would be as predicted in those books. Since the course of the natural world has rarely (if ever) been as predicted there, and this must have been obvious to the intellectually curious Mayans, therefore their beliefs were predominantly false and unsupported by the empirical evidence—thus the third premise of the argument also seems plausible. And the claim that these people were in massive error with respect to the objectivity and epistemic support of the *Chilam Balam*'s predictions follows from (1), (2), and (3).

Yet according to our argument, since the grounds for belief in such predictions were neither empirical nor purely rational, those beliefs would fall beyond the reach of common criteria of cognitive rationality of the sort listed above. If this is correct, then surely the Mayans' beliefs could have been proved to be false by ordinary, empirical means available to them, even though they showed no concern for such tests. But, as I shall argue now, it cannot be a requirement of rationality that agents regularly conduct such tests on beliefs that in fact rest on neither empirical nor rational justification. Otherwise, *most* of their beliefs would turn out to be irrational.

Why the Mayans' Massive Error Does Not Amount to Irrationality

Consider, for instance, the analogous case of moral beliefs. According to a plausible doctrine, such beliefs could be said to have descriptive content in spite of the fact that there is no reality that corresponds to them,[11] so they would fail any test of objectivity. Ordinarily, however, people not only do take their moral beliefs to correspond to an objective reality but also feel no need to carry out simple, empirical tests to determine whether this is so. Of course, were such tests to be performed, they would show that the moral-belief holders are commonly in error since, assuming that the natural world is all that exists, beliefs in moral properties could correspond to nothing in that world and therefore would be false.

Ordinarily, however, we do not judge moral beliefs (or their holders) to be irrational because of such massive failure of objectivity. And the agents' failure to use empirical means available to them to test those beliefs still does not make us think of them as irrational beings. There is, then, a presumption that in evaluating the rationality of such beliefs, common norms of minimal cognitive rationality are out of place. Although such norms do seem required for the rational evaluation of beliefs supported either empirically or by reason alone, they fail to reach moral beliefs, which may be thought of as subject only to norms of rationality internal to the kind of belief they are. But could not an "error theory" along these lines, if plausible for moral beliefs, also help in solving the puzzle about the Mayans' beliefs in astrological and prophetic predictions? These people certainly took most propositions in the books of *Chilam Balam* to correspond to events in the natural world, but since that acceptance was based on magical thinking, no such belief can amount to empirical belief. These predictions turned out to be predominantly false, not corresponding to anything in the natural world. However, far from entailing the irrationality of the Mayans' acceptance of them, that suggests that beliefs so formed would fall beyond the common norms of cognitive rationality altogether, whether empirical or a priori rationality.

Discussion Questions

1. Define weak rationality. How is that rationality analogous to animal rationality? What would be the consequence of saying that the Mayans had only rationality of the latter kind? Is that conclusion acceptable? Explain.

2. It is possible to interpret the Mayans' belief in the *Chilam Balam*'s predictions as only metaphorical? How? (Explain how that interpretation would go.) Discuss a possible objection.

3. At the beginning of the modern period, some people (following scripture) believed that the earth does not move, whereas others argued that it does move. Was this a real conflict? How was it

used in this chapter against relativism? And could the relativist reply to that objection? If so, how? If not, why not?

4. Based on the fact that different rules of reasoning may be used by people living in different societies, does it follow logically that there are no correct rules of reasoning? And is that the way cultural relativists argue? If not, is there any other argument they may offer to defend their view that rules of reasoning are relative?

5. How could relativists account for the Mayan belief in astrological and prophetic predictions? Would such predictions have truth values? Is the relativist committed to saying that, if the predictions were true for the Mayans, then they are true, period? And is it possible that a prediction can be false and also be true for the Mayans? If so, what consequences would that have for relativism?

6. The contextualist interpretation of Mayan prediction differs from the metaphorical one but is similar to that of relativists. Compare these three views with respect to the truth values of those predictions.

7. What definition of doxastic rationality is proposed in this chapter? When we say that certain beliefs are rational, are we describing those beliefs or evaluating them? Or are we doing both?

8. The Bridgehead view was rejected on the grounds that it cannot solve the puzzle about Mayan rationality. According to the perfect rationality interpretation of the view, the Mayans come out as irrational. But according to the weak rationality interpretation, they have only animal rationality. Reconstruct these arguments.

9. If we think it implausible that the Mayans had only weak rationality, what evidence could be invoked to show this implausibility? Would the Bridgehead view imply that conclusion? Explain.

10. Consider the following argument:

> Since the Mayans failed to perform empirical tests on their astrological predictions and prophecies, it follows that these predictions and prophecies could not have been the outcomes of rational thinking.

In light of the conclusion of this chapter, is this argument persuasive? If so, why? If not, what is wrong with it?

11. In this chapter, belief in the *Chilam Balam*'s predictions was held to be analogous to moral beliefs. Reconstruct that analogy.

12. Discuss the error theory about Mayan rationality proposed here.

Suggestions for Further Reading

Harman, Gilbert. 1996. "Moral Relativism." In G. Harman and J. Thomson, eds., *Moral Relativism and Moral Objectivity*. Oxford: Oxford University Press.

Lévy-Bruhl, Lucien. 1966. *Primitive Mentality*. Boston: Beacon Press.

Mackie, J. L. 1977. *Ethics: Inventing Right and Wrong*. London: Penguin.

Meiland, Jack W., and Michael Krausz. 1982. *Relativism: Cognitive and Moral*. Notre Dame, Ind.: University of Notre Dame Press.

Stich, Stephen. 1991. *The Fragmentation of Reason: Preface to a Pragmatic Theory of Cognitive Evaluation*. Cambridge, Mass.: MIT Press.

Wilson, Bryan R., ed. 1970. *Rationality*. Worcester: Basil Blackwell.

Notes

1. Steven Lukes, "Problems About Rationality," in Bryan R. Wilson, ed., *Rationality* (Worcester: Basil Blackwell, 1970), p. 211.

2. Martin Hollis, "Reason and Ritual," in Wilson, *Rationality,* p. 235. Emphasis mine.

3. Hollis, "Reason and Ritual."

4. Lucien Lévy-Bruhl, *Primitive Mentality* (Boston: Beacon Press, 1966). For a criticism of that position, see Lukes, "Some Problems About Rationality," pp. 202–203.

5. See, for instance, J. H. M. Beattie, "On Understanding Ritual," in Wilson, *Rationality*.

6. Hollis, "Reason and Ritual," p. 238.

7. Some think moral relativism is rationally defensible. See, for instance, David Wong, *Moral Relativity* (Berkeley: University of California Press, 1984), and Gilbert Harman, "Moral Relativism," in G. Harman and J. Thomson, eds., *Moral Relativism and Moral Objectivity* (Oxford: Oxford University Press, 1996).

8. Peter Winch, "Understanding a Primitive Society," in Wilson, *Rationality*, p. 104.

9. Hollis, "Reason and Ritual."

10. See Stephen Stich, *The Fragmentation of Reason* (Cambridge, Mass.: MIT Press, 1991). Against the bridgehead of rationality view, he argues that any system that could master complex metalogical proofs but fail to draw the most simple inferences of propositional logic would qualify for rationality.

11. See J. L Mackie, *Ethics: Inventing Right and Wrong* (London: Penguin, 1977).

3

NATIVE FOLK COSMOLOGIES VERSUS WESTERN PHILOSOPHY AND SCIENCE

And then the earth arose because of them, it was simply their word that brought it forth. For the forming of the earth they said "Earth." It arose suddenly, just like a cloud, like a mist, now forming, unfolding. Then the mountains were separated from the water, all at once the great mountains came forth. By their genius alone, by their cutting edge alone they carried out the conception of the mountain-plain, whose face grew instant groves of cypress and pine.

Popol Vuh, chapter 1

The fierce and bloody conflict that marked the Spanish and Portuguese conquest of America was of course a conflict of cultures as well as of individuals. In this chapter, we shall explore some aspects of that conflict with an eye to determining whether the indigenous peoples had reached an understanding of the natural world that could stand comparison with Western conceptions grounded in philosophy and science. To the extent that some ele-

ments of non-Western worldviews persist among indigenous societies of the Americas today, we too must ask about these radically
different ways of understanding the world; thus the possibility of
making such comparisons remains of significant interest to us.

There are, however, two separate issues here. Although the evidence examined in Chapters 1 and 2 does not show that indigenous
Latin Americans thought in ways sharply at odds with those of Europeans, whether they reached an understanding of the natural world
similar to that afforded by Western philosophy and science is a different question. Since the cultures that met in October 1492 were utterly alien to each other, it is plausible to think that their conceptions
of nature may also have differed so greatly as to be incommensu-
rable. Yet to explore this issue, we have no choice but to proceed
with the tools available in our culture, which are Western philosophy
and science; thus it seems we face a challenge. On the one hand, can
our conclusions about the cognitive achievements of a radically different culture be both justified and objective? And on the other,
would not any affirmative answer to that question amount to ethnocentrism in assuming our own ways of thinking to be preferable? It
will be shown, however, that there is a view, "cognitive pluralism,"
that avoids both skepticism and relativism about such comparisons
without falling into ethnocentric bias.

Understanding the Natural World:
Latin America and the West

The native peoples of Latin America have left abundant evidence of
their interest in the question of the origins of the natural world. For
instance, the Mayan book *Popol Vuh* is an attempt to provide an understanding of these origins (parts 1 and 4), together with a narrative
of their history with a detailed chronology of their kings down to
1550 (parts 2, 3, and 5). Although written during the mid-sixteenth
century, probably between 1554 and 1558, it is usually thought to
record teachings already in the oral tradition of the Quichés, a
Mayan people living northwest of what is today Guatemala City, before the arrival of Europeans. According to a plausible hypothesis,
the original *Popol Vuh*, now lost, was the work of several authors

and quite likely contained illustrations and hieroglyphs to supplement the narrative.[1] The modern English text is a translation of a Spanish manuscript in Chicago's Newberry Library that seems to have been composed between the years 1701 and 1703 by the parish priest of Chichicastenango (in highland Guatemala), Francisco Ximénez (sometimes spelled Jiménez). Beyond doubt, the *Popol Vuh* is among the most comprehensive documents showing how the Mayans understood the origins of the natural world.

In Western culture today, cosmological explanations of the origins of the universe are scientific accounts, belonging to the domain of astrophysics. To distinguish such explanations from those that do not belong to science, we shall refer to the latter as "folk cosmologies." Since mythical accounts of the origins of the universe of the sort offered in the *Popol Vuh* are not scientific explanations, they are clearly not cosmologies in the contemporary Western sense. But could these folk cosmologies amount to philosophical explanations, perhaps in a rudimentary form? If so, then at least one group of Latin American indigenous peoples appears to have developed a philosophical theory. However, not all folk cosmologies qualify as philosophical explanations, so we must look closely at the account given by such cosmologies to determine what kind of understanding is provided by them.

Folk Cosmologies in Latin America

Let us first consider the Mayan cosmological account offered in the *Popol Vuh*. In the beginning, it tells us, there was nothing but the gods of the sea ("The Maker," "The Modeler," "The Bearer," "The Begetter," "The Heart of the Lake," and "The Heart of the Sea") and those of the sky ("The Sovereign Plumed Serpent," "The Heart of the Sky," "The Heart of the Earth," "The Newborn Thunderbolt," "The Sudden Thunderbolt," and "The Hurricane"). These gods debated among themselves how to create the earth and its living things. The former emerged from the water, and the latter, by successive processes of sowing and dawning.

Creating people, however, was the most difficult challenge of all, for the gods intended them to be creatures capable of walking, working, praying, talking, and praising them, but they failed at first to achieve beings that could do all these things. According to the narrative, the gods succeeded only after four attempts. In the first attempt, the ancestors of modern reptiles were created, but they had no arms to work and were unable to speak. Next, the gods made beings out of mud, but these could not praise them, walk, or even keep their shape—which was lost when they came in contact with water. Then the gods tried making creatures out of wood who were to be the ancestors of our monkeys. Such beings could talk and multiply themselves but could neither move easily nor praise the gods, so they were ultimately destroyed by a hurricane. But in the fourth attempt, the Mayan gods at last succeeded in creating humans. These beings, made out of a dough of yellow and white corn taken from a mountain, could do everything their creators intended. The first people were four men, whom the *Popol Vuh* calls the "mother-fathers" of the Quichés, probably because they were believed to be the original four patriarchs of their ancestral lineages.

The Mayans were not the only native group of Latin America to leave a fully developed folk cosmology. The Nahuas, for example, had a strikingly similar cosmology. This ancient Aztec group believed that the

> first humans were made of ashes, and their end came as a result of water, which changed them into fishes. The second class of humans consisted of giants who, notwithstanding their great size, were . . . weak because . . . whenever they dropped to the ground, for whatever reason, "they fell forever." The people who existed during the third Sun, or Age of Fire, likewise had a tragic end: they were converted into turkeys. Finally . . . the people who lived during the fourth Sun went on to live in the mountains after the cataclysm that finished that age.[2]

Narratives such as these raise the question of whether such conceptions of the origins of the universe could stand comparison with those elaborated by Western scientists and philosophers. To answer this, we must briefly examine some Western folk cosmologies often taken as the precursors of science and philosophy.

Folk Cosmologies in the West

Both science and philosophy are usually considered to have their roots in ancient Greece in the teachings of Thales of Miletus (ca. 624–548 B.C.E.) and other ancient thinkers who flourished in Ionia, in Asia Minor, more than a century before Socrates. For these pre-Socratics, the origins of the cosmos or the universe were thought to be in one of the basic sublunar elements, from which everything else was taken to derive—viz., either water, fire, air, or earth (with some maintaining that all have together generated the cosmos).[3] Today, of course, it would not be to philosophy but to astrophysics that we would look to solve this problem. Although it seems that our best cosmological hypothesis at present, the big bang theory, does indeed offer such a solution, that in fact depends on how the problem is construed. According to this familiar theory, the origin of the universe was in the explosion of a primordial mass that sent pieces in all directions, thus generating the various galaxies with their millions of stars and planets.

Would the pre-Socratics be likely to accept the big bang as an adequate explanation? Certainly not, since what they wished to know were the origins of absolutely everything. Given that goal, it seems always possible to add a further question about origins until finally the question would fall beyond the scope of any sound cosmological account. Suppose, for example, that the big bang theory could solve the puzzle of what was the cause of the original explosion. Anyone who thought like the pre-Socratic philosophers would expect that the theory also should explain why there was something there at all, that primordial mass waiting to explode, rather than nothing—which the big bang theory cannot explain. Without that elucidation, the theory would appear not to provide a complete explanation of the origins of the cosmos.

Questions That Make Little Sense to Ask

Any other scientific hypothesis about such origins seems vulnerable to similar charges, so we may usefully recall a popular tenet of philosophers during the early twentieth century: that questions that are worth asking (i.e., that have cognitive value) are only those that could in principle be answered by science. If this is correct, then the pre-Socratics' inquiry, aimed at finding out the origins of absolutely everything, would not be worth pursuing. Although that tenet was later considered too strong, there is nonetheless something appealing in being able to reject questions about the natural world that make no sense to ask. We may then hold the weaker (and therefore more acceptable) position that theories about the world that raise questions unanswerable by even the best conceivable science available hardly serve to achieve cognitive goals of any sort. Such questions would belong to neither science nor philosophy since both of these are human practices undertaken to achieve certain cognitive goals. If we are correct about the pre-Socratics' theories, then they seemed to focus on questions that make little sense to ask—which probably led these thinkers to overlook other problems more within their reach, given the knowledge available. Furthermore, it is plain that their own attempted answers were not even close to the truth about the origins of the universe.

According to a common view, however, it was the pre-Socratics who created the discipline we accept today as philosophy. For example, the Mexican philosopher José Vasconcelos (1882–1959) believed that the ancient Greeks "founded the method of philosophy."[4] In Britain, Bernard Williams now insists that Greek thinkers are responsible for nothing less than having given us the legacy of philosophy, establishing the discipline's major fields. According to Williams,

> [t]he legacy of Greece to Western philosophy is Western philosophy. . . . The Greeks initiated almost all its major fields—metaphysics, logic, the philosophy of language, the theory of knowledge, ethics, political philosophy and . . . the philosophy of art. Not only did they start these areas of enquiry, but they progressively distinguished what would still be recognized as many of the most basic questions in those areas.[5]

In a recent introduction to the subject, A. C. Grayling agrees. "The Greeks," he writes, speculated about the origins, composition, and functioning of the physical universe. They discussed the ethical and political circumstances of mankind, and proposed views about their best arrangement. They investigated human reason itself, and the nature of truth and knowledge. In doing so they touched upon almost every major philosophical question, and their legacy to subsequent thought is vast.[6]

But it is ironic that those who asked questions that made hardly any cognitive sense and that provide no adequate solutions at all have entered the history of Western thought as the first philosophers. If the speculations of the pre-Socratics about the origins of the universe count as philosophy, must we not say the same about the folk cosmologies and the belief systems held by the ancient native peoples of Latin America?

Are Folk Cosmologies Philosophy?

Whether or not the doctrines of the pre-Socratic Greek thinkers are part of philosophy at all depends on what counts as philosophy. Construed in a broad sense, "philosophy" sometimes means the way of life of some person or group. It can then be said that there is an implicit philosophy in each of us and in every community.[7] Then it would seem plausible that the ways of life, not only of the pre-Socratics, but also of the Aztecs, the Mayans, and the Incas count as philosophies—and this use of the term departs from a more technical one that takes "philosophy" to refer to an intellectual practice requiring specific methods and the formulation of questions and theories of a certain sort. The latter usage captures the meaning of the term as we understand it today. In that narrow sense, it appears that neither the pre-Socratics nor any of the indigenous peoples of Latin America had philosophy.

Yet according to the Mexican philosopher Samuel Ramos (1897–1959), philosophy and science were common practices among some ancient groups of indigenous peoples. "The astronomy of the Aztecs and Mayas," Ramos contends, "although closely tied to religious ideas, represents beyond any doubt a rational effort to understand the universe."[8] Unfortunately, Ramos offers no original sources to support his view, so acceptance of it would amount, at most, to a bad argument from authority. But let us consider some reasons suggested by others to persuade us that philosophy and science did exist among those peoples.

Did Ancient Latin American Civilizations Have Any Philosophy?

A contemporary Mexican scholar who has studied the life and thought of Mesoamerican Indians, Miguel León-Portilla, has argued that philosophy (in the narrow sense) existed among an ancient Aztec group, the Nahuas. According to him, these people had not only isolated thinkers but wholly developed schools of thought conducted by wise men. Would the existence of such men be sufficient to show that the Nahuas developed *philosophical* theories? According to León-Portilla, some documents indeed provide "sufficient evidence that they [the Nahuas] were not satisfied by myths or religious doctrines."[9] Yet this statement, if correct, would fall short of supporting the claim that Nahuatl thought was philosophical. Consider an analogous case: Suppose we have evidence that a certain group of people were unsatisfied by theories that explain fire in terms of the presence of some mysterious substance called "phlogiston." By itself, that would be insufficient to show that they must instead have believed some scientific explanation of combustion such as, for example, Lavoisier's theory, since they may have either simply lacked an account to replace the unsatisfactory theory or perhaps accepted some other nonscientific explanation.

According to León-Portilla, there is written evidence of the Nahuas' questions about knowledge, truth, and morality—which constitute major philosophical issues. As evidence, León-Portilla offers some passages, generally embedded in longer literary pieces. Here is, for instance, one where the immortality of the soul is discussed:

> Are flowers carried to the kingdom of death?
> It is true that we go, it is true that we go!

Where do we go? Where do we go?
Are we dead there or do we still live?
Do we exist there again?[10]

If texts of this sort are the only basis of the claim that the Nahuas had philosophy, the evidence is too weak, showing no more than that they took an interest in questions which could be discussed philosophically. From such evidence we can infer the existence of neither philosophical theories nor professional philosophers among the Nahuas. To see this, recall some religious texts you have probably read: They may contain questions concerning, for instance, the existence of God and the possibility of life after death—each of which may indeed generate a philosophical discussion. But that is hardly enough to show that those texts are philosophical.

What Bernardino de Sahagún Saw in the Colonies

León-Portilla's position here, however, is consistent with the testimony of some during the Conquest, and shortly after, who noted the cultural achievements of native peoples in Latin America. One of these, Fray Bernardino de Sahagún, was a Franciscan priest who arrived in Mexico during the early days of the Conquest (1529) and came to have great knowledge of the Aztecs' intellectual practices. After learning the Nahuatl tongue, Sahagún wrote a survey of Aztec cultures, which he published under the title *General History of the Things of New Spain*. Devoting himself to the study of the Nahuas, he argued that their society had some wise men who enjoyed the status of a professional group. In fact, he took the skills of such men to be similar to those of Western philosophers and astrologers of his time.

It is unclear, however, what evidence supports Sahagún's conclusions. Did he think, like León-Portilla, that such men merely raised questions that perhaps could be answered by philosophy or even astrology? Or did he think that the existence of such men meant that the Nahuas, as a group, had philosophical concerns and fostered a professional group to help them deal with them? Since Western philosophy long coexisted with astrology (and worse), we may be sure that the existence of wise men in a certain society does not guarantee that their theories could count as philosophy. Whether we should accept Sahagún's conclusions about the Nahuas would depend upon both the sources of his views about the intellectual practices of their wise men and the reliability of Sahagún's own understanding of what could be considered "philosophical" and "wise." Did he, for example, take those men to be wise because the Nahuas believed them to be so? Or did he think that such men were wise because they actually thought out theories that had intrinsic merit, whatever the Nahuas may have believed about them?

Yet since the evidence for such claims is weak, we cannot know what to make of them in the absence of further scholarly research. We would certainly need more information about the conceptual framework of those who, like Sahagún, reported the existence of philosophy among the natives of Latin America. And knowledge of these scholars' empirical sources would also be relevant to the question of whether their reports should be taken as conclusive evidence of the existence of Amerindian philosophers. But note, finally, that in finding a connection between philosophy and wisdom, Fray Bernardino de Sahagún was endorsing a well-known Western tradition. What then is that connection?

Is Philosophy Universal?
Latin Americans Follow the West

In the narrow sense more usual today, "philosophy" denotes a particular intellectual discipline with a subject matter and procedure of its own. We need a precise definition so that it will be differentiated from other intellectual practices. The Mexican philosopher Antonio Caso (1883–1946) favored the traditional Western view: Philosophy is the "love of wisdom."[11] Attributed to Pythagoras, this definition in fact follows closely the etymology of the composite Greek word used in antiquity to refer to any intellectual discipline within what we would today call philosophy or natural science.

If wisdom is a condition for philosophy, then neither the indigenous people of Latin America nor the pre-Socratic Greeks could be said to have developed such a discipline. In both cases, the thinkers identified as wise men were devoted to problems that make little scientific sense, and their attempted solutions were false. That their theories would not qualify as philosophy by the traditional definition can be shown by a thought experiment. Imagine a person, Bert, who regularly holds false beliefs, pursues meaningless questions, and has unrealistic cognitive goals. In addition, suppose that there is evidence available to him so that, upon sufficient reflection, he could realize that his beliefs were groundless and his questions meaningless. Here, it would certainly be odd if *we* considered Bert wise and a lover of wisdom—whether or not his community took him to be so. But could not the same be said of ancient thinkers, such as the Mayans, Aztecs, and pre-Socratic Greeks? After all, we have seen that they asked questions about the origins of the universe that made little sense and that they concocted theories that were clearly false. If the analogy with Bert's case is sound, we must conclude that it is equally odd to ascribe wisdom, and therefore the practice of philosophy, to them.

Antonio Caso on the Philosophical Character

Perhaps this is only because "love of wisdom" as a definition of philosophy is far too vague. To gain some precision, we might follow Caso's conception where wisdom is accompanied by traits of character that practitioners of philosophy are supposed to share. According to him, what philosophers have in common is that, instead of pursuing worldly success, they engage in an activity that consists entirely of thinking. Here Caso probably means that philosophers value reflecting upon the beliefs they hold, which is certainly correct. But this does not preclude such reflection's being directed to some goals philosophers pursue either instrumentally (as a means) or in themselves (as ultimate ends). Making sure that beliefs are consistent among themselves and are supported by reasons exemplifies the former because it is a means to achieving true beliefs, which in turn illustrates the latter.

In Caso's view, because philosophy consists entirely in reflection, those who engage in it must have some other special traits of character. Not only is thinking rigorously about philosophical problems often difficult, but actual solutions to those problems are frequently beyond the philosopher's reach—so that engaging in philosophy is sometimes frustrating. (When Caso observes that heroism is one of the traits philosophers should possess, he shouldn't be taken literally.) Another character trait philosophers need is intellectual curiosity, "a constant and incorruptible spirit of adventure." Thus "[w]hoever aspires to an interior quietude of the mind, a strong stability, a soft and easy rest," cautions Caso, "should not preoccupy himself with a study of philosophical questions."[12]

If the etymological definition of philosophy as love of wisdom is too vague, the notion that such traits of character must be shared by philosophers is not better, for it is still unclear how it could make more precise just what philosophy is. Caso may have in mind something along the following lines. The philosopher's activity leads to wisdom because it is based on a special kind of reflection aimed at two goals: (1) formulating puzzles that make sense to investigate; and (2) solving them by theories or systems of beliefs that get closer to the way things are. Such aims, which we may call "cognitive relevance" and "plausibility," respectively, provide philosophy's connection with wisdom—because, as we have seen already, those who regularly pursue meaningless questions and who hold false beliefs hardly qualify as wise. But cognitive relevance and plausibility are difficult to achieve, so the practitioners of philosophy must possess certain other qualities as well (principally, heroism in the sense discussed above and intellectual curiosity) in order to practice their discipline. Moreover, for a theory to be philosophical, it must raise questions that are cognitively relevant at the time and that have some plausibility (i.e., some likelihood of being true).

Surely philosophy, like any intellectual activity undertaken for the sake of cognitive goals, must make use of optimific means, and they must in this case consist of the systematic use of the method of rational argumentation to elucidate and, when possible, to solve both conceptual and empirical problems. It is worth noting that philosophers have appealed to that method to examine questions that later turned out to be better settled by empirical science. For instance, the folk cosmologies of the pre-Socratics and Aristotle's physics invite doubts about whether questions more suited to the methods of science can be adequately resolved by those of philosophy. In our view, however, even though there is in principle no limit to the type of questions open to examination by philosophers, cognitive relevance seems to require that when a certain matter concerns the natural world, there should be no successful scientific competitors contemporaneous with a viable philosophical theory about it. If competitors of that sort were available, to persist in the method of rational argumentation alone would be dogmatic—and therefore nonphilosophical.

José Vasconcelos's "Super-Criterion"

Rational argumentation is perhaps what Vasconcelos had in mind when he conceived the notion of a "super-criterion" as the method of philosophy. According to him,

> [T]he world of the philosopher is to be distinguished from the methodology of the experimental science and from all specialized approaches, in that it is not limited to a single criterion but must combine all of them: a philosopher requires a super-criterion. He must constantly compare the discoveries of the mind with those of the senses, and with that which the emotions teach him.[13]

Vasconcelos thinks that the work of philosophers is distinctive in that it must appeal to an overarching set of standards to justify beliefs and theories. Such a super-criterion could be recast as follows:

> By combining empirical and conceptual procedures, philosophers employ an overarching method to reflect upon the beliefs they

hold and produce theories of the world and of human understanding that are both justified and plausible.

Vasconcelos is of course squarely within the Western tradition
that originated in ancient Greece, and there any such overarching
philosophical method is called "rational argumentation." Without
that method, no dialogue would be possible between people holding
different beliefs and theories. By appealing to rational argumentation, philosophers try to ensure that their beliefs at least (1) are supported by good reasons; (2) are grounded in the evidence; (3) are
consistent with each other; and (4) are the outcome of sound cognitive processes. Moreover, this method seems effective in discerning
which questions make sense to investigate at all, as well as in finding
the best possible solutions on the basis of the information available.

Argumentation as a Demarcation Criterion

Rational argumentation may also be a criterion for distinguishing
theories that are philosophical from those that are not. When rational argumentation is taken to be the essential method of philosophy,
nonphilosophical theories are those that use that method either
rarely or not at all. A broad spectrum of theories may then be sorted
out according to their use of rational argumentation: Some would
fall at the extremes if they are either highly philosophical or not
philosophical at all, and others would be placed in the middle as being only partly philosophical. Comparative judgments could be
made on this basis, enabling us to determine in principle whether a
given theory is more philosophical or less so relative to others. As
with science and nonscience, the demarcation would then be a matter of degree, contingent upon how much a given theory depends on
the method of rational argumentation.

The Ancestors of Philosophy in the West

We may now ask how much philosophy was in the pre-Socratics'
doctrines of the origin of the universe. Clearly, their concern could

also be construed as involving a fundamental question about the natural world that was empirical—in other words, answerable only by hypothesis and observation. The pre-Socratics attempted to use the method of rational argumentation as evidenced by the fact that their answers rested less on mythology and religion than on hypothesis formulated from empirical evidence. Their doctrines then would have amounted to empirical hypotheses that aimed to capture the way things are, and they were testable, at least in principle. Perhaps this is the reason Vasconcelos took such thinkers "to have founded the method of philosophy precisely in the attempt to subordinate external processes to the forms of the intellect, in contrast with primitive thought that assimilates the movement of the objects within the impulses and desires of our will."[14]

On the other hand, the pre-Socratics obviously never mastered the method of rational argumentation as developed by later philosophers in the West. Were they, for instance, aware that their task was to justify their beliefs by reasons grounded in the evidence then available? And did they keep an eye on the consistency of their doctrines, remaining methodologically skeptical about their ways of drawing conclusions? More scholarly work needs to be done before such questions can be given definite answers. Until then, we must conclude that the method of the pre-Socratics is only an ancestor of the more fully fledged rational argumentation of later thinkers and that they thus qualify only as "primitive" philosophers at most. But if this is plausible in their case, why then may we not say the same of those natives of Latin America whose elaborate explanations of the origins of the universe we discussed earlier? Are these wise men not primitive philosophers as well?

The Ancestors of Philosophy in Latin America

The folk cosmologies of the indigenous peoples of Latin America resemble those of the pre-Socratics in that both could be construed as attempts to answer a fundamental question concerning the origins of the natural world. However, for the former, available documents and testimonies show that the proposed answers rested predominantly on myth and religion. Consider, for example, parts 1 and 4 of the Mayan *Popol Vuh* and the Aztec explanation of the origins of the universe discussed above. Since such doctrines were clearly not based on hypothesis and observation, they fail to count as empirical theories, testable in principle and able to describe the actual origins of the universe. Thus the kind of justification of such folk cosmologies differs from that of those offered by the pre-Socratics, who made some use of the method of rational argumentation. Although the latter also undeniably incorporated elements of mythological and religious thinking, they clearly appealed to hypothesis and observation more than did the doctrines of the Mayans and Aztecs. Only the pre-Socratics' folk cosmologies actually had a chance of finding out the truth about our cosmic origins, were testable (though false), and thus were truly empirical theories.

Still, it is clear that there is no simple way of determining which of these theories could count as strictly philosophical and which could not. In fact, a common feature of all such folk cosmologies is that they were attempts to answer an empirical question in an era when they had no scientific competitors within their own cultures.

Philosophy Today in Latin America and the West

I have argued that the pre-Socratic Greek thinkers could be considered only primitive philosophers, with their doctrines at most counting as the precursors of mature theories of the origins of the universe. Although they seem to have introduced the method of rational argumentation (fundamental to philosophy), they never mastered it in the more developed form widely used by later philosophers and scientists. Today, for instance, philosophers must be capable of recognizing reasons *as reasons* and must think about the status of such reasons with regard to their role in knowledge and truth. Furthermore, contemporary philosophers are expected to reflect upon the beliefs (and theories) they hold, to make sure that they (1) are supported by good reasons; (2) are grounded in the available evidence; (3) are consistent with each other; and (4) are the outcome of sound cognitive processes. If these are the traits of mature philosophy, then it is plain that neither the folk cosmologies of the native peoples of Latin America nor those of the pre-Socratics qualify for it.

That the method of philosophy must be rigorously conceived follows from the discipline's definition of its intellectual goals, which are cognitive relevance and plausibility (recall that pursuit of meaningless questions and faith in predominantly false beliefs are incompatible with wisdom, which standardly defines philosophy). To show that criteria (1) through (4) are essential to the satisfaction of philosophy's goals, consider an analogy with the natural sciences. Even though notorious problems stand in the way of taking any scientific theory to be true, there is nonetheless a presumption suggesting that some theories are better than others. For instance, when the experts prefer scientific psychology over astrology and evolutionary biology over creation science, does it make sense to maintain that such preference is altogether capricious and unwarranted? Certainly not, for psychology and evolutionary theory can be shown to have certain useful features lacking in astrology and creation science. Such features are valuable because they have good track records: The theories that maintain good track records have proven to be better at explaining and predicting than others that lack them (which is why they are often known as "values" or "virtues"). Accuracy in prediction, explanatory power, simplicity, consistency, and refutability are but a few of the most commonly identified virtues of scientific theories. These are often divided into those that are instrumental (adequate for solving puzzles, accurate predicting, and so forth) and those that are evidential (indicative that the theory is true or approximately true). We may now assert through analogy that in philosophy theories resulting from reasoning that follows steps (1) through (4) are more likely to have the instrumental and evidential good traits—which we have argued are cognitive relevance and plausibility. At the same time, the presence of those virtues could also be said to confirm the soundness of such reasoning. However, it should be kept in mind that not all circles are vicious.

Discussion Questions

1. The *Popol Vuh* is an attempt to account for the origins of the cosmos, but is it a philosophical text? And what about the folk cosmologies of Christianity, Judaism, and Islam?

2. In Christianity, Judaism, and Islam, God has certain properties that are incompatible with the conception offered in the *Popol Vuh*. Select two of these properties and compare.

3. Is the belief that supernatural forces have the powers ascribed to them in the *Popol Vuh* less rational than the belief in the powers ascribed to God by Christianity, Judaism, or Islam? If so, why? If not, why not?

4. According to testimony of some Spaniards during the Iberian Conquest, certain ancient indigenous peoples in Latin America had groups of professional wise men. Would that show that they also had philosophical and scientific theories? If so, why? If not, why not? What would it take to accept those testimonies as reliable?

5. It is sometimes claimed that organized groups of people cannot exist "without their own philosophy."[15] In which sense is the term *philosophy* being used here? If we agree with this claim, are we then committed to saying that anything goes in matters philosophical?

6. A common objection to cognitive relativism is precisely that it seems to entail that anything goes. Evaluate that objection. Is the cognitive pluralist vulnerable to a similar criticism? Explain.

7. According to Antonio Caso, the Pythagorean definition "love of wisdom" captures what philosophy really is. Is that an adequate definition? If so, why? If not, could it be amended? How?

8. Arguably, if philosophy is defined as "love of wisdom," then neither the cosmologies of the pre-Socratic Greek thinkers nor those of Latin American native people qualify as philosophy. Why? (Reconstruct the argument for this conclusion.)

9. According to Caso, what are the defining character traits that philosophers must have?

10. José Vasconcelos states that philosophy is an activity that follows a special method. What is his proposed super-criterion? Under a charitable interpretation, are the ideas underlying Vasconcelos's criterion plausible?

Suggestions for Further Reading

Caso, Antonio. 1971. "Philosophical Heroism." In John Haddox, ed., *Antonio Caso: Philosopher of Mexico*. Austin, Tex.: University of Texas Press.

Craine, Eugene R., and Reginald C. Reindorp, eds. 1979. *Preliminary Study to The Codex Pérez and the Book of Chilam Balam of Maní*. Norman, Okla.: University of Oklahoma Press.

Grayling, A. C., ed. 1995. *Philosophy: A Guide Through the Subject*. Oxford: Oxford University Press.

León-Portilla, Miguel. 1963. *Aztec Thought and Culture*. Norman, Okla.: University of Oklahoma Press.

————. 1992. *The Aztec Image of Self and Society*. Salt Lake City: University of Utah Press.

Northrop, F. S. C., ed. 1949. *Ideological Differences and World Order: Studies in the Philosophy and Science of the World's Cultures*. New Haven: Yale University Press.

Ramos, Samuel. 1943. *Historia de la filosofía en México*. Mexico City, Mexico: Imp. Universitaria.

Sahagún, Fray Bernardino de. 1982. *General History of the Things of New Spain*, Books 4 and 6. Salt Lake City: University of Utah Press.

Tedlock, Dennis. 1996. *Popol Vuh: The Mayan Book of the Dawn of Life*. New York: Simon & Schuster.

Vasconcelos, José. 1967. *Tratado de metafísica*. In John H. Haddox, ed., *Vasconcelos of Mexico*. Austin, Tex.: University of Texas Press.

Winch, Peter. 1970. "Understanding a Primitive Society." In Bryan R. Wilson, ed., *Rationality*. Worcester: Basil Blackwell.

Notes

1. That hypothesis could explain a certain use of demonstrative terms in the copy that remains, which would otherwise be quite odd. See Dennis Tedlock, ed., *Popol Vuh: The Mayan Book of the Dawn of Life* (New York: Simon & Schuster, 1996).

2. Miguel León-Portilla, *The Aztec Image of Self and Society* (Salt Lake City: University of Utah Press, 1992), p. 4.

3. For Anaximander, it was none of these but something he called *apeiron*—"the unbounded."

4. José Vasconcelos, *Tratado de metafísica*, in John H. Haddox, ed., *Vasconcelos of Mexico* (Austin, Tex.: University of Texas Press, 1967), p. 91.

5. See Bernard Williams's "Greek Philosophy," in M. I. Finley, ed., *The Legacy of Greece* (cited in A. C. Grayling, ed., *Philosophy: A Guide Through the Subject* [Oxford: Oxford University Press, 1995], p. 338).

6. Grayling, *Philosophy*, p. 1.

7. It is sometimes thought that there are a plurality of philosophies since different groups of people have systems of beliefs that vary greatly. We shall discuss a relativist argument for that conclusion in Chapter 4. But note that "philosophies" is used in that argument in the broad sense that equates it with "ways of life." *Cf.* Clyde Kluckhohn, "The Philosophy of the Navaho Indians," in F. S. C. Northrop, ed., *Ideological Differences and World Order: Studies in the Philosophy and Science of the World's Cultures* (New Haven: Yale University Press, 1949).

8. Samuel Ramos, *Historia de la filosofía en México* (Mexico City, Mexico: Imp. Universitaria, 1943), p. 11.

9. Miguel León-Portilla, *Aztec Thought and Culture* (Norman, Okla.: University of Oklahoma Press, 1963), pp. 8–9, 23, and ff.

10. Angel Maria Garibay, *Historia de la literatura Náhuatl* (cited in Miguel León-Portilla, *Aztec Thought and Culture*, p. 220).

11. Antonio Caso, "Philosophical Heroism," in John Haddox, ed., *Antonio Caso: Philosopher of Mexico* (Austin, Tex.: University of Texas Press, 1971).

12. Caso, "Philosophical Heroism," p. 79.

13. Vasconcelos, *Tratado de metafisica*, p. 81.

14. Vasconcelos, *Tratado de metafisica*, p. 91.

15. Kluckhohn, "The Philosophy of the Navaho Indians, " p. 356.

4

THE LEGACY OF 1492: PLURALISM, RELATIVISM, AND THE CLASH OF CULTURES

Five senses, then, to gather a small part of the infinite influences that vibrate in Nature, a moderate power of understanding to interpret those senses, and an irregular, passionate fancy to overlay that interpretation—such is the endowment of the human mind. Nothing less than to construct a picture of all reality, to comprehend its own origin and that of the universe, to discover the laws of both and prophesy their destiny. Is not the disproportion enormous? Are not confusions and profound contradictions to be looked for in an attempt to build so much out of so little?

George Santayana, Interpretations of Poetry and Religion

The desire to understand the natural world, including the need to gain some knowledge of its origins and the course of future events, seems to be an interest common to different groups of people. That may in part explain why cultures develop religion, myth, rites, and even art. A view along these lines was expressed by the

Spanish-born philosopher George Santayana—who, in reflecting upon the situation of the human mind in the natural world, noted that

> The resources of the mind are not commensurate with its ambition. . . . We have memory and we have certain powers of synthesis, abstraction, reproduction, invention—in a word, we have understanding. But this faculty of understanding has hardly begun its work of deciphering the hieroglyphics of sense and framing an idea of reality, when it is crossed by another faculty—the imagination.[1]

Santayana clearly believes that different faculties may be put to work to satisfy the human need to understand the natural world. Intellectual ones are responsible for rational understanding of that world, and their more sophisticated results make up what we call philosophy and science. But the need to understand may also trigger our imagination, in some cases producing such elaborate cultural realizations as religion, myth, and poetry. Santayana's views suggest that, as with knowledge and truth, there is more than one kind of understanding.

The plausibility of this is not difficult to see. We may recall that understanding is often more directed toward coming to terms with fundamental events of the natural world that affect our lives than toward achieving rational explanations and predictions of those phenomena. We have seen that people in different cultures have made efforts to understand the origins of the universe, but other contingencies of the natural world, such as those of birth, death, and sex, have also attracted widespread interest among human thinkers. A contemporary English philosopher of the social sciences, Peter Winch, argues that these essential elements of human life constitute a fundamental concern in every society. They operate as limiting notions in that any "conceptions of good and evil in human life will necessarily be connected with such concepts."[2] Winch notes that this position is traceable back at least to the Italian social thinker Giambattista Vico (1668–1744), for whom "all nations, barbarous as well as civilized, though separately founded . . . keep three customs: all have religion, all contract solemn marriages, all bury their dead."[3]

Let us say more modestly that most cultures have shown concern with understanding basic questions of human life, such as the origins of the universe and of life, death, and sex. In this way, we can recognize that there are some concerns common to nearly all cultures, without endorsing the existence of cultural universals. It is, after all, not easy to prove that some concept, belief, or preference is important for *all* groups of people.

What Would Santayana Say About Magic Thought and Prayers?

Santayana is in a position to hold that if the folk cosmologies of the Latin American Indians were not conducive to true and epistemically justified beliefs about the origins of the universe, that does not amount to denying that they might, instead, have arisen to fulfill other needs. Compare the use of prayer by Christians seeking, for example, God's intervention in events concerning their own health and welfare. Some of them surely believe that such intervention has sometimes occurred in miraculous ways. And to them, it seems not to matter that physical events generally follow their own natural courses, showing no sign of supernatural intervention in response to prayers. Since such believers continue, in spite of this, to offer their prayers, completely undisturbed by the empirical evidence, their situation is in fact as puzzling as that of the Mayans and Aztecs who believed in totally unsupported folk cosmologies. Arguably, even though in neither case could the practice be said to have achieved a rational understanding of past and future events of the natural world, the folk cosmology seems to have been implemented to provide practitioners with understanding of another sort. It is not surprising that different groups of people may have very different understandings of fundamental phenomena of the natural world since their conceptions of such limiting notions as birth, death, and sex vary radically from group to group.

According to Winch, "the importance of something to [a person] shows itself in all sorts of ways: not merely in precautions to safeguard that thing. He may want *to come to terms* with its importance to him in quite a different way: *to contemplate* it, *to gain some sense of his life in relation to it*." If this is correct, then even though the Mayan and Aztec texts may indeed count as sufficient evidence of these people's having accepted many doctrines that fail to be supported by reason, we need not deny that they cared about fundamental questions of the natural world and that their beliefs about them apparently fulfilled other needs. The beliefs may, for instance, have been formed because, like the prayers of Christians, they help those who accept them in expressing their "attitude to contingencies; one, that is, which involves recognition that one's life is subject to contingencies, rather that an attempt to control these."[4]

In light of Winch's view, one possible account of why the Mayans believed in the *Popol Vuh*'s folk cosmology may be as follows. There is conclusive evidence that this group cared greatly about understanding their surroundings since many documents testify to their efforts to measure, to calculate, and to predict various phenomena of the natural world. To them, certainty and order also mattered quite a bit, and so failure to understand the origins of the universe would probably have disturbed them greatly. Yet if this is plausible, it also explains why they cared so much about predicting future events in nature—a practice that, as we have seen in Chapter 1, led them to accept the astrological and prophetic predictions of the *Chilam Balam*. Similarly, the folk cosmology of the *Popol Vuh* may have brought certainty and order to the Mayans, who would otherwise have been disturbed by the unknown natural events at the beginning of their chronology and earlier. A very tentative hypothesis is that through belief in their folk cosmologies, these ancient peoples of Latin America attempted to impose a coherent schematic account on events in the natural world that would otherwise have been perceived by them as uncertain and chaotic. This hypothesis draws on some historical evidence[5] suggesting that certainty and order were held as fundamental by them.

Could Magic Really Help in
Understanding the Natural World?

It may be argued that, given historical circumstances, even if the ancient Latin American indigenous peoples did have an interest in achieving a rational understanding of nature, it was beyond their reach. For example, the Mayans and the Aztecs did not have the scientific theories and technologies required to devise accurate theories of the origin of the natural world or to allow really accurate predictions of future events. We have already seen that there are at least two different ways of going about understanding that world, namely,

> *Attitudinal Understanding of Events* =
> Typically, the outcome of practices leading to the acceptance of some fundamental phenomena of the natural world, such as its origins and human birth, death, and marriage.
> *Rational Understanding of Events* =
> The outcome of practices typically conducive to explaining and predicting some phenomena of the natural world, where these need not be events that directly affect the lives of people engaged in those practices.

Religion, myth, rite, and perhaps certain kinds of art now may be seen in a new light. Although they do not serve directly to fulfill cognitive ends, they tend nonetheless to contribute to the acceptance of certain important phenomena of the natural world, thus providing what we have called "attitudinal understanding" of those phenomena. As Santayana and Winch rightly insist, cognitive ends are but some of the goals humans care about. At the same time, it seems clear that only rational understanding can lead to the satisfaction of cognitive ends. Thus we can accommodate the indisputable fact that in nearly every culture humans are inclined to engage in intellectual practices that enable them to achieve some rational understanding of the natural world.

Of course, such understanding, unlike attitudinal understanding, is not restricted to phenomena that directly affect people's lives. In fact, there is a long and varied history of people's showing intense intellectual curiosity in phenomena so remote in either time or space (or both) that they could hardly be said to affect the course of their lives at all. Whether primitive chickens had teeth, for example, is surely not a question directly affecting our lives today, yet it is a matter of significant interest to paleontologists.[6]

It appears, then, that the native peoples of Latin America may not have differed so greatly from Westerners in the ways they went about understanding the natural world. Both made attempts not only at an attitudinal understanding of the natural world—by which they aimed (as we all still do) at coming to terms with the major contingencies of life—but also at a rational one. The Mayans' folk cosmology and magical predictions exemplify the former, but their astronomical calculations and systems of measurement show that they attempted the latter as well. Similarly, although Western philosophy and science are evidence of interest in a rational understanding of the natural world, that astrology exists in the West shows clearly that Westerners also engage in the sort of understanding that cannot fulfill any cognitive need.[7] Moreover, astrology in the West is far from an atypical case, for it coexists and competes with numerous similar practices, none of which could even begin to provide rational understanding of anything at all. (Think, for instance, of creation science, biorhythms, pyramidology, phrenology, and scientology.)

Relativism Revisited: The Linguistic Argument

If we are to accept different kinds of understanding, why not be pluralist also about philosophy and science, acknowledging that some ancient cultures of Latin America produced theories of the natural world that could qualify as philosophical and scientific? Although our account is in fact pluralist about understanding (for it allows that different people may go about understanding the natural world in ways that vary considerably), it need not be relativist. According to the cognitive relativist, if what philosophy and science actually are may likewise vary, depending on where and when the theories that make them up are proposed, then it would be the case that the Mayans' and the Aztecs' folk cosmologies count as philosophy. This view was introduced in Chapter 1, where we discussed some arguments both for and against it, none of which could be shown as conclusive.

Here I shall show that pluralism about understanding does not entail cognitive relativism—that is, the former may be true whereas the latter may be false. Relativism, however, proves attractive when invoked to determine whether non-Western cultures have had philosophy and science, in part because of a very common feature of our public language. In English, for instance, some words clearly change their meanings and references with variations in the context of their use. Thus *probability* means "frequency of occurrence" in some contexts but "strength of belief" in others. And when someone tells me, "I'll meet you at the bank," I rely on the context to know whether the person is making an appointment at a financial institution or someplace by the river.

According to this linguistic argument for cognitive relativism, if words such as *probability* and *bank* vary in this way, could not the same be said of *philosophy* and *science*? Then thinkers such as Bernardino de Sahagún, Samuel Ramos, and Miguel León-Portilla would be correct in using those terms to describe the cosmologies and related works of the indigenous peoples of Latin America. At the same time, José Vasconcelos, Bernard Williams, and A. C. Grayling would not be wrong in maintaining that the ancient Greeks invented the subject since (the relativist must say that) what the subject in fact *is* varies from culture to culture.

 But, under a closer scrutiny, any argument along such lines would fail, even when its premise seems clearly true, since it is beyond doubt that the meanings of certain strings of sounds or marks may vary with context. That by itself shows only that if the context changes in certain ways, some sounds or marks such as *bank* could be used to express different concepts and to refer to different things. It would be a mistake to infer, on the basis of such trivial linguistic phenomena alone, that there is no single, universal concept *bank*, which picks out instances of the same type of object in relevantly similar contexts—for example, either riverbanks or financial institutions. If this is correct, it would likewise be wrong to conclude, entirely on the basis of contextual variation in how people use the term, that there is no *philosophy*, conceived as a single, universal discipline. Were Sahagún to have a debate with Vasconcelos about that discipline, they would likely be talking about different things when each of them utters the locution "philosophy." But this is a trivial feature of language use, which can support no relativist conclusion about what constitutes science and philosophy.

A Contribution from Cultural Anthropology

A more interesting argument for relativism stems from the insights of some anthropologists working in the early twentieth century in the United States—Franz Boas (German-born, 1899–1942) and Ruth Benedict (1887–1948). They believed that a common obstacle for Westerners in studying remote cultures was their lack of toleration, and therefore they recommended that cultural anthropologists avoid passing judgments on such cultures. Others working in the same field followed suit, ultimately developing a view that became known as cultural relativism. One of its more thorough proponents, Melville Herskovits (1895–1963), often urged that "our body of tradition is but *one of many* such bodies—just as we today recognize that man is but one unit of the biological series."[8]

The claim is uncontroversial in assessments of, for example, what counts as having good manners and as being properly dressed. Clearly, not only do these vary greatly from culture to culture, but people who think that there is only one acceptable way of doing such things could rightly be accused of ethnocentrism—the view that the ways of life of one's own culture are better than those of other cultures. The cultural relativist often takes examples involving rules of courtesy and codes of dressing to argue for his "tough-minded philosophy," which requires the replacement of ethnocentrism with the thesis that

> All cultural judgments are based on experience, and experience is interpreted by each individual in terms of his own enculturation.[9]

Yet each of the claims made in this thesis, when considered independently, is in fact quite trivial. Each is easily acceptable, and therefore "soft." The first claim (that all cultural judgments are based on experience) seems sensitive to the concern of Boas and Benedict, which led to their suggestion that observers should avoid ethnocentric bias in evaluating a different culture. The second claim (that experience is interpreted by each individual in terms of his own enculturation) appears to be a simple recognition that *any* such evaluation would rest on the observer's own experience. That is, there is no neutral way of judging the practices of an alien culture since the terms of any such evaluation must presuppose one's own assumptions and conceptual schemes. Note that this does not logically imply that such evaluations would lack objectivity. So, if that is what the relativist really has in mind in his second claim, he owes us an argument to support it. And why, exactly, does Herskovits take his cultural relativism (a combination of cognitive and moral relativism) to be a "tough-minded philosophy" at all?

Avoiding Ethnocentrism

It can only be because Herskovits seeks to avoid ethnocentrism, and he reasons that, since evaluations of cultures other than one's own are made in terms of one's own assumptions and conceptual schemes, any such evaluation therefore must fall into ethnocentricism. His argument then would run as follows:

1. All evaluations of a culture other than one's own are made in terms of one's own assumptions and conceptual schemes.

Therefore,

2. All evaluations of a culture other than one's own are ethnocentric.
3. Ethnocentrism is wrong.

Therefore,
4. It is wrong to make any evaluation of a culture other than
    one's own.

Construed in this way, the relativist's argument is invalid—that is,
his premises could be true but the conclusions false. This amounts
to saying, first, that there is no entailment between premise (1) and
conclusion (2)—or, equivalently, that (2) does not follow deductively from (1). Clearly, when any person evaluates the ways of life
of other cultures, she must use her own assumptions and conceptual
schemes. But it is simply false that her judgments must always be
ethnocentric. Without much imagination, we could think of a person who, unlike the ethnocentric, sometimes praises the ways of life
of other cultures. And it is not farfetched to imagine someone (probably someone you know) who is the reverse of an ethnocentric: She
always praises the ways of life of societies she thinks of as exotic
and criticizes those of her own. Thus, not only does (2) fail to follow from (1), but it also seems false; therefore it cannot lend support to the conclusion of the above argument.

Getting Tough-Minded

Note that Herskovits is certainly tough-minded when he takes cultural relativism to have a consequence that is both evaluative and
normative—viz.,

> *NR* It is wrong to pass judgments on any culture other than one's
> own.

Since *NR* may be taken to amount to a prescription telling us that
we ought to abstain from doing something that is wrong, the cultural relativist claim does, under that construal, certainly appear
provocative and therefore tough-minded. For our present purposes,
the view entails that it is wrong to pass judgment on the question of
whether the native peoples of America had philosophy and science
since there is no possible neutral standpoint from which to make

those judgments. Clearly, we could not help using our own notions of what those disciplines are. Yet if this is correct, then a similar argument must also be run for other disciplines, for the same could be said of astronomy, chemistry, biology, physics, and each of the other sciences. We would then be committed to holding that what the sciences are varies from culture to culture, so it would be more appropriate to speak of "astronomies," "chemistries," and so on. Now something has gone wrong in this argument, for relativism in this form appears to lead to an absurd conclusion. Do we really think that anything goes in matters scientific? By parity of reasoning, we should also have to say that anything goes in matters philosophical.

Pluralism Without Cultural Relativism

An open-minded view of what counts as philosophy and as science need not be based on conceding the truth of cultural relativism. A cognitive pluralist, for example, could take philosophical and scientific theories to be artifacts that differ from other human-made tools in that the former are devised to facilitate the performance of intellectual tasks—among which figure prominently the rational understanding of theoretical questions and the solving of scientific puzzles. A pluralist may hold that although human tools in general vary greatly according to where and when they are made, some of them that are created to facilitate the performance of common practical tasks resemble each other sufficiently so that in spite of their diversity, they can be identified as axes, hammers, knives, and the like.

In this case, pluralism seems a correct view. Not all groups have gone about the business of making knives and axes in the same way, nor have all achieved the same degree of artistry in producing them. Moreover, pluralism does not entail that anything goes. Since axes are made for chopping, we can say not only that steel axes are better at it—and could thus be considered a step forward in development compared to those made out of stone—but that electric ones are an improvement compared to other mechanical axes. Under optimal circumstances of use (sufficiently sharpened, handled by those who know how to use them, and so on), such objects exhibit varying degrees of efficiency at performing their functions, with some of them being more primitive versions of the others. Here pluralism seems plausible, for it concedes the existence of cross-cultural differences while allowing common evaluations of ordinary tools in terms of their efficiency at performing certain tasks.

Similarly, with philosophical and scientific theories, different groups of people will formulate them in ways that differ greatly. But as with practical tools, a pluralist approach to philosophy and science need not entail that anything goes. To see this, recall that to be a tool of a certain kind (ordinarily conceived), an object must in principle be able to perform some defining functions under optimal circumstances. Now imagine a remote tribe who makes gigantic, ax-shaped sculptures to be used in some religious ceremonies. Furthermore, suppose that the tribe's world is quite similar to ours in other respects and that such sculptures could not be used for chopping, even under optimal circumstances, since they are too big and are made out of a clay, a material far too soft for that purpose. The obvious intuition here is that even though the sculptures may have religious and aesthetic uses, they are not axes as such tools are ordinarily conceived. This seems to support the view that practical tools are defined by their dispositional properties: What makes an artifact an ax instead of a knife or a spade is that, under optimal circumstances, it would be useful in performing a certain function (viz., chopping).

Surely, the view that the ancient Aztecs went about making practical tools in ways that differed radically from, say, those of early modern Westerners is pluralist. But is it relativist? A relativist view of tools would hold that the defining function of practical tools may vary according to context, so that what axes, knives, and other tools really are depends upon the culture where they were made, and there is no universal concept of an ax or a knife. At some point, such relativism becomes untenable. In our example, if the members of the tribe were to believe as a result of an illusion that their sculptures really were axes, their belief would be false. Those objects simply cannot count as axes because, given the assumptions of our thought experiment, they could never perform the defining function of axes, even under optimal circumstances. And if we were to discover that the tribe has in fact a broader concept of axes (e.g., one that denotes all ax-shaped objects), we should still not have to concede that relativism is true. Rather, we may conclude that we had been misunderstanding such people all along.

Completing the Analogy

How, exactly, does all this bear on intellectual artifacts such as philosophy and science? Pluralism here is the view that different cultures approach philosophy and science in different ways. Moreover, it holds that not all cultures have in fact developed similar artifacts of this sort and that (where comparisons are possible) some have formulated better intellectual tools than others. In this view, philosophical and scientific theories are, like tools, also defined in terms of their functions, but here the sort of usefulness in which their role is defined is less practical than cognitive. Consider axes and knives again: What makes a piece of steel a knife rather than an ax is its disposition to perform a certain characteristic function under optimal circumstances. By analogy, what makes a body of beliefs a philosophical theory rather than a myth is the role it would play in ideal conditions with regard to certain cognitive goals of human beings. Once we agree on what the goals of philosophical and scientific theories are, then we have found the key to defining those intellectual artifacts.

In this pluralistic view, it could be acknowledged that the ancient Aztecs pursued fundamental human cognitive goals in ways that differed radically from those of, for instance, early modern Westerners. But does that entail relativism? Recall that the latter is the thesis that the defining functions of intellectual tools may vary from culture to culture so that what philosophy and science *are* may likewise differ radically. In fact, a definition of either term could never be said to hold universally but would rather always be relativized to the groups that practice them. Thus the relativist concludes that there is no universal sense of *philosophy*, but only a great variety of *philosophies*. Yet if our analogy with practical tools is sound, pluralism without relativism is an available option that allows cultural variation without leading to the absurd conclusion that anything goes in matters philosophical and scientific.

Philosophy, Science, and World Cultures

What account can a pluralist give of the origins of such intellectual artifacts as philosophy and science? As we have seen, these are usually thought to be the legacy of ancient Greece, whose thinkers first produced rationalist and physicalist theories of the origin of the universe and later showed increasing interest in the more general questions of determining what exists, what can be known, and how we should live. It is also well known that other cultures, such as the Chinese and the Indian, made contributions to the development of philosophy and science. Then why not consider that the cultural achievements of ancient Latin American peoples such as the Mayans and Aztecs may have contributed to that development?

We have seen that according to Sahagún, León-Portilla, and some others, there was philosophy among the natives of Latin America, but their evidence was in fact too weak to support that conclusion. Clearly, the doctrines of the *Popol Vuh* and other documents left by these indigenous peoples are cultural achievements that attest to their material, intellectual, emotional, and religious ways of life, and it seems uncontroversial to hold that they made up diverse cultures with achievements meriting equal consideration with those of other cultures. Why, then, is such consideration never given?

Francisco Romero: Not All Cultures Are Created Equal

The Argentinian philosopher Francisco Romero (Spanish-born, 1891–1962) offers a possible answer:

> The fact that, out of the many cultures which have appeared in history, only three survive—the Indian, the Chinese, and the Occidental—seems to suggest that these three possess some particular advantage over the others. In my judgment, this superiority

consists in the fact that the three, in contrast to all others, contain an answer (each a radically different one, of course) to the most profound and permanent questions and needs of man. Man is not only the one being that objectifies, he is also a being that objectifies endlessly and untiringly, and he needs the goal and lodestar of a supreme and absolute object to set his mind at rest. Every culture is likely to have aspired to satisfying this need. But while others were unable to supply more than myths, which in the course of time wear out and lose their charm, or halfway goals that proved unsatisfactory, the three mentioned above have each found a great clue or goal which has determined their organization.[10]

This assertion plainly implies that the cultures of the indigenous peoples of Latin America, among others, were inferior compared to the Indian, the Chinese, and the Occidental cultures. If Romero is right, the consequence would indeed be unfortunate, for then the pervasive neglect of indigenous Latin American cultures would be entirely justified. But before conceding Romero's claim, let us look at his reasons.

The "Species Chauvinism" Objection Against Romero

What shall we say are the necessary conditions for a group of people to create a culture? Must they include the development of art, religion, laws, political institutions, technology, science, and philosophy? If so, then since, as we have seen, the indigenous peoples of Latin America did not have *all* of these, it would follow that they did not have a culture. Yet a conception of culture that makes it equivalent to such cultural achievements puts the cart before the horse. We may instead follow Romero in holding that cultures are a necessary condition for such achievements as art, laws, or philosophy to arise. In his view, cultures are the media where those elements of civilization can flourish.

But Romero's views on culture are more troubling when he takes this notion to serve to differentiate humans from other animals.

"The inner world of an animal is dim," writes Romero, "and the larger part of it remains hermetically sealed. The human world, on the other hand, grows ever clearer, opens up more and more, and develops into a world of explicit contents which are largely communicable."[11] Romero aims to differentiate humans and other animals by invoking the notion of intentionality, which was very important to medieval thinkers but later largely forgotten until the work of Franz Brentano in the late nineteenth century.[12] In one way, this seems reasonable, for we humans are crucially intentional animals. Intentionality applies to phenomena that have meaning, have content, or simply are about something. A characteristic of all human cultures is that we develop very complex systems of communication and use them to utter sounds or write strings of marks that usually have meanings, have contents, or are about things. But some of our mental states seem likewise to be intentional, for we have thoughts, beliefs, desires, fears, and hopes, and these have contents—since they are always the thought, belief, or the fear that something is the case. Moreover, we have created paintings, statues, movies, religious rituals, and theories of many different kinds, all of which indeed have contents: They are about something.

It is not clear, however, that the line separating humans from other animals can be drawn this way. Certain nonhuman animals seem to use intentional systems of communication, and there is no shortage of experts arguing that they have mastered codes that amount to languages. Moreover, why think that cats and dogs, for instance, do not have any mental states possessing content at all? Do we really want to assert that they are unable to entertain beliefs and desires? Romero's views on intentionality appear to lead to "species chauvinism."

He could avoid this objection, however, by acknowledging, as he has, that the "animals nearest to man seem to execute some objectifications," although they do so "precariously and sporadically."[13] For Romero, the first stage in developing a culture is when the intelligence of certain agents transforms the input of sensations into perceptions of objects—a process he calls "objectifying." This is followed by the agents' development of intentional systems of signs. In this view, then, until reality has been "objectified and fixed in signs with objective meaning" by some agents and accepted within their group, no culture can develop.

Now Romero is in a position to grant that nonhuman animals may be able to create intentional communities (i.e., they may indeed develop systems of signs that are eventually accepted for communication within their group) and even achieve what he calls "objective culture" (i.e., the result of the process by which a being's intelligence transforms perceptual input into objects). But he could nonetheless insist that nonhuman animals lack intentional consciousness (such as self-awareness and critical reasoning), which arguably amounts to a "primary," and perhaps exclusive, feature of humans. Since this last point is plausible, Romero seems to avoid being trapped by the "species chauvinism" objection. His problems are not over, however, since he must now respond to another objection that may present him with an uphill battle. We still want to know, what grounds are there for thinking that some cultures are superior to others?

Is There a Natural Selection of Cultures?

To call a culture superior is to make a certain evaluative claim about it: It is to claim that it has some "good-making" properties. And, for Romero, evaluative properties such as those of being a superior culture or an inferior one seem to be cashed out in terms of natural selection, for they are clearly connected to the concept of fitness for survival. Romero assumes that fitness for survival is indicative of cultural superiority, so in his view, the cultures of the native peoples of America come out as inferior. In the passage quoted above, we are told that the disadvantage or inferiority of some cultures is evident from their inability to provide anything more than myths when it comes to understanding the fundamental questions humans ask about their world. Suppose that an adequate explanation is one that truly gives an answer. His argument then seems to be as follows:

1. Only cultures that have produced adequate explanations of the most fundamental human questions are fit for survival.
2. Myths give no adequate explanation of the most fundamental human questions.

Therefore,

3. Cultures that have nothing more than mythological explanations of the most fundamental human questions are not fit for survival.
4. The cultures of the ancient indigenous peoples of America had nothing more than mythological explanations of the most fundamental human questions.

Therefore,

5. The cultures of the ancient indigenous peoples of America were not fit for survival.

Although it may appear that this argument rests on evolutionary theory of natural selection, its premises would find no support in any serious version of Darwinism. So the odds are that they rely heavily on some historicist variety of evolutionism. Romero is not alone, however, in trying to ground his views (about culture, in this case) in natural selection. Many twentieth-century philosophers appeal to that notion in their attempts to justify various theories and methods. For example, the American philosopher W. V. O. Quine, among others, seems to believe that certain kinds of reasoning (for example, induction) may be justified by the realization that "[c]reatures inveterately wrong in their inductions have a pathetic but praiseworthy tendency to die out before reproducing their kind."[14]

Romero's appeal to natural selection, as well as Quine's and those of many others, carries little weight. Not only is there no scientific evidence that natural selection works as envisaged by these thinkers, but all the available scientific information points to a quite different conclusion. For one thing, in evolutionary biology, natural selection is but one of many processes that determine whether a species survives.[15] Even if we ignore this complication, we find that Romero's argument is beset by larger problems. Why does he think that there is a connection between a certain culture's having adequate explanations of questions important to humans and its being more fit for survival? The passage cited earlier fails even to begin to make a plausible case for the existence of any such connection.

In addition, it leaves us completely in the dark about the alleged connection on the other end. How does a culture's having only mythological explanations to important questions leads to its becoming extinct? In fact, it is not difficult to see that there is no causal connection of that sort since belief in myths may actually have survival value. For example, in remote tropical regions of Paraguay and northern Argentina, many descendants of an indigenous group, the Guarani, still believe in an ancient myth according to which on a certain afternoon of a summer day, the sun knowingly and intentionally brought about some tragedy to those exposed to it. Since for many centuries the Guarani have accepted the absolute veracity of this myth, they generally refuse to be under the sun at noon and during the siesta hours (the early afternoon). Surely anything that results in staying away from the sun in the summer at the time of day when it is at its peak, and especially in the tropics, may safely be said to have survival value. For we now know that the chances of getting skin cancer, eye damage, headaches, and other ailments are reduced by such avoidance. This example, then, seems to run counter to Romero's assumption about the negative correlation between myth-believing and survival because it shows that belief is some myths may actually enhance the prospects for survival.

It is clear now that Romero's argument is suspicious, for although there are some practices like those of the Guarani that appear to belie it, there is no clear evidence in the offing to support it. Moreover, it may be argued that the assumption is objectionable on moral grounds since it entails that certain cultures are superior and others inferior, and in matters cultural, such claims often rest on nothing more than ethnocentrism. As discussed above, this is a form of prejudice that may easily undermine our judgments about alien cultures. "The primary mechanism that directs the evaluation of culture," warns Herskovits, "is *ethnocentrism*. Ethnocentrism is the point of view that one's own way of life is to be preferred to all others. . . .

[I]t characterizes the way most individuals feel about their own culture, whether or not they verbalize their feeling."[16]

In fact, the cultures of the indigenous peoples of Latin America have been disparaged by a long and varied tradition of ethnocentrism, and it is difficult to avoid the suspicion that Romero's position (at least, when he reasons as in the above passage) falls within it. And if his position is ethnocentric, it must be rejected. A more cautious attitude would be to conclude that the ancient indigenous peoples of Latin America had cultures that were rich and insightful in ways that deserve respect. We need only recall their achievements, documented in many written texts such as the books of *Chilam Balam* and *Popol Vuh* as well as in the testimonies of those who, like Sahagún and León-Portilla, have made significant contributions toward preserving the cultural patrimony of these people.

Discussion Questions

1. Following a suggestion by George Santayana, we have in this chapter distinguished two kinds of understanding. Summarize that distinction and give two examples of social practices that illustrate each kind.

2. Santayana posits that imagination is sometimes needed to interpret the content of sense experience and thus to produce a picture of reality. But does imagination aim at cognition? What does *cognition* mean, anyhow? In light of the distinction between attitudinal and rational understanding, where would you place imagination?

3. Peter Winch offers an account of Christian prayer that could be extended to explain the magic beliefs of Latin American native peoples. What would that further account say? Do you find that explanation reasonable?

4. According to cultural anthropologists, ethnocentrism must be avoided in passing judgment on the ways of life of other ethnic groups. But what, exactly, is ethnocentrism? Give an example of a common ethnocentric judgment about people of Hispanic culture, together with a reason against that judgment.

5. In "Cultural Relativism and Cultural Values" (p. 26), Melville Herskovits rejects descriptions of traditional societies as "simple,"

"savage," and "primitive" on the grounds that these terms amount
to disparaging evaluations of the groups in question. He writes,

> Some of the characteristics held to distinguish "primi-
> tive" or "savage" ways of life are open to serious ques-
> tion. What, for example, is a "simple" culture?. . . The
> natives of Peru, before the Spanish conquest, made ta-
> pestries of finer weave, dyed in colors less subject to de-
> terioration, than any of the deservedly prized Gobelin ta-
> pestries.

If the tapestries of the natives of Peru were in fact more finely
wrought than European Gobelins, what would that show about
the complexity of the societies where such works were produced?
Evaluate this argument.

6. Cultural relativists take their view to be "tough-minded." But is it
    really? If yes, why? If not, why not?

7. Relativism about philosophy has been criticized on the grounds
    that it leads to an anything-goes mentality regarding what can
    count as philosophical. Formulate the objection.

8. In "Man and Culture," Francisco Romero holds that animals do
    not really see objects at all but are instead in the situation we hu-
    mans are in when we contemplate a painting from close up—see-
    ing nothing but color blotches. This claim, however, seems vulner-
    able to the "species chauvinist" objection. What is that objection?
    In light of it, could Romero still maintain his claim?

9. Romero argues that "intentionality in itself suffices to open a gulf
    between man and animal" ("Man and Culture," p. 399). What
    does *intentionality* mean here? Could it be used as a criterion to dis-
    tinguish humans from other animals? If so, how? If not, why not?

10. According to Romero ("Man and Culture," p. 405), Indian cul-
    ture cares about the "cosmic sense of the whole," while Chinese
    culture puts the emphasis on social reality. He writes,

> Only the Occident is concerned with the concept of time;
> only the Occident really has history. . . . The process of
> history has been defined by the greatest Occidental
> thinkers as a march toward "humanity" . . . or toward
> freedom, or again as a progressive realization of the
> most exalted values.

Does this passage contain any argument? If not, what are the consequences for Romero's view?

11. As the above passage makes clear, Romero seems to think that there is only one conception of history and that only the West has it. Is that claim reasonable? How could Romero support it? Could the relativist agree with Romero on this?

12. Is Romero's claim about history vulnerable to any objection? If so, state it. If not, explain why you agree with him. Could Romero be a cognitive pluralist about history? Discuss.

Suggestions for Further Reading

Benedict, Ruth. 1934. *Patterns of Culture*. Boston: Houghton Mifflin.

Dascal, Marcelo. 1991. *Cultural Relativism and Philosophy: North and Latin American Perspectives*. Leiden: E. J. Brill.

Herskovits, Melville J. 1972. *Cultural Relativism: Perspectives in Cultural Pluralism*. New York: Random House.

León-Portilla, Miguel. 1966. "Pre-Hispanic Thought." In Mario de la Cueva, *Major Trends in Mexican Philosophy*. Notre Dame, Ind.: University of Notre Dame Press.

Northrop, F. S. C., ed. 1949. *Ideological Differences and World Order: Studies in the Philosophy and Science of the World's Cultures*. New Haven: Yale University Press.

Olivé, León. 1991. "Conceptual Relativism and Philosophy in the Americas." In Marcelo Dascal, *Cultural Relativism and Philosophy*. Leiden: E. J. Brill.

Ramos, Samuel. 1943. *Historia de la filosofía en México*. Mexico City, Mexico: Imp. Universitaria.

Romero, Francisco. 1949. "Man and Culture" In F. S. C. Northrop, ed., *Ideological Differences and World Order*. New Haven: Yale University Press.

———. 1950. "The Human Personality and the Cosmos." *The Humanist* 5:210–213.

———. 1964. *Theory of Man*. Berkeley: University of California Press.

Sahagún, Bernardino de. 1982. *General History of the Things of New Spain*, Books 4 & 6. Salt Lake City: University of Utah Press.

Santayana, George. 1989. *Interpretations of Poetry and Religion*. Cambridge, Mass.: MIT Press.

Notes

1. George Santayana, "Understanding, Imagination, and Mysticism," in *Interpretations of Poetry and Religion* (Cambridge, Mass.: MIT Press, 1989), pp. 7–8.

2. Peter Winch, "Understanding a Primitive Society," in Bryan R. Wilson, ed., *Rationality* (Worcester: Basil Blackwell, 1970), p. 111.

3. Giambattista Vico, *The New Science*, paragraphs 332–333 (cited in Winch, "Understanding a Primitive Society," p. 111).

4. Winch, "Understanding a Primitive Society," pp. 104–105. Emphasis mine.

5. See Eugene R. Craine and Reginald C. Reindorp, *Preliminary Study to the Codex Pérez and the Book of Chilam Balam of Maní,* and Miguel León-Portilla, *Aztec Thought and Culture* (Norman, Okla.: University of Oklahoma Press, 1963) and *Endangered Cultures* (Dallas: Southern Methodist University, 1990).

6. In 1980, E. J. Kollar and C. Fisher reported the results of experiments to prove that chickens retain, in latent state, their genetic capability for developing teeth. For an interesting discussion of that report, see Stephen J. Gould, *Hen's Teeth and Horse's Toes* (New York: W. W. Norton, 1983).

7. It has recently been argued that astrology may in fact be an ancestor of scientific psychology since it constitutes an attempt to predict human behavior on the basis of certain (false) cause/effect connections. See Paul Thagard, "Why Astrology Is a Pseudoscience," in P. Asquith and I. Hacking, eds., *Proceedings of the Philosophy of Science Association* 1 (1972), pp. 223–234.

8. Melville J. Herskovits, "Culture: Definition and Values," in *Cultural Relativism: Perspectives in Cultural Pluralism* (New York: Random House, 1972), p. 10. Emphasis mine.

9. Herskovits, "Culture: Definition and Values," pp. 11 and ff.

10. Francisco Romero, "Man and Culture," in F. S. C. Northrop, ed., *Ideological Differences and World Order* (New Haven: Yale University Press, 1949), p. 403.

11. Romero, "Man and Culture," p. 391.

12. Franz Brentano was a German philosopher (1838–1917), the founder of "act psychology," or intentionalism.

13. Romero, "Man and Culture," p. 399.

14. "Natural Kinds," reprinted in W. V. O. Quine, *Ontological Relativity* (New York: Columbia University Press, 1969), p. 126.

15. For a good discussion of natural selection and epistemic justification, see Stephen Stich, *The Fragmentation of Reason* (Cambridge, Mass.: MIT Press, 1991).

16. Herskovits, "Cultural Relativism and Cultural Values," in *Cultural Relativism,* p. 21.

5

THOMISTIC PHILOSOPHY AND THE CONQUEST: HUMAN RIGHTS IN THE NEW WORLD

The bow-using Caribs . . . and most of those who live along the coast, eat human flesh. They do not take slaves, nor are they friendly to their enemies or foreigners. They eat all men that they kill and the women they capture, and the children they bear—if any Carib should couple with them—are also eaten. The boys that they take from foreigners are castrated, fattened, and eaten.

Gonzalo Fernández de Oviedo y Valdés,
Natural History of the West Indies

The Europeans and Indians who met in Latin America in 1492 could hardly have been more different in their customs and worldviews. They looked upon each other in much the way we would with alien beings from a distant galaxy. Given this apparent incompatibility, a violent encounter may have been unavoidable. But could those differences provide moral justification for the Europeans' waging war against the native peoples of the New World?

And when the actions taken by colonial powers led directly to outcomes where natives were deprived of their freedom, property, and lives, did not that amount to a violation of fundamental human rights? In this chapter, we shall consider the morality of the Iberian Conquest and ask whether an appeal to radical cultural diversity could justify the depredations carried out in its name.

Human Rights: A Moral Dilemma

Lest we rise too hastily to condemn Spain and Portugal for their actions during the Conquest, we must ask what, if anything, those who perpetrated them were morally permitted (or even obliged) to do when confronted with peoples whose practices appeared openly repugnant. As is well known, according to popular chronicles of the Conquest, the indigenous peoples of Latin America often engaged in human sacrifice and cannibalism. The Aztecs, the Incas, and the Caribs are portrayed as ordinarily killing and eating their prisoners of war, including women and children. It was long assumed that such narratives lacked credibility since their authors were mostly Spaniards and Portuguese participating in the Conquest. But now there is evidence that many of these stories are at least approximately true. Giving some *conquistadores* and colonists the benefit of the doubt, we may well believe that they were horrified at the practices they saw among the natives. Should we not then conclude that their interference was ethically permissible and even mandatory?

Clearly, we are faced with a dilemma when we attempt to ask whether the Conquest could be justified morally. On the one hand, the actions of many *conquistadores* and colonists plainly violated the Indians' rights to freedom, property, and life. Yet the Europeans' intervention with certain practices of the natives may have been ethically justified, for under normal circumstances, if an action is wrong, then there are moral grounds for interference.

Ordinarily, claims to life have the force of a universal right. But then, given that human sacrifice and cannibalism as practiced by some groups of Indians violated that right, the colonists' interference with those practices was at least *prima facie* justified—in other words, it was justified in the absence of more stringent considerations to the contrary. The argument runs as follows:

1. Violation of any universal human right is morally repugnant and provides a *prima facie* moral justification for interference.
2. If killing people for the purpose of human sacrifice (cannibalism and the like) violates a universal human right, then that practice provides a *prima facie* justification for interference.
3. Killing people for the purpose of human sacrifice (cannibalism and the like) violates a universal human right.
4. Some Latin American Indians killed people for the purpose of human sacrifice (cannibalism and the like).

Therefore,

5. The Europeans' interference with that practice was *prima facie* morally justified.

The first and second premises of this argument are grounded in a common intuition about universal human rights or "natural rights" (as they were called at the time of the Conquest). It is often thought that people have certain rights just because they are people and that such rights are moral ones since they remain even when they may not be protected by positive law, which comprises the statutes established by legislative authority within nations. Rights of this sort have been defined in various ways, but for our purposes here we shall assume that

> An individual (or a group) has a right if and only if she has a justified claim with the normative force of limiting the actions of others in a certain way.[1]

The notion of a right is crucial to Western thought, yet it has long been a point of controversy as well. Philosophers who have written about rights may be divided roughly into three distinct groups. "Absolutists" believe that rights are fundamental moral claims that are unconditional since they hold no matter what. "Universalists" take them to be important moral claims that hold under normal circumstances, though with possible exceptions. And "skeptics" think that rights are empty concepts—perhaps the products of medieval imagination. The above argument is incompatible with the empty concept view of skeptics since it rests on the common intuition that there are human rights. At the same time, the argument need not commit to absolutism, for it is compatible with the universalist position that, under special circumstances, a human right may be outweighed by other moral considerations. Thus, to say that an individual has the right to life is to maintain that no one is justified in killing her—unless the circumstances are such that other reasons outweigh that right. And since people are commonly said to have a right of that sort, premises (1) and (2) in the above argument seem well supported.

But (3) is also plausible because the killing of prisoners of war, especially for the purpose of human sacrifice or cannibalism, is clearly a violation of the right to life of the victims. If there is a right to life, then under normal circumstances, it holds universally—it is, in other words, possessed by humans no matter where or when they live. Thus any actions that violate that right are (at least *prima facie*) morally wrong. Would not we, today, object to any society's having such a practice on the ground that it amounts to cruel treatment of human beings and a flagrant violation of their right to life? And would not we further claim that the existence of any such practice provides a sound moral reason justifying intervention—and even the use of force, if required—to stop it? But then, because there is evidence supporting premise (4)—and we may assume that some Europeans acted out of a genuine belief that human sacrifice and cannibalism were violations of the natural rights of humans—it is difficult to see how their attempt to interfere with those practices could be morally unjustified. This argument seems sound, so we must accept its conclusion.

The reasoning here may yet be faulty since it ignores another morally relevant consideration. Assuming that the means chosen to achieve a certain end do matter in moral evaluation, can it be permissible to interfere with an action that is morally wrong by doing what is also morally wrong? To justify the conquest and colonization of Latin America with the argument offered above, the *conquistadores'* and colonists' own actions must be clearly better compared with the practices they were attempting to prevent.

Although it is easy to criticize the ethnocentrism of the *conquistadores* and the colonists, it is in fact possible to find arguments on their behalf. Some have held that, on the whole, Europeans brought civilization to the New World and that *that* good outweighed any harm visited upon the native peoples. Proponents of this view have further claimed that the natives were incapable of suffering harm or moral injury at all, simply because, given their "barbaric" practices, they could not count as full-fledged people. Yet this claim seems to rest on the dubious assumption that beings whose ways of life differed from Europeans' ways of life could not qualify as human. And it also presupposes that only the latter could be the bearers of rights—and therefore subjects of moral injury when deprived of them. Clearly these assumptions are open to objection, and in fact, the first was at the center of heated philosophical disputes in the sixteenth century.

It did not go unnoticed by some intellectuals of the early modern period that the natives of the New World did have the faculty of reason, then considered the defining element of human nature. Some philosophers and members of the clergy argued that claims to the contrary were based on nothing more than prejudice, lacking any support in the available evidence. Once it was acknowledged that the natives were human beings, then what argument, if any, could be offered for regarding the conquest of the natives as something good for them? The facts seem to speak for themselves, for they show beyond dispute that the Iberian Conquest led to the wholesale massacre, dispossession, and subjugation of the Indians and the destruction of their traditional ways of life.

A belief popular at the time, however, had it that any such depredation was only instrumental harm that was fully justified by the greater good of eternal salvation. Provided that the natives were converted into the Roman Catholic faith, perceived as a good in itself that could outweigh any directly caused bad result, they actually had been made better off, no matter what they had lost. Although religious conversion seems to have been an important motive of the Iberian Conquest, the notion that it could somehow be a reason to justify moral injury does not hold up under closer examination. The grounds for pursuing such a conversion are open to rational criticism, for, unless some highly disputable theological doctrines are assumed, why think that belief in the teachings of the Roman Catholic Church was a good for the indigenous peoples at all? They, after all, already had their own religions before the arrival of Europeans, so the assumption required to justify conversion (viz., that the religion of the latter was to be preferred) must also be supported by plausible reasons. Yet could any such reason be offered?

Finally—given that in deliberations about the moral status of actions it is not only ends that matter but also the intentions of agents and their means—any assessment of the morality of the Conquest must consider how the actions of the Spaniards and the Portuguese should be assessed on those counts. Before turning to these, we shall first look more closely at the claim that the Europeans and the indigenous cultures were radically different.

Conflict of Cultures and of Religions, Too

Spain and Portugal undertook the conquest of Latin America as an exercise of devotion to the Christian faith. It was, many believed, a sacred war, similar in relevant respects to the religious crusades of the Middle Ages and to the later campaigns of the Spaniards to expel the "infidel" from the Iberian Peninsula. When the Catholic monarchs of Spain decided to sponsor Christopher Columbus's expeditions to foreign lands, they surely thought of those trips as fulfilling a religious purpose, the expansion of the Roman Catholic faith. Columbus[2] himself apparently intended his mission (in what he erroneously believed to be the Indies) as aiming, at least in part, at the religious conversion of the natives—often writing in his various journals and letters that he had been designated directly by God to act as His instrument in that undertaking.

Beyond doubt, then, the conflict that ensued with Columbus's expeditions was one of religions. But, as illustrated in his numerous references to the customs and appearance of the inhabitants of the "Indies," the conflict also involved the values and ways of life of entire peoples. Further evidence of radical cultural difference can be found in popular chronicles of the events and discoveries in the New World—with those of Bernal Díaz del Castillo (Spanish, 1492—ca.1581) and Gonzalo Fernández de Oviedo y Valdés (Spanish, 1478–1557) at the top of a very long list.[3]

Columbus enthusiastically chronicled his own discoveries of radical cultural differences in his diaries, often registering disappointment over the natives' appearance and issuing harsh judgments on their ways of life. Even when he appears to be praising a group of Indians, closer attention to his words invariably shows that he is in fact criticizing their culture, their character traits, or their physical appearance. For example, his observation that they "give everything they have for a very low price" and are "very free from wickedness and unwarlike"[4] are misleading to contemporary readers since they seem to suggest that Columbus is expressing approval of some qualities of the natives. But when understood in the proper historical context, it becomes clear that they are rather intended as criticisms. Within Columbus's worldview, generosity and peacefulness amounted to inferior qualities, incompatible with characteristics that Europeans of the end of the fifteenth century thought it desirable for men to have. As Beatriz Pastor Bodmer points out, among these were individualism and belligerence, both required by the spirit of enterprise that was expected of men of action in the early modern period.[5]

Some of Columbus's opinions on the customs and character traits of the natives are more straightforward, with no contextual information needed to see them as evidence of a deep conflict of cultures. In many passages of his journals and letters, it is transparent that (like many other Europeans), when confronted with the ways of life of the indigenous peoples, he reacted with amazement and disapproval. In one entry, he writes,

[A]ll go naked, men and women, as their mothers bore them. . . .
They have no iron or steel or weapons, nor are they fitted to use

them. This is not because they are not well built and of handsome
stature, but because they are very marvelously timorous. . . . I
have sent ashore two or three men . . . and as soon as they have
seen my men approaching, they have fled, a father not even waiting for his son. . . . It is true that, after they have been reassured
and have lost this fear, they are so guileless and so generous with
all that they possess, that no one would believe it who has not
seen it. . . . They are content with whatever trifle of whatever kind
that may be given to them, whether it be of value or valueless.[6]

Europeans soon learned that some Indians had practices of a
more shocking sort. The information that the Caribs were fierce
combatants in war and even eaters of human flesh reached Europe
in the narratives of many travelers, beginning with Columbus himself. He concluded that those peoples were similar to other natives
in that they all seemed malformed and strange. According to him, it
was chiefly the ferocity of the Caribs that distinguished them from
other groups of Indians, whom he perceived as "cowardly to an excessive degree."[7] In addition, Columbus often showed his contempt
for these peoples in general by referring to them in terms ordinarily
used to designate animals and even inanimate objects: They were
"cattle," "beasts," and "things." He counted them as if they were
indeed animals, using the common expression "heads of" women or
men. That Columbus saw these creatures as fit only for involuntary
servitude becomes apparent:

> It was so that yesterday there came to the side of the ship a boat
> with six youths, and five came on board the ship: I ordered them
> to be kept and will bring them with me. And afterwards I sent to
> a house which is near the river to the west, and they brought
> *seven head of women*, small and large, and three children. I did
> this, in order that the men might conduct themselves better in
> Spain, having women of their own land, than if they had not. . . .
> So that, having their women, *they will be willing to do what is
> laid upon them.*[8]

Of course, to those who shared Columbus's assumptions and prejudices, questions about the morality of enslaving the Indians did not arise since they too remained skeptical about whether such beings were human. Recall that for Europeans of the early modern period, only humans could have rights; thus it is not surprising that the enslavement of Indians began shortly after the encounter of 1492 and continued in some Latin American countries until the late nineteenth century. Columbus himself brought natives to Europe to be sold as slaves, and he openly recommended that Spaniards take advantage of them by organizing a trade, writing about this in the spirit of a businessman whose only concern is to turn a profit. But he was not alone in advocating the enslavement of the indigenous peoples and the destruction of their cultures, as the writings of others of the time make clear.

Was the Conquest Morally Justified?

Even as the Conquest was unfolding, however, there were also those who denounced it. Among them, some who thought it was wholly justified were nevertheless horrified at the violence and greed of many *conquistadores* and colonists. One eloquent critic was Garcilaso de la Vega (Peruvian, 1539–1620), son of an Inca princess and a Spanish conqueror who was thus familiar with the ways of both cultures. Garcilaso, born in Cuzco during the first decade of the conquest of Peru, was by education and by choice sympathetic to the European worldview. He left his country to fight with the Spanish army in Europe and remained to live out his days in the southern Spanish province of Andalusia, never returning to Peru. His major work, *Royal Commentaries of the Incas*,[9] recounts the history of the Inca empire from its origins to the death of Tupac Amaru in 1572. Unable to find a publisher in Spain, Garcilaso sought one in Portugal instead, and the first part of this work finally appeared at Lisbon in 1609. But the second part, finished in 1616, proved equally unattractive to publishers who were perhaps reluctant to publish the work of a *mestizo*, and it was published only posthumously in 1616–1617 in Cordova, Spain. Although these and other episodes made him bitter about his second-class citizen status in Spain, where his half-Indian heritage clearly hurt him professionally, he nonetheless justified the conquest of Latin America in his writings for a mostly European readership.

Garcilaso's major work is notable for its sympathetic account of the emergence of the Inca empire, and was based on stories he had heard firsthand in his mother's house (where he developed a keen interest in the history of the Peruvian Incas). His devotion to the Incas is evident in the idealized treatment of their culture he offers in the *Royal Commentaries*, the latter part of which also includes subtle criticisms of the gratuitous violence and greed of many Spaniards in the conquest of Peru. But his condemnation of their abuses is most explicit in his account of the execution of the Inca prince Tupac Amaru, whose memory is honored in Peru even today. In a dramatic chapter,[10] Garcilaso accused the local Spanish authorities of concocting blatantly false charges against the prince for no other reason than to spread fear among the Indians in order to prevent possible uprisings.

Garcilaso's work, however, provides only a stirring historical account of the Conquest. His main purpose was not to offer a philosophical discussion of the moral problems raised by the actions of *conquistadores* and colonists but only to fashion a vivid chronicle of the violent clash of cultures and the abuses of human rights that marked the Conquest. For a philosophical assessment of these events, we shall have to look elsewhere.

Were the Indians "Natural Slaves"?

Not all Iberian intellectuals of the period were averse to discussing the moral and philosophical issues raised by the Conquest. Prominent among those who offered philosophical arguments attempting to justify it was the Spanish philosopher and clergyman Juan Ginés de Sepúlveda (ca.1490–1573).[11] His views clearly conflict with our moral intuitions; he believed that waging war against the Indians and forcing them into slavery were permissible. Given some com-

monly acknowledged principles of international relations, it is difficult to see how invasions of other nations' lands and war against
their peoples could be morally justified unless special reasons were
provided. In the case of the Iberian Conquest, we may well ask,
what special reason could there have been to justify abuses of that
magnitude? As Columbus and many others documented in their
writings, the Indians were generally peaceful and hospitable to Europeans, at least at the outset. Thus no such reason seems available
to justify waging war against these native peoples.

Moreover, the so-called *encomiendas* enforced by the Spaniards
and Portuguese to enslave the Indians appear well beyond moral
justification by even the most recondite philosophical argument.
Encomiendas were contracts that allowed representatives of the
Iberian authorities in Latin America to distribute Indians among
conquistadores and colonists as slaves in the mines, construction
projects, and other works often requiring heavy labor. In exchange,
the owners of *encomiendas* were to instruct the Indians in the Roman Catholic faith. Not surprisingly, this system motivated slave-
hunting expeditions against natives who resisted it. Sometimes these
raids were not in response to Indian resistance but simply to satisfy
the greed of colonists and *conquistadores*. Whatever good may have
been accomplished by the Spanish and Portuguese Conquest, it is
clear that it largely rested on social arrangements of this sort and involved actions that we would now agree were immoral. These actions were plainly in violation of the most basic rights of nations
and of peoples and were in conflict with fundamental rights of individuals that we would claim for ourselves.

In waging war against the Indians and in depriving them of their
liberty, the Spaniards and the Portuguese also expropriated Indian
lands and properties. Some argued that this was permissible since
the Indians had no standard form of government or social organization. In that case, defenders of the practice argued, they could have
neither ownership of the land nor other property rights. Yet this line
of reasoning would have met with challenges even at the time, for
some were already suggesting that property was a natural right. If
that is so, then it would be a right possessed equally by all human

beings—and the Indians would thus be legitimate owners of their lands and other properties. Aware of this argument, Sepúlveda attempted to justify the expropriations by denying that the natives were fully human. Given this assumption, and the ancient Greek doctrine that barbarians are "natural slaves," he took himself to have succeeded at last in providing the definitive grounds needed to justify the Conquest.

To Sepúlveda, the Indians' ways of life and their character traits suggested that they could not in fact be counted as full-fledged people because it was in their nature to be barbarians. A crucial step in his reasoning is the appeal to the doctrine of natural slaves, often ascribed to Aristotle (384–322 B.C.E.), one of the most influential philosophers in the Western tradition. Like many sixteenth-century followers of Aristotle, Sepúlveda held that some people are natural slaves of others whose nature is more civilized. He took certain features of an ethnic group to be essential to (or constitutive of) their nature and believed that when those features suggested that they were natural barbarians, then it followed that they were suitable for slavery. By claiming that the Indians were barbarians, Sepúlveda thought he had found a concrete reason that justified war against them, their enslavement in *encomiendas,* and the seizing of their lands.

This way of thinking is clearly morally repugnant, suggesting Sepúlveda's argument has gone wrong. But how? First, it makes a generalization about the Indians, who in fact amounted to many different groups. Generalizations of that sort are suspicious, often resting on nothing more than ethnocentric prejudice—which, as we recall, is the bias of preferring one's own ways of life over those of others. In response to this objection, Sepúlveda would probably point to empirical evidence supporting his generalization. Although he never visited the New World, he must have been familiar with the many chronicles of the Conquest and the testimonies of travelers reporting human sacrifice, cannibalism, and other objectionable practices among the Indians. Such practices, Sepúlveda might well insist, are plainly the mark of the barbarian. Note, however, that not all Indians engaged in those practices unless he could cite an objectionable custom practiced by all the indigenous groups, he would be in no position to generalize about them.

Yet it is also true that there were other customs that most natives observed, such as their lack of private property, their nonstandard forms of social organization, and their habits of dress (more often *undress*) that were deeply offensive to many Europeans. Sepúlveda may well have had some of these in mind when he imagined the "barbaric" Latin American Indians as fit exemplars of the Aristotelian natural slave. We may reconstruct the argument as follows

1. There is empirical evidence of barbaric practices among the indigenous peoples of Latin America.
2. People who engage in barbaric practices are natural slaves.
Therefore,
3. The indigenous peoples of Latin America are natural slaves.

In the twentieth century, cultural anthropologists have provided evidence to discredit this sort of thinking as naïve, showing such terms as "barbarian" and "barbaric" to represent strong ethnocentric bias, presupposing that those so identified are in some sense savage, primitive, or simply inferior by comparison with other people.[12] But a charitable view of Sepúlveda's reasoning could replace those terms with moral concepts, such as "harmful" and "wrong," which qualify actions leading to a violation of human rights. According to some contemporary research, the Aztecs, the Incas, and other groups of indigenous peoples in fact performed human sacrifices regularly, and other Indians killed their prisoners of war as part of their practice of cannibalism, with children and women often being among the victims. If there are any rights at all, then such customs plainly violated them, caused harm, and were therefore morally wrong. The best argument available to Sepúlveda could then be recast as follows:

1. There is empirical evidence that some groups of Indians regularly engaged in practices that are morally wrong.

2. People who regularly engage in practices that are morally
    wrong are natural slaves.
Therefore,
3. Some groups of Indians were natural slaves.

It is sometimes suggested that the Spanish and Portuguese chronicles of the Conquest were essentially a kind of propaganda in support of the European invaders and, as such, made exaggerated—and
even wholly fabricated—claims about the existence of human sacrifice and cannibalism among the natives. That such practices did exist among them, however, has now been confirmed by sound evidence provided by late-twentieth-century anthropologists, and so
the first premise of this argument seems true. (Note, however, that
the premise falls short of a universal generalization ranging over *all*
Latin American indigenous peoples and therefore makes a weaker
claim than what Sepúlveda may have originally had in mind—yet
the claim is for that reason more plausible.) The argument is valid;
thus, if the second premise is also well supported, then the conclusion appears unavoidable. But that premise rests on the Aristotelian
doctrine that some people are natural slaves, and is there any really
persuasive reason to believe that?

Note that to support (2), Sepúlveda could only offer an argument
from authority. Since arguments of that sort can be either good or
bad, we need to determine which category this falls in. To serve as a
basis for a cogent argument from authority, Aristotle must be acceptable as an expert on the subject of cross-cultural evaluation.
Otherwise, the premise would be based on nothing more than a fallacious argument from authority and therefore be useless in proving
anything.

Was Aristotle an expert on judgments about the ways of life of
people outside his own group, the Greeks? Aristotle was extremely
well read in all of the literature available to educated Greeks of his
day. He undoubtedly knew works of many disciplines and was familiar with travel narratives compiled by soldiers and explorers in
journeys to distant lands. Nevertheless, a closer look at his writings
reveals that he made numerous ethnocentric claims with regard to

non-Greeks and provided no empirical evidence for any of them. For example, he took northern Europeans to be excessively impulsive, unintelligent, and disorderly people who could not be governed. Even though he thought that Asians are clever and highly intelligent, he also judged them to be weak people, very suitable for slavery.[13] When he turned to an assessment of his own group, his views were quite different: They were temperate, intelligent, and, by nature, free people made to live in well-governed societies. Thus it seems most unlikely that an appeal to Aristotle for unbiased, expert testimony could succeed in supporting a claim that involves cross-cultural evaluation. It then follows that our stronger version of Sepúlveda's argument, even when construed in the most charitable way possible, has an unsupported premise and is therefore unsound.

The Theory of Natural Slaves in Context

Where, then, shall we place Sepúlveda in the history of the intellectual dispute about the morality of the Iberian Conquest? It may appear that he was merely defending the official view held by the leaders of the Conquest in his own country—the Spanish authorities of his time. Because we have demonstrated the unsoundness of Sepúlveda's argument, we may conclude that we have thereby shown the unsoundness of the official view. In fact, however, Sepúlveda's reasons never enjoyed popularity among the highest Spanish authorities during his lifetime. His was always a contested view, and he was challenged by Fray Bartolomé de las Casas (Spanish, 1474–1566) in a famous mid-sixteenth-century public debate in Valladolid, Spain, where both engaged in a battle of arguments about the morality of the Conquest.[14] Not only did Sepúlveda notoriously lose that debate; but he then struggled to find a publisher for his increasingly unpopular position.

Others holding different views had more influence with the Spanish crown, which seems to have been eager in the early stages of the Conquest to know what sort of actions were morally permissible in that vast undertaking. Spaniards were relatively inexperienced in expansion overseas, so they faced many new questions raised by the changing world order. Was war against aboriginal peoples ever justified? Did the Indians have legitimate ownership of the American land? What about other rights? And could they become Christians? Beginning with Queen Isabella the Catholic (1451–1504), who supported Columbus's explorations but also insisted that the natives must not be enslaved, such questions bedeviled not only the crown but also its ministers and the scholarly authorities of the Church. Isabella's husband, King Ferdinand the Catholic (1452–1516), who ruled alone after her death, sought the counseling of philosophers on moral issues raised by the Conquest—creating institutions for that purpose and granting audiences to those who, like Bartolomé de las Casas, had firsthand knowledge of what was happening in Spanish America. Even the powerful Holy Roman Emperor Charles V (1500–1558) had similar concerns as evidenced by his granting audiences with philosophers and requesting a philosophical study to be conducted by Francisco Vitoria (Spanish, 1488–1546), then professor at the University of Salamanca.

In this way, royal involvement in the discussion of moral controversies that arose during the Conquest gave the philosophical debate in the Iberian Peninsula unprecedented encouragement. Compared to other European rulers of the early sixteenth century, and to Spanish rulers of later periods, these exceptional monarchs played a significant role in promoting the development of what we would today call applied philosophy.

Sepúlveda Defeated by a Non-Scholastic Alternative

Although Sepúlveda's views won no hearing with the highest Spanish authorities of his time, they nonetheless expressed common ethnocentric prejudices that were to prevail in Spain later on, when Phillip II (1527–1598) became king. Such views must be rejected, but not just because they made a fallacious appeal to Aristotle's authority. They are also vulnerable to a different sort of objection: Why should we think that a people's ways of life are evidence of an essential nature? On the basis of the same information available to Sepúlveda, several other hypotheses were possible—and that was as clear to philosophers and clergymen within the tradition of the Roman Catholic Church as to other thinkers outside that tradition. The former shared with Sepúlveda a certain manner of reflecting upon philosophical questions known as "Scholasticism."

Thinkers of this methodological persuasion often engaged in meticulous disputes and reasoned by appealing to religious and philosophical authorities. This method has its roots in some medieval schools of law that were active in Italy but rapidly spread among Catholic philosophers and moral theologians throughout Europe. Two prominent early modern Dominican philosophers, Bartolomé de las Casas and Francisco Vitoria, were led by the Scholastic method to conclude that the Latin American Indians had certain rights and that there were no good grounds for the Conquest, at least in the way it was being pursued. But, as we have already seen, other Scholastics held views that were either openly sympathetic to the Conquest or could be invoked to justify it—not only Sepúlveda himself but later the distinguished Jesuit philosophers Luis Molina (Portuguese, 1536–1600) and Francisco Suárez (Spanish, 1781–1888). Of course, apart from one's method of reasoning, it also matters what basic premises one accepts, and these may lead to different conclusions despite a similarity in method. Before turning to the premises of these rival Scholastic thinkers, let us consider how Sepúlveda's argument could be challenged by thinkers outside his tradition.

In *The New Atlantis,* the empiricist philosopher Francis Bacon (English, 1561–1626) offered such a challenge to Sepúlveda. He appears at first to have harbored prejudices similar to Sepúlveda's since he also judged the Latin American Indians to be "rude" and "ignorant," yet for him such features did not indicate a nature suitable for slavery. He took them instead to be a sign of their youth as a people, arguing that the Indians were "younger a thousand years, at the least, than the rest of the world." Although Bacon also considered them "simple" and "savage" people—on the ground that they have failed "to leave letters, arts, and civility to their posterity"—he again drew no conclusion about the essential nature of their ethnic group. He instead sought external factors that may have accounted for their backwardness, finally blaming the time that had passed "between the universal flood and their particular inundation."[15] Unlike Columbus and many others, Bacon displayed no amazement at the nudity of the Indians and refused to see in it an essential weakness of their moral character. Here again his explanation appeals to external factors—viz., to supposed changes in their physical environment. Having earlier lived in the mountains, wearing "skins of tigers, bears, and great hairy goats," the natives later "came down into the valley, and found the intolerable heats which are there, and knew no means of lighter apparel," thus "they were forced to begin the custom of going naked."[16]

Although speculations of this sort may lack scientific support, they are nonetheless sufficient to show that reasoning of the kind proposed by Sepúlveda is uncharitable even by the standards of the time. Nothing follows about the nature (or the internal character) of a people from the fact that their ways of life are radically different from those of the observer. Surely the differences could in part be determined by factors external to the individuals that make up the group, including their history as a people and the physical and social features of their environment.

Montaigne and the Relativist Alternative

Another alternative to Sepúlveda's account is that of the French thinker Michel de Montaigne (1533–1592). Like many Europeans of his time, Montaigne learned from popular chronicles of the practices of human sacrifice and cannibalism among some natives of the New World. He seems also to have had firsthand testimony of a visitor to Brazil and personal conversations (through an interpreter) with some Indians. In his essay "On the Cannibals,"[17] Montaigne was especially interested in certain warfare customs of a Brazilian tribe (probably the Jivaros). He writes,

> Each man brings back the head of the enemy he has slain and sets it as a trophy over the door of his dwelling. For a long period they treat captives well and provide them with all comforts which

they can devise; afterwards the master of each captive summons a great assembly of his acquaintances; he ties a rope to one of the arms of his prisoner . . . and allow[s] his dearest friend to hold the prisoner the same way by the other arm: then, before the whole assembly, they both hack at him with their swords and kill him. This done, they roast him and make a common meal of him, sending chunks of his flesh to absent friends. This is not done for food—as the Scythians used to do in antiquity—but to symbolize ultimate revenge.[18]

According to Montaigne, moral assessment begins at home. Thus before making any judgments about these practices, he first evaluated comparable practices in the West. In Spain and Portugal at the time of the Conquest, Montaigne reminds us, the Inquisition burned people alive while animals were biting them. "[T]here is more barbarity," writes Montaigne, "in . . . lacerating by rack and torture a body still fully able to feel things, in roasting him little by little and having him bruised and bitten by pigs and dogs . . . than in roasting him and eating him after his death."[19] It would seem, then, that Spanish and Portuguese thinkers who, like Sepúlveda, attempted to justify the practices of the Inquisition while at the same time repudiating the customs of Latin American Indians are vulnerable to the objection that they had a double standard. It is hard to resist the conclusion that Montaigne was well ahead of his time in recognizing this double standard.

Yet he takes this objection to suggest further that "there is nothing savage or barbaric about those peoples [the Brazilian Indians], but that every man calls barbarous anything he is not accustomed to; *it is indeed the case that we have no other criterion to truth or right-reason than the example and form of the opinions and customs of our own country.*"[20] This view amounts to an inferential leap beyond the double standard objection because it makes the more extreme claim that what is "true" or "right" is determined by the customs acceptable within a certain culture. Those notions, in this view, are relative and can be properly paraphrased in terms of "truth for" and "right reason for" a certain culture. Clearly, Montaigne is now proposing a version of moral relativism:

1. Different groups of people have different and sometimes in-
    compatible practices and beliefs about what is right or true,
    and
2. Such practices and beliefs may all be equally correct.

The thesis in (1) might be trivial, but its conjunction with (2) is
not. Yet (2) follows from Montaigne's claim that culture determines
what practices or beliefs are correct. Against that claim one can say
that although culture does seem to determine (at least in part) what
people believe is right, believing that actions of a certain sort are
right is not the same as those actions actually being right. Consider,
for example, the case of racial persecution in Europe before and
during World War II. Surely, although many people in Germany believed then that such persecution was right, that did not make it
right. The history of popular moral beliefs in different cultures provides numerous cases of this sort. Therefore, even if (1) above were
plausible, the stronger assumption needed for (2) is vulnerable to
such counterexamples.

Moreover, it appears that sometimes customs change as a result of
moral criticism. Given the relativist theses, how could those changes
be explained? After all, if what is right is determined by the prevail-
ing beliefs of the culture one lives in, the changes need not happen at
all. Why bother trying to alter practices within one's own culture if,
as Montaigne holds, whatever people think is right or true within
their own culture *is* thereby right or true? In a relativist view of this
sort, it would actually be *wrong* to strive for changes in the customs
sanctioned by one's culture. But that unavoidable conclusion would
again clearly be vulnerable to counterexamples. Furthermore, it
would have to be wrong in some universal sense, but Montaigne's
point appears to be the claim that there is no such sense.

To defend the above theses, a relativist might argue that they lead
to toleration of other peoples' beliefs and customs. But then he
would have to explain how that could be a reason for him, given his
central claim, for he seems to assume that toleration is something
universally good—which it cannot be, according to his own theory
(because nothing is universal). Arguably, the relativist here is sub-
scribing to the principle that

   T The beliefs and customs of other cultures must be tolerated.

Since *T* is a generalization that, if true, holds universally, the principle is not available to the relativist, whose theory commits him to the claim that for some cultures the negation of the thesis must be true or right. Therefore, if the relativist happens to belong to one of the latter, he would have to be quite intolerant.

Moreover, once radically diverse cultures have met, toleration may not always be the best advice, morally speaking. What were Europeans obliged to do when confronted, for instance, with the warfare customs of Brazilian Indians as described by Montaigne? In a case of that sort, there seem to be good moral grounds for intervention, for if there are any rights at all, such practices clearly violate the most basic rights of the victims. Now the relativist seems committed to advocating *non*intervention,[21] arguing that Europeans had no right to intervene because they were in other peoples' territories. As Bernard Williams has noted, that would already presuppose a universalist claim—that one has no right to intervene with morally wrong actions when one is in other peoples' territories. The presence of Spaniards and Portuguese in Latin America during its conquest may be likened to a kind of trespassing since they were, so to speak, on someone else's property without having any right to be there. Imagine a burglar who has just broken into a house with the intention of stealing silverware but who is surprised to find a truly horrible murder about to be committed by the resident. If the burglar were to intervene to prevent it, would we not justify that interference, whether or not the burglar was trespassing?[22]

In addition, relativists of Montaigne's persuasion seem committed to denying that there are any universal human rights. Thus, if a society recognizes no such rights, then there are none in that society. This has the consequence that, within that culture, no moral harm could be done to people by, for example, depriving them of their freedom or life—and therefore no interference by outsiders would be justified in trying to stop it. But this is in conflict with common intuitions about the universality of at least certain basic human rights, such as the rights to life and personal liberty. Furthermore, if there were no such rights, it is difficult to see how, in the case of concern here, we could condemn either the enslavement or the widespread massacre of Latin American Indians during the Conquest.

Finally, Montaigne's reasoning seems vulnerable to a double standard objection in reverse, for although he refrains from criticizing morally questionable practices when these are accepted in traditional societies (such as that of the Brazilian Indians), he roundly condemns similar actions when they happen in the West. That is, where both societies have customs that seem equally repugnant, Montaigne's "primitivism" inclines him to be more charitable to those of the primitive culture. For example, he takes the great disparity in wealth and power among social classes in Western societies[23] to be somewhat less justified than the practices of cannibalism and human sacrifice among the Brazilian natives. No doubt both seem deeply unjust, but how could comparative judgments of this sort be substantiated? Such disparities in the West are a different kind of issue altogether from the morality of the Brazilian Indians' warfare customs.

Las Casas's Scholastic Defense of the Rights of the Indians

As we have seen, the moral justifiability of actions undertaken in the early part of the Iberian Conquest was of concern to the Spanish crown, which seems to have been interested in knowing what philosophers of the time thought about it. Emperor Charles V, for example, sought the help of Francisco Vitoria, a prominent Dominican moral theologian and professor of philosophy at the University of Salamanca, assigning to him the task of investigating some moral issues raised by the Conquest. But, like his predecessor Ferdinand II, he also sought answers in the arguments of another Dominican theologian and philosopher, Fray Bartolomé de las Casas, who employed the Scholastic method in reasoning about such issues and was notable for his indefatigable pursuit of solutions to those problems of applied moral and political philosophy. His numerous trips across the Atlantic in a vigorous campaign against the abuses of the Conquest earned him respect as "The Apostle of the Indians." He honored that title in his writings and in life, both as an active priest in Latin America and as a self-appointed attorney representing the Indians in Spanish institutions.

His progressive views, however, had developed slowly over time. When las Casas arrived in America in 1502 as a young man, his family owned an *encomienda*, which he inherited later in addition to other properties from his father. In 1510 he was ordained a priest, and four years later he surprised the local authorities by giving up his *encomienda* and beginning a campaign for the rights of Indians. Clearly he had been moved by what he saw in the Spanish colonies and had reflected upon some sermons he heard from Dominican friars who were already denouncing the enslavement of Indians and refusing to give confession to colonists and *conquistadores* who owned *encomiendas*.

In his writings, las Casas famously attacked the views of those who denied that the Indians were fully human. They were people too, he insisted, and therefore had natural rights to life and personal liberty. He was convinced that they could be peacefully converted to Roman Catholicism and could work with Spaniards under conditions other than slavery. To demonstrate these possibilities, he devised collaborative projects with the natives. For example, he organized a community (or "mission") in Venezuela with clergymen, Indians, and Spanish colonists. Although that community faced strong resistance from authorities and colonists, and ultimately failed after only a year (1520–1521), other missions in various parts of Latin America later succeeded in proving las Casas's project to be a feasible alternative to the existing unjust system.

During the early stages of the Conquest, las Casas's views about the Indians were influential not only with the Spanish authorities but also with the Roman Catholic Church, where they inspired some official documents. Offered the crucial post of bishop in Peru, an important center of colonization, he rejected that position but later served for a brief period (from 1544 to 1547) as bishop of what is today the Mexican city of Chiapas, then called "Chiapa" and attached to the captain generalcy of Guatemala. He seems to have been more interested in writing and traveling to defend the rights of the Indians than in achieving a high position within the Church, yet his influence with the Spanish authorities led to an important decision by the Council of the Indies, the main Spanish institution that regulated the Conquest. According to historians, it was las Casas's ideas that were the foundation of the so-called New Laws (1542) that came to regulate the Spanish colonies, banning the *encomienda* system—although, to las Casas's disappointment, the laws were rendered ineffective in practice by the resistance of *conquistadores* and colonists and were later abandoned altogether.

Las Casas's success, however, is evident in his relations with the Crown and in his numerous publications. Unlike some prominent contemporaries, he published in Spain during his lifetime, and his work was translated into other European languages. Moreover, his ideas were known to at least two monarchs, King Ferdinand II and Emperor Charles V, who granted him audiences and with whom his views appear to have carried some weight. In 1518, a year after Emperor Charles V moved to Spain, he was presented with two opposite views on the question of whether a peaceful conversion of the Indians could be achieved. On the one hand, las Casas argued that those peoples were kind and could make good Christians, provided that peaceful means instead of force were used to persuade them. On the other, one of his numerous rivals, Gonzalo Fernández de Oviedo y Valdés (Spanish, 1478–1557), maintained instead that only some Indians were as described by las Casas. Oviedo y Valdés, who also had firsthand knowledge of the New World, insisted that many natives were belligerent and unsuitable for peaceful conversion. But las Casas prevailed and gained the emperor's support. As a result, Oviedo y Valdés faced difficulties, even years later, in getting his famous *General and Natural History of the Indies* published in Spain.[24]

Las Casas believed that the Indians would adopt the Christian faith if persuaded by peaceful means and that their interests could be made compatible with those of *conquistadores* and colonists.[25] To that end, he proposed ideal communities of Spaniards and Indians, to be organized throughout Latin America. This project was insightful since such communities worked well in different parts of

Latin America. Prominent among them was the mission organized by the Jesuits in Paraguay, which survived for more than a century and was forced to close only when Spanish authorities—perhaps fearful of the rise of Jesuit power in Europe—sought to expel them from Spanish and Portuguese territories in the New World. The Paraguayan mission attracted thousands of Indians who would otherwise have lost their freedom and even their lives to the greedy Portuguese slave hunters and plantation owners of the region. Las Casas inspired communities of this sort with the social and political ideas he offered in his *Memorial of Remedies for the Indies*.[26] An early utopian theory, written to persuade Emperor Charles V, it appeared in 1516, some months before the publication of Sir Thomas More's more famous work, *Utopia,* which coined the word and may have had considerable influence on it. In the Netherlands at the time, las Casas made some copies of his *Memorial* available to the king's advisers, and in that way his proposal for Latin America seems to have come later to the attention of Erasmus and other thinkers, including More.[27]

Las Casas was deeply involved in controversial issues of applied moral and political philosophy, so he had many rivals who were stung by his extraordinary rhetorical power. His *Short Account of the Destruction of the Indies* (1542),[28] which is said to have inspired the New Laws, certainly made him some passionate enemies. Translated into several European languages, this essay caused a "battle of books" in France, with some arguing for and others against las Casas's incisive report of the horrors of the Iberian Conquest. Whether or not he exaggerated the harm done to the Indians (as his critics claimed), he drew attention to moral problems that some of his contemporaries wished to ignore and thus initiated a progressive tradition of moral, political, and social thought that continues, both in the Iberian Peninsula and in Latin America, to the present day. During his lifetime, he was popular not only with the Indians but apparently even among some *conquistadores.* One of them, Alvar Núñez Cabeza de Vaca (Spanish, ca.1490–ca.1557),[29] is said to have argued that the Indians could become Christians and subjects of the Spanish crown only if they were won by kindness. Alonso de Ercilla y Zúñiga (1533–1594), a Spanish *conquistador* and poet, may have been influenced by las Casas in his narrative poem *La Araucana*[30]—where he held that the simple and honest indigenous peoples of Chile never encountered greed until the arrival of the Spaniards.

Some of las Casas's enemies accused him of being morally inconsistent because he famously signed a petition to the Spanish authorities recommending the importation of slaves from Africa to Latin America. Although las Casas probably acted out of a desire to protect the Indians, and soon conceded publicly that signing the petition was a mistake, that would fall short of justifying his action in this case. Even so, those who disregard his apology are clearly uncharitable, for it is beyond question that las Casas opposed slavery of any sort, as he made explicit in his "Condemnation of African Slavery" (1552).[31]

Other critics have simply attacked las Casas as a person rather than attacking his arguments, completely ignoring his challenging reasons and the soundness of his fundamental convictions. For example, his rival Fernández de Oviedo y Valdés is said to have described him as a simple and greedy man. It was also rumored that las Casas was a spy for rival European powers seeking to undermine the pervasive influence of Spain. But to have any force, objections to las Casas must address his *arguments* rather than his *person*. (Otherwise, any objection of that sort counts as nothing more than the fallacy known as *ad hominem*.) These accusations have never been substantiated, and they fall short of what would be needed to challenge las Casas's views.

By the end of the sixteenth century, important ideological changes had been introduced by King Philip II, partly in response to a deep financial crisis, and the enemies of las Casas had begun to gain influence in the Iberian Peninsula. Spaniards then lost sympathy altogether with the plight of the Indians in Latin America—recognizing that their enslavement had been a continuous source of revenues for Spain. Yet las Casas's ideas survived, and even today his work is revered by thinkers concerned with moral, social, and political justice in Latin America. Not surprisingly, his views figure prominently in progressive movements within the Roman Catholic Church and have been especially influential in the development of what is now called "liberation theology."[32]

Lascasianism: A Philosophy or a Political Agenda?

Like many Iberian thinkers of his time, las Casas advocated the conversion of the Indians to Catholicism, but he did so with the conviction that

1. The Roman Catholic faith could be rationally supported; *and*
2. The Indians were fully rational beings, and therefore humans.

The first claim las Casas took for granted, but he saw correctly that the second claim challenged a prejudice widely held at his time and so offered a forceful defense of it. Those who denied that the Indians were fully rational used to point to such Indian practices as human sacrifice, cannibalism, and idolatry, yet according to las Casas, these were compatible with the Indians' being fully rational. He further argued that their practice of human sacrifice was indicative of the intensity of their religious commitment.[33] Since they were devoted believers, they offered to their gods the best they had, which was human life. It is unclear, however, whether las Casas intended this line of reasoning as merely an explanation of the Indians' practice or as a moral justification of it.

Yet the latter surely was his intent when he proposed that the Indians were in "probable error." According to this doctrine, given that beliefs underlying the practice of human sacrifice turned out to be false, those who held them were in *error*. But, since those beliefs were recommended by the wise men of their society, who were held wise precisely because their opinion was *usually* right, therefore the Indians were in *probable* error. This account seems to preserve their rationality, for believing what is, on the basis of one's total evidence, probably true is after all a rational attitude. And the opinion of wise men counted as *prima facie* evidence for the Indians' belief. Recall that appeals to authority are not fallacious when they rest on the opinion of those who are experts in the subject under consideration. But because any argument of that sort is inductive, the premises, even when true, would fall short of guaranteeing the conclusion. It follows that las Casas may be correct in holding that the Indians were justified in their beliefs even though it was in fact false, so they were in error. If this is what he intended in his doctrine of probable error, and he could further show that those wise men were in fact experts in the relevant subject matter, then it would seem plausible that the Indians' empirical beliefs about human sacrifice were epistemically justified. Yet those beliefs could neither amount to knowledge (because they were false) nor provide any moral ground for that practice (because its justification would then be epistemic).

In the doctrine of probable error, as elsewhere, las Casas's reasoning followed the familiar Scholastic method, appealing frequently to the authority of ancient and medieval philosophers in support of his position and offering detailed discussions of issues that seem not obviously relevant to the subject at hand. Educated in the Catholic tradition, he accepted the views of the Dominican philosopher Thomas Aquinas (Italian, 1225–1274). These views are usually known as "Thomism." They were devised by Aquinas on the basis of revisions and enlargements of ideas first proposed in antiquity by Aristotle and comprised a body of doctrines about reality, knowledge, and morality. Thus Thomism may be described fairly as a kind of Christianized Aristotelianism.

Las Casas's endorsement of Thomism is not surprising since this was (and still is) the official philosophy of the Roman Catholic Church. When he set out to determine the fairness of the Conquest, then, he did so by invoking a central Thomistic doctrine, that of natural law theory, which is commonly used by Catholic philosophers in their moral deliberations. This theory holds that *it is in the natural order of things* that the principles of morality are grounded. Hence, it was thought suitable, for example, to solve the conflicts that arose in the modern era between the rights of individuals and those of the emerging states since the positive law that sanctioned the latter was itself dependent for its justification on the more fundamental natural law. Whether in the writings of thinkers who, like Sepúlveda, denied human rights to the indigenous peoples or those who, like las Casas, granted them, most early modern Iberian philosophers embraced the fundamental tenets of natural law theory and constructed questions of rights in terms of it.

After the seventeenth century, however, natural law theory came to be challenged by a rival view, legal positivism, which maintained instead that the only binding laws were those issued by human sovereigns and were thus subject to no higher constraints. But natural law theory has continued to have many followers even up to the present day,[34] surviving the most trenchant criticisms, which are still usually framed in positivist terms.

At the time of the Conquest, several versions of natural law theory had been developed, yet many Iberians clung stubbornly to Aquinas's original version, which was already obsolete in other parts of Europe. In fact, the history of natural law theory goes well beyond Aquinas, having its origins in the writings of Cicero (106–43 B.C.E.) and in the concept of privilege, or liberty, available in Roman jurisprudence. Privileges were held to be self-evident, inalienable, indefeasible, and valid beyond the positive laws issued by humans. Scholastic thinkers (i.e., the philosophers of the Church) adapted this jurisprudential concept to moral theology, incorporating it in a theory of moral (and not merely legal) human rights. That theory was developed during the Middle Ages through a rather mundane controversy over property rights. Members of a Roman Catholic order, the Franciscans, wished to have the right to use certain properties without having ownership over them so that their conduct in this respect would be consistent with their vows of poverty. They thus initiated a controversy about whether individuals could have certain privileges, and this culminated in the natural law theory of rights, with Aquinas figuring prominently among its proponents.

In the early modern period, that theory evolved further in response to moral problems that arose during the early stages of the Iberian Conquest. In the hands of Sepúlveda, natural law was cited in an attempt to justify the Spanish invasion and conquest of the

New World. Yet there were others (e.g., las Casas and Vitoria) who invoked the theory to argue for the wrongness of waging war against the Indians and violating their rights to freedom, property, and life. By the end of the sixteenth century, however, the financial crisis in Spain had given rise to a new attitude among the authorities, who now expressed clear hostility toward critics of their conduct in Latin America.

Not surprisingly, there were some philosophers eager to use their rhetorical skills in the service of Spanish and Portuguese imperialism. They devised new versions of the natural law theory to rival those prevalent among the Dominicans so as to make it compatible with the moral justification of slavery and colonialist expansion. For example, to Luis Molina and Francisco Suárez, a right was a property owned by an individual (or a group of people) and, as such, could be traded or given up by its owner(s). In this view, then, all rights are alienable. Thus, those who seek to justify the abuses of the Conquest need not deny that the Indians were full-fledged rational beings; rather, they might hold that as a people the Indians had traded (and therefore forfeited) their rights to property and to freedom in exchange for some other goods. Once they had done that, they had entered a contract, and it was then too late to change their minds. This is a stratagem that conflicts with a fundamental principle of charity in interpretation, for why think that the Indians (or any other group) had forfeited their rights?

Finally, it is important to bear in mind that las Casas did not make a substantial contribution to the development of natural law theory. Although there is abundant evidence that he had significant successes, producing actual improvements in the lives of the indigenous peoples, he was not chiefly concerned with philosophical theories. As a clergyman of his time, he was educated in philosophy and wrote on applied issues of that discipline, yet his interests were mainly those of a man of action concerned with the situation of the Latin American Indians. Our study, however, is also interested in theoretical contributions to natural law theory, as it was affected by the events in the New World, and for that we must look elsewhere—to the work of Francisco Vitoria and the Dominican school of Salamanca.

Vitoria: Humanism About
International Law and Natural Rights

Like other humanist philosophers and clergymen, Francisco Vitoria was interested in problems concerning justice, human rights, and international law. He studied Thomism in Paris between 1507 and 1522 and later taught in Spain at the University of Salamanca. Developing his own distinctive interpretation of Aquinas, while adding certain refinements through arguments he had worked out, Vitoria devised a philosophical position that became known as "Vitorian Thomism"—a name now used to designate not only his own philosophy but also that of his followers in the Dominican school of Salamanca. Among the most significant parts of his philosophical work are his writings on rights. When the Spanish authorities asked Vitoria to determine which, if any, were the rights of the indigenous peoples, he of course appealed to Aquinas's version of natural law theory.[35] In this view, rights are objective because they consist of whatever is in accordance with natural law and thus in accordance with justice. The requirements of natural law are themselves objective because they are rooted not only in the natural order of things, but also in the laws of reason (i.e., the principles of logic), and these apply in the same way for all rational beings. From the epistemic point of view, rights are justified moral claims that are self-evident (i.e., to understand any such claim is to recognize immediately that it is true) and indefeasible (i.e., there are no considerations that could outweigh them).

Vitoria, however, also takes rights to be capabilities or faculties that people have, thereby introducing a more subjective conception that was to be developed later by modern thinkers. Here lies a tension with Aquinas's objective view, according to which individuals do not own their rights—conceived as "what is just,"[36] or "determined by the law." Rather, rights are inalienable: They cannot be given up because they are not properties owned by people. One may have a right without having a power or dominion. For example, a student may have certain rights with respect to her teachers, even when she has no power or dominion over them. According to the objective view, then,

> An individual has a right if and only if she has a *just claim*—that
> is, a claim in accordance with what is sanctioned by the law.

The connection between "right" and "what is just or determined
by the law" is evident in Latin languages, where the same word can
be used to convey either. Thus in Spanish we say "*derechos
humanos*" to refer to "human rights" but also "*derecho penal*" to
mean "penal law."[37] Given the textual evidence, Vitoria seems, on
the whole, to have had in mind this objective conception of rights.

If a moral right is whatever is determined by the law, which laws,
exactly, are those relevant to establishing the moral rights of humans? In Vitoria's tradition, they are natural laws, sanctioned by
God as objective norms governing human action. Although God is
invoked here, the view is secular because the natural law does not
strictly depend on the existence of a divine power. Since such law instead concerns what is in human nature, clearly secular natural law
theories of human rights have underwritten famous documents such
as the American Declaration of Independence and the Bill of Rights,
the French Declaration of the Rights of Man, and the United Nations Declaration of Human Rights.

If Vitoria's objective view is correct, then human rights are determined by the (natural) law, and therefore no human being should be
denied such rights.[38] Following Aristotle and Aquinas, he took it
that each type of thing that exists, whether organic or not, has a distinctive nature (something that makes it what it is) and a final end
(something toward which the thing is inclined). Our nature and inclination as humans is to be rational, and we develop toward
achieving that nature beginning from birth and continuing throughout our lives. Natural law prescribes that we act according to reason, and our having rationality thus puts us above other earthly
creatures, over whom we have rights and dominion (or justified
property claims). Such rights are therefore also inalienable and valid
beyond the positive law issued by human beings. It follows that beings who lack the faculty of reason can have no rights or dominion.

When the Spanish authorities sought Vitoria's help in examining
the philosophical question of whether the Conquest could be
morally justified, he framed this question in terms of natural law

theory and thus needed to determine first whether the Indians were full-fledged human beings. Sepúlveda had argued that they were not and that they therefore failed to qualify for rights to liberty or to property. In his view, the Europeans' waging war against the natives and their enslavement in *encomiendas* was justified. But Vitoria, having the arguments on both sides of the debate, reached a quite different conclusion.

On the question of whether waging war against the Indians could be justified, he drew a distinction between just and unjust wars.[39] If "slaughter of the innocent"[40] is contrary to natural law, he reasoned, then at least under normal circumstances, war against other nations would be morally wrong. Since he also finds that "it is contrary to natural law for one man to dissociate himself from another without a good reason,"[41] it follows that "[t]he Spaniards may lawfully carry on trade among the native Indians, so long as they do not do harm to their country."[42] To Vitoria, the Indians' possible rejection of the Gospel "furnishes no ground for making lawful war on them and seizing in any other way their lands."[43] If they allow the Spaniards to preach the Gospel and to travel in their lands and establish trade, there would then be no grounds for waging war against them. Vitoria's position, however, was qualified. Among special circumstances justifying war against foreign nations, he listed the customs of cannibalism and human sacrifice (for which Spaniards might lawfully intervene without requesting the permission of the Pope) and also violations of the rights of persons to travel freely, to acquire citizenship, to practice their religion, and to defend themselves.

Unfortunately, Vitoria was influenced by the ethnocentrism of his time. Such prejudices are clear when he writes about the Indians, yet his work also shows that he condemned the injurious deprivations of those peoples' rights, and his biases never led him to justify the abuses of the Conquest. The following passage illustrates this conflict in Vitoria's own thoughts:

> It is, however, to be noted that the natives being timid by nature and in other respects dull and stupid, however much the Spaniards may desire to remove their fears and reassure them

with regard to peaceful dealings with each other, they may excus-
ably continue afraid at the sight of men strange in garb and
armed and much more powerful than themselves. And therefore,
if under the influence of these fears, they unite their efforts to
drive the Spaniards out or even to slay them, the Spaniards might,
indeed, defend themselves but within the limits of permissible
self-protection, and it would not be right for them to enforce
against the natives any of the other rights of war (as, for instance,
after winning the victory and obtaining safety, to slay them or de-
spoil them of their goods or seize their cities) because on our hypothesis the natives are innocent and are justified in feeling
afraid. Accordingly, the Spaniards ought to defend themselves,
but so far as possible with the least damage to the natives, the
war being a purely defensive one.[44]

Regarding the right to property, Vitoria argued that the Indians
were legitimate owners of their lands and had genuine political authority in them. In support of this, he noted that they had their own
organized government before the arrival of the Spaniards and that
rights to property are not compromised by lack of allegiance to the
Roman Catholic faith. According to Vitoria, once the division of
lands in the world has been made, natural law sanctions that division. Furthermore, although he takes the Indians' faculty of reason
to be undeveloped, that, he thinks, does not entail that they lack the
right to property. "Inasmuch as the Indian aborigines are not of unsound mind," he writes, "they are not precluded from being true
owners on the pretext of unsoundness of mind."[45] In his view, then,
Spaniards have violated a fundamental right of these people in seizing their lands and other properties.

On the other hand, to determine whether the Indians had rights to
life and to liberty, Vitoria examined four reasons commonly offered
in his time for denying them—that people could not claim these
rights who were either (1) sinners, (2) infidels, (3) irrational, or (4)
insane. Against each of these, he argued by appeal to the views of
some authorities and to counterexamples, which show that none of
them amounts to either a necessary or a sufficient condition justify-

ing violations of those rights. Conditions (1) and (2) were rejected because they involved matters of divine law and therefore could have no bearing on human rights, which were the subject of natural law. Although (3) and (4) would probably strike us today as insufficient reasons for denying basic human rights, this was not obvious to most Iberian thinkers of the sixteenth century, according to whom free will and self-mastery were required for having those rights. Vitoria accepted this view, as well as some ethnocentric beliefs about the diminished rationality of the Indians, for he had never traveled to the New World and thus was probably influenced by reports offered in the popular chronicles of his time.

We may expect, given conditions (3) and (4) and the common belief among Iberians that the Indians were not fully rational beings, that Vitoria would have held them ineligible for the basic rights to life and to liberty. But in fact he thought the information available about them was insufficient to judge them either irrational or insane. They were therefore legitimate bearers of those rights and would be harmed if deprived of their lives or their personal liberty. Thus, like other Dominicans, Vitoria opposed the enslavement of the Indians and the slave trade in general. He admitted that only under very extreme circumstances may human beings enslave themselves (for instance, when they are forced to trade their freedom for their lives), and he saw no grounds for thinking that the Indians were in such circumstances.

Vitoria thus developed a rather sophisticated humanist theory of rights that suited the moral and social concerns of sixteenth-century Dominican clergymen. Later, that theory was to be challenged by modern conceptions inspired by the work of Hugo Grotius, Molina, and Suárez, among others. It is no surprise that, during the Counter-Reformation, Jesuits reacted against socially oriented views such as those of Dominicans, whom they accused of Protestantism. The Jesuits defended a psychological doctrine of rights first suggested by the Portuguese philosopher Molina and further elaborated by the Spaniard Suárez. Countless public debates between representatives of these orders dominated the Iberian intellectual scene between 1580 and 1610.

By the turn of the century, the social and political ideals of Dominicans had come under fire from the modern doctrine that was ultimately to replace it, according to which rights are faculties or powers owned by individuals. In this view, only certain kinds of creatures (those who possess such faculties) could suffer when they are deprived of their rights. Moreover, individuals could give up their rights, to trade them for goods that they considered more important, and even entire groups of people may legitimately engage in such trades. This doctrine had clear implications for the practice of slavery, for once contracts have been established, each party must keep its promise, and then if one party were to trade its liberty for some good, it would be too late for them to change their situation. Given this doctrine, it could be argued that the Indians, the Africans, and other enslaved peoples of the world had voluntarily sold themselves, trading their freedom for something else.

Yet this line of reasoning is, again, open to objections. Why should we think that people would trade their freedom voluntarily? The view plainly conflicts with a sound principle of charity in interpretation and thus seems highly suspect. If there is nothing that could be offered to support it, it must be rejected. But the history of ideas has not always followed reason. During the seventeenth century, the humanist theory of rights held by the Dominicans lost popularity in the Iberian Peninsula as the modern Jesuit rival gradually won the upper hand. We, of course, may feel inclined to lament this as a retrograde development that only added impediments to the increase of human liberty. But if we expect the course of history to lead always toward social progress, we shall often be disappointed.

Discussion Questions

1. Because the Vikings arrived in America around the year 1000, they are sometimes said to have discovered the continent. But a regular relationship between America and Europe began only with Christopher Columbus's trip in 1492, and the name "America" was first used in the introduction of a book on cosmography that appeared in 1507, honoring Amerigo Vespucci's awareness of a new continent, the result of his various explorations after 1500.

Suppose we want to say that some European "discovered" America; who should get the credit for this? The Norse, Christopher Columbus, or Amerigo Vespucci? If an individual (or a group) discovers that something is so, then it must actually be the case, and the individual (or group) must be aware of having acquired new knowledge about it. That is, "discovery" is a success term, implying that what is discovered is true and that the agent has acquired new knowledge. On the basis of this assumption, determine how to answer the above question.

2. Until the beginning of the sixteenth century, European geographers believed that the earth consisted of only one big mass of land surrounded by water, the so-called Island of the Earth. After Vespucci's evidence, many people changed their beliefs on the matter. Quite possibly, then, at different times, some took the Island of the Earth theory to be true, while according to others it was false. Could relativism help in solving this contradiction? How? Is it really a contradiction according to relativists?

3. In this chapter, justifying some of the things done in the name of the Spanish and Portuguese Conquest was presented as a moral dilemma. What, exactly, is this dilemma?

4. Juan Ginés de Sepúlveda believed that there are absolute, inviolable human rights—that is, that humans, by their very nature, have some justified claims with a certain normative force that no other considerations could ever defeat. At the same time, he held that the Latin American Indians did not have any such rights. Are his views consistent? If so, how? If not, why not? Explain.

5. Sepúlveda's justification of the enslavement of the Indians rests on an argument from authority. Although such arguments may sometimes be good, Sepúlveda's is fallacious. Reconstruct his argument and show why it is a fallacy.

6. Explain how Francis Bacon's speculations about the ways of life of the Indians may serve to undermine the doctrine that they were natural slaves.

7. State Michel de Montaigne's double standard objection and describe a case that may be vulnerable to that objection.

8. Can moral relativists accommodate the notion of universal human rights? If so, how? If not, why not?

9. Montaigne supports the credibility of one of his witnesses by noting that, unlike intellectuals (or "cosmographers"), he was a simple man who "has nothing on him on which to build such false

discoveries or make them plausible."[46] This argument is weak since the simplicity of a person has no bearing on the accuracy of his report. Show its weakness by providing a counterexample.

10. According to Montaigne,

> Those "savages" [the Indians] are only wild in the sense that we call fruits wild when they are produced by Nature in her ordinary course: whereas it is fruit which we have artificially perverted and misled from the common order which we ought to call savage. It is in the first kind that we find their true, vigorous, living, most natural and most useful properties and virtues.[47]

What claim is being made here? Is it consistent with Montaigne's primitivism? And why do you think the term "savage" is in quotes?

11. Montaigne takes the great disparity in wealth and power among social classes in Western societies to be somewhat less justified than the practices of cannibalism and human sacrifice among the Brazilian natives. Discuss this view.

12. "In the fascinating book by Bernal Díaz del Castillo," Bernard Williams writes,

> there is an account of what they [the *conquistadores* led by Cortez] all felt when they came upon the sacrificial temples. This morally unpretentious collection of bravos was genuinely horrified by the Aztec practices. It would surely be absurd to regard this reaction as merely parochial or self-righteous. . . . But what, after all, is one supposed to do if confronted with a human sacrifice?— not a real question for many of us, perhaps, but a real question for Cortez.[48]

As an attempt to justify some morally objectionable actions of the *conquistadores* (especially their way of interfering with native practices), how effective is this argument? Could you offer a reply?

13. Reasoning in accordance with the tenets of natural law theory, Francisco Vitoria and Bartolomé de las Casas reached conclusions that were incompatible with those of Sepúlveda, who used the

same theory. How is this possible? Is the theory contradictory? Explain.

14. Las Casas held that the Indians could be converted to Catholicism by peaceful means. State some assumptions behind this claim and assess its plausibility.

15. According to the humanist version of natural law theory endorsed by las Casas and Vitoria, natural rights are objective. What does this mean? Explain.

16. Are you an absolutist, a universalist, or a skeptic about human rights? Define each view.

17. Vitoria argued that although waging war against the Indians was wrong, some wars are justified. What conditions must be present in cases of the latter sort? What reasons would he offer against the enslavement of the Indians?

18. According to Vitoria, it is self-evident that "there can not be a just war where no wrong has previously been done."[49] Do you agree? What does "self-evident" mean here?

19. Las Casas maintained that the Indians were in "probable error" when they engaged in the practices of human sacrifice and idolatry. What is meant by the doctrine of probable error? Reconstruct and evaluate his argument based on that doctrine.

20. There is a substantial difference between the moral justification of an action and an explanation of the motivations behind the action. When las Casas appealed to the intensity of the Indians' religious beliefs, was he justifying or explaining their practice of human sacrifice?

21. Can you see a crucial difference between the humanist version of natural law theory and that of modern Scholastic thinkers such as Luis Molina and Francisco Suárez?

22. According to Molina and Suárez, individuals and groups of people could give up their rights to trade them in exchange for other goods they valued more highly. This view was invoked to justify slavery, but does the argument work? What major objection was raised against it in this chapter?

Suggestions for Further Reading

Aquinas, Thomas. 1988. *On Law, Morality, and Politics.* W. Baumbarth and R. Regan, eds. Indianapolis, Ind.: Hackett.

Bacon, Francis. 1909. *Essays, Civil and Moral; and The New Atlantis by Francis Bacon. Areopagitica; and Tractate on Education by John Milton; and Religio Medici by Sir Thomas Browne.* New York: P. F. Collier & Son.

Boff, Leonardo, and Clodovis Boff. 1987. *Introducing Liberation Theology.* Maryknoll, N.Y.: Orbis.

Columbus, Christopher. 1960. *The Journal of Christopher Columbus.* New York: C. N. Potter.

Díaz del Castillo, Bernal. 1928. *The Discovery and Conquest of Mexico.* London: Percy Lund, Humphries.

Finnis, John. 1980. *Natural Law and Natural Rights.* Oxford: Clarendon Press.

Guttiérrez, Gustavo. 1993. *Las Casas: In Search of the Poor Jesus Christ.* Maryknoll, N.Y.: Orbis.

———. 1999. "The Task and Content of Liberation Theology." In Christopher Rowland, ed., *The Cambridge Companion to Liberation Theology.* Cambridge: Cambridge University Press.

Hart, H. L. A. 1955. "Are There Any Natural Rights?" *Philosophical Review* 64:175–191.

Himelblau, Jack J. 1994. *The Indian in Spanish America: Centuries of Removal, Survival, and Integration.* Lancaster, Calif.: Labyrinthos.

de la Vega, Garcilaso. 1966. *Royal Commentaries of the Incas.* Austin, Tex.: University of Texas Press.

las Casas, Bartolomé de. 1990. *Memorial of Remedies for the Indies.* V. N. Baptiste, ed. Lancaster, Calif.: Labyrinthos.

———. 1992a. "The Only Way." H. Rand Parish, ed. *Bartolomé de las Casas: The Only Way.* Mahwah, N.J.: Paulist Press.

———. 1992b. *A Short Account of the Destruction of the Indies.* London: Penguin.

———. 1993. *Witness: Writings of Bartolomé de las Casas.* George Sanderlin, ed. Maryknoll, N.Y.: Orbis.

las Casas, Bartolomé de, and Juan Ginés de Sepúlveda. 1994. "Aquí se contiene una disputa o controversia." In Jack J. Himelblau, ed., *The Indian in Spanish America: Centuries of Removal, Survival, and Integration,* vol. 1. Lancaster, Calif.: Labyrinthos.

Montaigne, Michel de. 1946. "On the Cannibals." In *The Essays of Michel de Montaigne.* London: Allen Lane.

O'Gorman, Edmundo. 1961. *The Invention of America: An Inquiry into the Historical Nature of the New World and the Meaning of Its History.* Bloomington, Ind.: Indiana University Press.

Oviedo y Valdés, Gonzalo Fernández de. 1969. *Natural History of the West Indies*. Chapel Hill, N.C.: University of North Carolina Press.

Pastor Bodmer, Beatriz. 1992. *The Armature of Conquest: Spanish Accounts of the Discovery of America, 1492–1589*. Stanford: Stanford University Press.

Sepúlveda, Juan Ginés de. 1951. *Democrates segundo o de las justas causas de la guerra contra los indios*. Madrid: Consejo Superior de Investigaciones Científicas.

Suárez, Francisco. 1944. *De Legibus ac Deo Legislator*. Oxford: Clarendon Press.

Vitoria, Francisco de. 1917. *De Indis et de Ivre Belli Relectiones*. Washington, D.C.: Carnegie Institution.

Williams, Bernard. 1982. "An Inconsistent Form of Relativism." In Jack W. Meiland and Michael Krausz, eds., *Relativism: Cognitive and Moral*. Notre Dame, Ind.: University of Notre Dame Press.

Wong, David. 1984. *Moral Relativity*. Berkeley: University of California Press.

Notes

1. See H. L. A. Hart, "Are There Any Natural Rights?" in *Philosophical Review* 64 (1955), pp. 175–191. A rival view of rights, which takes them to be benefits a person may have, is found, for instance, in David Lyons's *Rights, Welfare, and Mills' Moral Theory* (Oxford: Oxford University Press, 1994).

2. Christopher Columbus (1451–1506) sought support for the "Enterprise of the Indies" first in Portugal and then in Spain, where he finally persuaded the Catholic monarchs after eight years of earnest argument. That he had landed in a new continent was never realized by Columbus himself, but his trips, unlike those of the Vikings (ca. 1000), marked the beginning of regular contact between the Americas and the rest of the world.

3. Bernal Díaz del Castillo, *The Discovery and Conquest of Mexico* (London: Percy Lund, Humphries, 1928) and Gonzalo Fernández de Oviedo y Valdés, *Natural History of the West Indies* (Chapel Hill, N.C.: University of North Carolina Press, 1969). See also the selection in Jack J. Himelblau, *The Indian in Spanish America*, vol. 1 (Lancaster, Calif.: Labyrinthos, 1994).

4. Christopher Columbus, *Journal of Christopher Columbus* (New York: C. N. Potter, 1960), pp. 56–57.

5. See, for instance, Beatriz Pastor Bodmer, *The Armature of Conquest: Spanish Accounts of the Discovery of America, 1492–1589* (Stanford: Stanford University Press, 1992), pp. 20–42.

6. Columbus, *Journal*, p. 194.

7. Columbus, *Journal*, p. 200.

8. Columbus, *Journal*, p. 6. Emphasis mine.

9. Garcilaso de la Vega, *Royal Commentaries of the Incas* (Austin: University of Texas Press, 1966).

10. Garcilaso, *Royal Commentaries*, bk. 8, chapter 19.

11. The *locus classicus* for this view is Juan Ginés de Sepúlveda's *Democrates segundo o de las justas causas de la guerra contra los indios* (Madrid: Consejo Superior de Investigaciones Científicas, 1951).

12. Melville J. Herskovits, for example, explicitly rejects the use of terms such as "barbarian" and "primitive" to refer to people of traditional societies. See his *Cultural Relativism: Perspectives in Cultural Pluralism* (New York: Random House, 1972).

13. See Aristotle, *Politics*, Part 7, 1327b, edited by Richard McKeon (New York: Random House, 1947).

14. An English translation of this debate is available in Bartolomé de las Casas and Juan Ginés de Sepúlveda, "Aquí se contiene una disputa o controversia," in Jack J. Himelblau, ed., *The Indian in Spanish America*, vol. 1 (Lancaster, Calif.: Labyrinthos, 1994).

15. Francis Bacon, *Essays, Civil and Moral; and The New Atlantis by Francis Bacon. Areopagitica; and Tractate on Education by John Milton; and Religio Medici by Sir Thomas Browne* (New York: P. F. Collier & Son, 1909), p. 167.

16. Bacon, *The New Atlantis*, pp. 167–168.

17. Michel de Montaigne, "On the Cannibals," in *The Essays of Michel de Montaigne* (London: Allen Lane, 1946), pp. 228–241.

18. Montaigne, "On the Cannibals," p. 235.

19. Montaigne, "On the Cannibals," pp. 235–236.

20. Montaigne, "On the Cannibals," p. 231. Emphasis mine.

21. In *Moral Relativity* (Berkeley: University of California Press, 1984), David Wong argues for the compatibility of a certain form of relativism with intervention in cases of morally inadmissible actions. But what reason, if any, is available to the relativist to claim that some action of people in remote cultures is morally inadmissible?

22. Bernard Williams, "An Inconsistent Form of Relativism," in Jack W. Meiland and Michael Krausz, eds., *Relativism: Cognitive and Moral* (Notre Dame, Ind.: University of Notre Dame Press, 1982), pp. 172–173.

23. According to Montaigne, some Indians gave him testimony that ". . . they had noticed that there were among us [Westerners] men fully bloated with all sorts of comforts while their halves were begging at their doors, emaciated with poverty and hunger: they found it odd that those destitute halves should put up with such injustice." See "On the Cannibals," pp. 240–241.

24. See the introduction to Oviedo's *Natural History*.

25. For example, in "The Only Way," las Casas offers several arguments for the peaceful conversion of the Indians. See *Bartolomé de las Casas: The Only Way*, edited by H. Rand Parish (Mahwah, N.J.: Paulist Press, 1992a).

26. las Casas, *Memorial of Remedies for the Indies*, edited by V. N. Baptiste (Lancaster, Calif.: Labyrinthos, 1990).

27. See Baptiste's introduction to las Casas's *Memorial*.

28. las Casas, *A Short Account of the Destruction of the Indies* (London: Penguin, 1992b).

29. "Cabeza de Vaca" (literally, "cow's head") was a hereditary title of Alvar Núñez, who explored the American Southwest, reaching Texas, New Mexico, probably Arizona, and even California. He narrated his adventures in these parts of the world in *Los naufragios* (*The Shipwrecked Men*, 1542). See English translations by Thomas Buckingham (1851), reprinted in F. W. Hodges, *Spanish Explorers in the Southwestern United States* (1907) and in I. R. Blacker and H. M. Rosen, *The Golden Conquistadores* (1960).

30. Ercilla began writing his epic poem in Chile, where he fought against the Araucanian Indians (1556–1563). This work, considered one of the best Spanish historical poems, has three parts, published in 1569, 1578, and 1589. Translations available in English include those by Walter Owen (1945) and C. M. Lancaster and P. T. Manchester (1945).

31. See las Casas, "Condemnation of African Slavery," in *The Only Way*.

32. See, for instance, Gustavo Gutiérrez, *Las Casas: In Search of the Poor Jesus Christ* (Maryknoll, N.Y.: Orbis, 1993) and Leonardo Boff and Clodovis Boff, *Introducing Liberation Theology* (Maryknoll, N.Y.: Orbis, 1987).

33. las Casas, "A Defense of Human Sacrifice," in George Sanderlin, ed., *Witness: Writings of Bartolomé de las Casas* (Maryknoll, N.Y.: Orbis, 1993), pp.162–167.

34. See, for instance, John Finnis, *Natural Law and Natural Rights* (Oxford: Clarendon Press, 1980).

35. Thomas Aquinas, *On Law, Morality, and Politics*, edited by W. Baumbarth and R. Regan (Indianapolis, Ind.: Hackett, 1988).

36. The connection between what is "right" and what is "just" is clear in Latin, where one word, *ius,* is the root of both terms.

37. Compare a similar dual meaning of *Recht* in German.

38. This is in fact an argument deployed by las Casas and Vitoria in their respective defenses of the rights of the indigenous peoples of Latin America.

39. In his *Relectiones,* especially in "De Indis," Francisco Vitoria condemns waging war against the Indians, though in "De Jure Belli," he provides reasons for just war. See Vitoria, *De Indis et de Ivre Belli Relectiones* (Washington, D.C.: Carnegie Institution, 1917).

40. For Vitoria, it is self-evident that "there can not be a just war where no wrong has previously been done," *Relectiones,* p. 157.

41. Vitoria, *Relectiones,* p. 153.

42. Vitoria, *Relectiones,* p. 152.

43. Vitoria, *Relectiones,* p. 157.

44. Vitoria, *Relectiones,* pp. 154–155.

45. Vitoria, *Relectiones,* p. 115.

46. Montaigne, "On the Cannibals," p. 231.

47. Montaigne, "On the Cannibals," p. 231.

48. Williams, "An Inconsistent Form of Relativism," pp. 172–173.

49. Vitoria, *Relectiones,* p. 157.

6

IBERIAN SCHOLASTICISM AND
ITS CRITICS: FROM COLONIAL
RULE TO INDEPENDENCE

*The colonial world was a projection of a society that had al-
ready grown mature and stable in Europe. It showed almost no
originality whatever. New Spain did not seek or invent: it applied and adapted. All its creations, including its own self, were
reflections of Spain. And the ease with which the Hispanic
forms gradually admitted the modifications demanded by neo-
Hispanic realities does not negate the conservative character of
the colonial world.*

Octavio Paz, *The Labyrinth of Solitude*

During the modern era, the philosophical and scientific views of
Spain and Portugal were transplanted to their colonial domin-
ions in other parts of the world. This process affected the intellectual practices of Latin Americans, adding a misguided sense of their
own indigenous identity and inspiring some resistance to the European views of their colonial masters. Although such challenges ultimately failed to subvert those views, they revealed certain traits in

the intellectual character of Latin Americans that have resurfaced again and again—for example, their remarkable curiosity to learn and their tendency to discuss critically, both of which were in evidence from the earliest days of the colonies. In this chapter, we shall see that a phenomenon often referred to as "cultural dependence," which first appeared in the colonial period and persisted for more than three centuries, also left an indelible mark in their character. Even after Latin Americans gained political independence from Spain and Portugal, their intellectual practices retained a tendency to mirror major trends of European thought. Since communication with Europe was then sporadic, they sometimes came to champion theories already discredited there. This inclination, however, also met with criticism. During the period of independence in the nineteenth century, for example, when a reflection on the distinct historical, cultural, and ethnic makeup of the emerging nations was essential, some Latin Americans such as Simón Bolívar considered the problem of whether imported models could accommodate their nations' diverse ethnic and historical backgrounds.

The issues raised in this chapter concern primarily questions related to the processes of colonial rule and political and social organization after independence. In spite of their specificity, they are to some extent analogous to other issues that have arisen in later times. Although historical, cultural, and environmental factors had a bearing on the intellectual practices of Latin Americans during the wars of independence, comparable factors still affect them today. And, as we shall see, that Latin American culture should develop as part of Western culture was self-evident to some thinkers of the nineteenth century—notably, Domingo F. Sarmiento—but to others, it represented an abiding concern and remains so today.

The Scholastic Paradigm

The colonial period in Latin America comprises some three centuries, from Columbus's arrival in 1492 to roughly 1810, when Argentina and Colombia declared their independence, thus igniting the fires of revolution that were soon to sweep the region. During that period, the indigenous peoples' worldviews had some indirect influence on the architecture and other visual arts cultivated in the colonies, where the ornate baroque style of Spain and Portugal remained the dominant artistic form. But the Indians left hardly any mark on the colonial practices of science and philosophy, perhaps because their own intellectual development was tragically interrupted by the Iberian Conquest. Furthermore, to the Spaniards and the Portuguese, the Indians' approach to scientific and philosophical problems seemed hopelessly primitive compared with their own medieval Christian philosophical methodology known as Scholasticism.

More than a method, this complex system of argumentation was a cluster of theories and fundamental assumptions about which questions were important at the time, including strategies to settle them and views about what entities and values were to be assumed in the practice of science and philosophy. Following contemporary usage (especially in the work of Thomas Kuhn[1]), we may say that such clusters amount to "paradigms" that are the governing conceptual frameworks in terms of which theories come to be articulated. In different periods, experts may accept different, and even incompatible, paradigms. When a so-called normal or prevalent paradigm is perceived as unable to solve the questions of concern to a community of experts, then uncertainty among them increases, and this may lead to a period of crisis or intellectual revolution. The experts must then articulate a new paradigm—that is, they must provide a novel way of seeing things, so that the original puzzles that triggered the crisis are resolved, at least provisionally.

Scholasticism was the normal paradigm in Europe during the medieval period, but in the early modern period, new discoveries and inventions generated uncertainty about its effectiveness in solving the puzzles then regarded as most important. This precipitated a crisis, which finally resulted in the replacement of Scholastic science and philosophy with a new paradigm grounded in modern physics, astronomy, and cosmography in science, and empiricism and rationalism in philosophy. The modern revolution spread rapidly in Europe in part because of the work of such well-known figures as Nicholas Copernicus (Polish, 1473–1543), Galileo Galilei (Italian,

1564–1642), Isaac Newton (English, 1642–1727), René Descartes (French, 1596–1650), John Locke (English, 1632–1704), and many others.

In Spain and Portugal, few philosophers and scientists took notice of the revolution engulfing other parts of Europe. In a region where the iron-clad authority of the Church was undisputed, these more conservative thinkers continued to accept Scholasticism until at least the end of the seventeenth century. And that paradigm, now undoubtedly obsolete in most of Europe, was slowly but steadily transplanted to Latin America. Crucial events in that process during the colonial period were the creation of some academic institutions where Scholasticism could be expounded, such as the Royal Pontifical University (founded 1553) in Mexico, and the University of Córdoba (1613) and the Royal Studies of Buenos Aires (1773) in Argentina.

Scholasticism was also brought to Latin America in the written work of its most salient Iberian representatives. In Chapter 5, we saw that Francisco Vitoria and Bartolomé de las Casas were humanists who endorsed that paradigm. Their conception of human rights came to be supplanted later by other theories inspired by the views of Luis Molina and Francisco Suárez, Scholastic thinkers prominent in their own day in promulgating that paradigm throughout the Iberian intellectual world. In common with other thinkers of the Church, Vitoria, las Casas, Molina, and Suárez had a certain manner of reflecting not only upon philosophical questions but upon empirical ones as well. Typically, they attempted to solve them by engaging in meticulous disputes and rational argumentation, relying heavily on the Scriptures and the received wisdom of antiquity and medieval thought in the writings of Plato, Aristotle, Augustine, Thomas Aquinas, and many others. When Scholastics debated a subject, they usually held the opinions of such authorities as beyond challenge, sometimes invoking them to settle the dispute. Not surprisingly, Scholastics would often disagree about how to interpret a certain authority with accuracy, so their debates sometimes ended up as little more than lengthy exegetical discussions.

The methods of Scholasticism first appeared in the Middle Ages to address issues of law and politics but soon spread to philosophy and moral theology, notably in the work of Pierre Abelard (French, 1070–1142) and Peter Lombard (Italian, ca.1100–ca.1160), among others. Scholasticism then became the lingua franca of philosophical writing and scholarly disputation until the fifteenth century.

As we have seen, in the early modern period, experts had begun to question whether that paradigm could properly account for the results of the experiments and discoveries that had by then been made. An increasing awareness that it could not led to a period of crisis, and ultimately Scholasticism was replaced by a new paradigm. As they attempted to accommodate modern inventions and discoveries, the experts came to believe that for any theory about the world to be taken seriously, it must rest on something more than an appeal to authority and exegetical discussion. Rather, it must be supported by empirical evidence. When Scholasticism was compared with the new paradigm of empirical science (or philosophy),[2] the limits of the former became apparent.

In the course of intellectual revolutions, however, subverting a certain received view is likely to involve power struggles among partisans of the conflicting paradigms, simply because each party wishes to have control—for example, over academic institutions and publications. During the early modern period, such struggles centered around whether Scholasticism or modern philosophy should prevail. Finally, at the end of that revolutionary period, it was clear that Scholasticism was defeated in most academic institutions of Europe, where modern cosmography, Newtonian physics, and the theories known as "rationalism" and "empiricism" had come to be accepted as the building blocks of modern science and philosophy.

But in the Iberian Peninsula, mainstream thinkers turned their backs on that paradigm and continued to follow a Scholastic methodology, not only in their philosophical disputations but in their scientific investigations as well. Initially (as we saw in Chapter 5 in our examination of the dispute between las Casas and Sepúlveda), some moral and social issues created by the encounter of 1492 figured prominently among those questions. Later thinkers such as Molina and Suárez were concerned with similar problems, which they likewise expected to settle by Scholastic methods—as became evident in their attacks on Vitoria and the Dominican school of Salamanca, even though they were no less Scholastic in their approach to discussions of natural rights and international law. By the seventeenth century, Iberian Scholastics (more precisely, "neo-Scholastics") developed an interest in other areas of philosophy, reaching agreement, for instance, on some contested questions of Aristotelian metaphysics. After the defeat of the Dominican school of Salamanca and certain changes in the political climate of the Iberian Peninsula, questions concerning rights, justice, and other issues of moral and political philosophy began to lose their priority in the mind of Scholastics, who had become more interested in problems of metaphysics and related branches of philosophy. Only rarely did Scholastics make an effort to accommodate the novel empirical evidence stemming from recent discoveries and inventions within their views.

At the same time that Spanish and Portuguese philosophers were engaging in appeals to authority and in exegetical discussions to settle their disputes, intellectuals in other parts of Europe were excited by new discoveries of the natural sciences. They believed that the reigning theories in both the sciences and in philosophy must take account of the new discoveries—as they could do only by proceeding according to good reasons and empirical investigations. To these thinkers, it was beyond doubt that Scholasticism was unable to explain much of the new, empirically based evidence and that it must therefore be replaced by modern science and philosophy. As early as the mid-sixteenth century, this process was already well under way in some academic centers of Europe. Yet in Hispanic America, Scholasticism was at the same time only just taking hold. It would continue to dominate Latin American thought until the period of independence in the early nineteenth century. Needless to say, any attempt to think about the problems of modern science and philosophy during the colonial period was counted as subversive by mainstream intellectuals, and their proponents were targets for censure or worse.

José de Acosta Versus Aristotelian Science

Colonial Hispanic America, at least at the outset, was—by our standards—an intellectually closed society, where rebels against Scholasticism, whether in science or philosophy, were regarded by the authorities as unwelcome pests. In late-sixteenth-century Peru, a Jesuit missionary, José de Acosta (ca.1539–1600), came into this hostile environment, launching a challenge to that paradigm. He held that certain philosophers, among whom he numbered some ancient and medieval authorities most respected by Scholastics, had made substantial mistakes with regard to empirical questions of geography. At the time, such questions belonged to cosmography, a discipline then thought crucial to cartography, which studied all physical aspects of the earth, such as its shape, distribution of land and water, relative distances, and climate. (Cosmography, of course, as well as other empirical sciences, was still considered part of the discipline of philosophy—which, in the writings of Acosta, is spelled with a capital "P.") Furthermore, he argued that those philosophers were in error not only in *what* they had said about such empirical questions but also in *how* they had sought to answer them since they had relied entirely on mere speculation. In his *Historia Natural y Moral de las Indias (The Natural & Moral History of the Indies)*,[3] he insisted that empirical questions could in fact be resolved only where sound reasoning is based on good evidence from observation.

As we have seen, this view had already come to be accepted as the scholarly consensus in most countries of Europe since philosophers and scientists had generally become convinced that, otherwise, crucial puzzles raised by recent discoveries and inventions may remain unresolved. That such a view should be endorsed by a *Hispanic* thinker of the late sixteenth century, such as Acosta—who was himself trained in the medieval, Scholastic tradition—was indeed unusual. Born in Spain, he entered the Society of Jesus in 1570 and a year later was sent to the New World as a missionary in Peru. Some sixteen years in this post allowed him to gain firsthand acquaintance with various regions of South America, an experience he recounted in his *Natural & Moral History,* composed on his return to Spain and published in 1590. In this book, available in English in 1604, Acosta defied the authority of ancient and medieval thinkers in matters of cosmography and in doing so departed boldly from the standard procedure among Iberian Scholastics of his day, which was to treat ancient and patristic writings as proof-texts. It simply never occurred to them that such eminent authorities could have been mistaken in those matters.

According to Acosta, the geographic discoveries of his contemporaries and his own experience in South America offered overwhelming evidence against some doctrines about the natural world held by Aristotle, Augustine, and certain "Doctors of the Holy Church." In his *Natural & Moral History,* he set out to use that evidence in a series of refutations by counterexample. In the style common among philosophers of the time, he first advanced an opinion or summarized a certain subject matter in the title of a chapter, often appending his own views on the issue. Some such titles read: "That the Heaven is round on all parts, moving in his course of itself"; "Containing an Answer to that which is objected in the holy Scriptures against the roundness of the earth"; "Of the fashion and form of Heaven, at the newly found world"; "The reason why S. Augustine denied the Antipodes"; "Of Aristotle's opinion touching the new World, and what abused him to make him deny it"; "Of the opinion which Plato held of the West Indies"; and "That the burning Zone abounds with waters and pastures, against the opinion of Aristotle, who held the contrary."[4]

As these titles make clear, a substantial portion of the *Natural & Moral History* concerns issues of cosmography related to the discovery of a "new world," focusing on what that discovery showed about the shape of the earth, the number of continents, and life and climate of the "torrid zone" (viz., the portion of America that is between the Tropics of Cancer and Capricorn). Acosta's chief objection to the Iberian Scholastics of the time was that they were attempting to ground claims about physical geography, an empirical matter, on mere speculations. Recall that Scholastics ordinarily appealed to authorities whose opinion rested mostly on aprioristic reasoning. But such an approach to cosmography was simply untenable for Acosta. Although he did not object to *all* attempts to solve puzzles involving such matters by relying on testimony, he did question the value of mostly a priori testimony. He trusted (and often cited) the testimony of explorers and navigators whose knowledge was based on direct observation and whose experiences overseas he judged relevant to settle certain cosmographic issues.

Among other ancient confusions that Acosta set out to expose were some mistaken beliefs about the continents. He noted, for example, that ancient authorities had long speculated about the existence of a continent apart from Asia on "the other side" of the Atlantic Ocean, at what Europeans used to refer to as "the Antipodes." Some believed that no considerable mass of earth could exist at the Antipodes, others that there could be lands that would have a climate so horrendously hot—especially in the tropics or "the burning zone"—that no life whatsoever could prosper there. Some even speculated that Antipodeans walked on their heads with their feet on the air. Acosta was well aware that some of his dogmatic contemporaries would still believe such absurdities, but he hoped that his own firsthand account of South America would persuade fair-minded readers. "[W]hatever they say," wrote Acosta, "we live now in Peru, and inhabit that part of the world . . . [and] do not find ourselves to be hanging in the air, our heads downward, and our feet on high."[5]

In arguing against such hypotheses, Acosta held fast to his empiricist principle: He proceeded entirely on the basis of what he had observed. Such a methodology appears to have been a matter of settled conviction, for in various passages of the *Natural & Moral History*, he expressed the view that beliefs about the world should be based on empirical evidence, whether this be acquired firsthand or from the testimony of others. "[E]xperience should be of more force than all Philosophical demonstrations," he declared. Accordingly, the roundness of the earth was proven not only because "we who now live in Peru *see* it visibly," but because it had been conclusively shown by the crew of Magellan's ship *Victoria*, who first circumnavigated the globe. To them, he thought, was due "the honor and praise to have best discovered" that epoch-making cosmographic fact.[6]

And what of the belief, held since antiquity, that the Antipodes were uninhabitable because of the hot climate of the "burning zone"? Aristotle himself seems to have been among those who believed this, but Acosta is undaunted: "[A]lthough he was a great Philosopher, yet he was deceived in this point."[7] Invoking his own experience again, Acosta submitted that, in the Antipodes, the region between the tropics was "very well peopled and inhabited by men and other sorts of creatures, being a region of all the world the most fruitful of waters and pastures, and very temperate. . . . To conclude, we must believe that the burning zone is well inhabited, although the ancients have held it impossible."[8]

Naturally, to hold that Aristotle, Augustine, and the "Doctors of the Holy Church" entertained mistaken views of the world must have seemed quite subversive in the eyes of his contemporaries, the Iberian Scholastics. Perhaps to protect himself from censure by the Church, Acosta attempted to excuse the authorities' misconceptions about empirical matters by invoking their devotion to issues of greater importance, which at the time were of course those concerning "revealed religion"—the supernatural. In the first book of his *Natural & Moral History*, before discussing some of their mistaken beliefs, Acosta made it clear that, in his view, "whatever the Ancients say or hold . . . *it must not trouble us*, for . . . it is well known and verified that *they have not been so studious in the knowledge and demonstrations of Philosophy.*"[9] On the other hand, he also maintained that "those vain Philosophers of our age are much more to be blamed . . . [because] having attained to the knowledge of the being and order of creatures, and of the course and motion of the Heavens, have not yet learned . . . to know the Creator of all things."[10]

Whom did Acosta have in mind? His contemporary empiricists, the rationalists, or both? Needless to say, Acosta was not alone here: At the time, philosophers in each of these camps were criticized on similar grounds by officials of the Church. René Descartes, the first great rationalist philosopher of modern times, who flourished in the decades following the publication of Acosta's *Natural & Moral History*, was roundly attacked for his views. Although he was a devoted Roman Catholic himself, that did not prevent his writings' being banned by the Church—a condemnation that was not to be lifted until centuries after his death.

Acosta's Concerns in Perspective

In his writings about the natural world, Acosta seems to us strikingly modern when judged by the standards of his time. He was always mindful of avoiding conclusions not based on empirical evidence. In addition to his own experiences in South America, he clearly prized the information made available by the great early modern voyages of exploration. The Spanish circumnavigation of the earth (1520–1522), for example, he thought demonstrated something already suspected since antiquity: the roundness of the earth. That voyage was also important to Acosta because it settled a disputed question in proving that the Americas were indeed an independent continent, entirely separate from Asia. This was, of course, not a new idea, having been suspected by some experts since the first reports of the encounter of 1492. The Italian-born Spanish humanist Peter Martyr (1459–1526), for instance, was reluctant to refer to the lands visited by Columbus as "the Indies," coining instead the phrase *orbe nove*, possibly the origin of our expression, "New World."

Acosta was surely right in recognizing the importance of the circumnavigation of the globe and other exploratory journeys of the time in shedding new light on the relative proportion of lands and water on the earth and the existence of the Americas as a separate landmass. Before those expeditions, various misconceptions on these matters were prevalent among Europeans, a fact that has led some later scholars to question whether it is strictly correct to say that Europeans "discovered" a new world. In the early 1960s, Edmundo O'Gorman, a philosopher and historian of Latin America, examined some such misconceptions and took them as evidence for the view, now popular, that the Americas were not discovered but rather invented.[11] Of course, it is true that people lived there already when Columbus arrived, and that he himself died without ever realizing that he had landed in a new, free-standing continent, completely detached from Asia. Moreover, the work of Acosta, who often speaks of a newly discovered "world," makes clear that the notion of "continent" itself is a modern one and the result of some theoretical adjustments that were made after the most important expeditions. But these facts seem insufficient to make the case that America was invented. For note that both "invent" and "discover" are success verbs implying the acquisition of some knowledge. Yet if a thing was invented, then it did not exist before the intervention of a certain agent, while if it was discovered, then it did (though this was previously unknown to the agent). Now of course a committed idealist will hold that there is nothing that exists independent of the mind or language—so we participate in creating our reality rather than discover it ready-made—and perhaps this was O'Gorman's view. But from the perspective of the first Europeans to encounter the strange new world we now know as the Americas, the notion of discovery would seem more accurate in describing their achievement.

In any case, it was plainly only after revered ancient and patristic authorities had been shown to be spectacularly wrong about the geography of the earth that real progress could be made in understanding the actual configuration of continents and seas. For this reason, the contribution of Spain and Portugal toward articulating a new paradigm in matters cosmographic was of great importance. Even in the grip of Scholasticism, these cultures fostered a curiosity about the world that led to their sponsoring the crucial journeys of discovery that in turn brought a drastic change of view to world geography. Having already secured most of their own territories in the European peninsula known since antiquity as Iberia or Hispania, Spain and Portugal now turned to overseas explorations with the aim of extending their colonial domains through the annexation of new lands.

In this they were quite successful. It was Vasco da Gama (1469–1524), a Portuguese navigator sponsored by Manuel I of Portugal, who commanded the first fleet of Europeans to reach India by sea

(1497–1499). In Spain, the Catholic kings' decision to sponsor Columbus's trips led to important geographic discoveries that set the stage for further expeditions. In the face of powerful foreign opposition, Charles V supported Ferdinand Magellan (Portuguese born, ca.1480–1521) in his search for a passage from the Atlantic to the Pacific in South America that would enable him to circumnavigate the globe. After finding this passage off Cape Horn on October 21, 1520, in the strait that now bears his name, Magellan made his way up the west coast of South America and then westward into the islands of the South Pacific, only to meet his death there at the hands of native Polynesians. Yet one of his vessels, the *Victoria*, commanded by Juan Sebastián del Cano (Spanish, ca.1476–1526), completed the voyage on September 6, 1522, thereby accomplishing the first circumnavigation of the globe—and under the flag of Spain. Thus, as a by-product of their imperial expansion, Spain and Portugal made a material contribution to the modern revolution in cosmography. Through the discoveries of explorers sailing abroad in their names, they made available for the first time evidence that was crucial in the articulation of the paradigm that would replace ancient and medieval ways of thinking about geography and reorient the sciences to a modern view of our planet.

Sor Juana: Could Women Think in Colonial Mexico?

It will come as no surprise to the reader to learn that the major protagonists of philosophical and scientific work in Hispanic America, from the colonial period to this day, have been men. For women pursuing intellectual activities of any sort, the Iberian colonial world presented formidable barriers to education and creative expression. It is then remarkable that in the colonial society of Mexico, a nun, Juana Inés de la Cruz, was able to achieve considerable success in those activities as a literary writer and a feminist thinker. Her experiences will be of interest to us chiefly because of the way in which they illustrate the limitations of that society, with its Scholastic paradigm, in accommodating some modern needs expressed by intellectuals of the time, among whom Juana Inés figured prominently. Thus we shall take her most important contribution to rest less in the literary merits of her writings than in her rebellion against certain strictures of that society, and we must try to determine which aspects of her contemporaries' Scholasticism were challenged by her work. Juana Inés has often been singled out as a pioneer in asserting the intellectual rights of women, so it is important to see also what sort of feminist demands were actually made by her. Yet to do this, we must first explore her life.

Born in San Miguel Nepatlan in 1651, Juana Inés de Asbaje y Ramírez de Cantillana, or simply Sor (Sister) Juana, tragically died in 1695 in Mexico City while ministering to the nuns of her convent stricken by an outbreak of the plague. She grew up on a farm in the south of Mexico, the child of a woman who seems to have been more independent than her peers in the colonial society, bearing several children out of wedlock and running the farm on her own. When Juana Inés was still a girl of about ten, her mother took up with a man and sent her to live with her grandfather in Mexico City. But this turn of events appears to have been fortunate in the end, for according to Sor Juana's own account, her grandfather had a library where she could satisfy an intellectual curiosity that, as she acknowledged, would have been unusual in any child of her age, but especially so in a girl. In an autobiographical note,[12] Juana Inés declared that instead of playing with dolls, she had been interested in reading and writing from the age of three. Later, she had learned Latin by means of a few lessons and even had contemplated trying to attend the university disguised as a man. When that scheme failed, she had to content herself with being an autodidact, a project in which she achieved great success. Not only her writings but also the testimony of contemporaries suggests that Sor Juana acquired in that way a considerable classical erudition and some knowledge of the sciences.

But chronicles of the time also describe her as a beautiful and smart young woman who was soon to become a favorite of the Mexican viceregal court, where she spent some years after living with wealthy relatives in Mexico City (who had taken her in upon the death of her grandfather). In spite of her success at court, at the age of sixteen she renounced that life to enter a convent, probably because of her intellectual leanings and the realization that, since she was an illegitimate daughter with no dowry, she had no status in the eyes of colonial society and thus could not qualify for a marriage of the kind that might allow her to pursue her interests. On the other hand, a community of nuns would provide the right environment for continuing with her project of self-education and literary writing. Thus, in 1667 she entered the order of Discalced Carmelites. The obligations of monastic life there, however, seem to have been more severe than she anticipated, and she soon left to return to the life at court. Two years later she again took vows, this time in the less severe Hieronymite order, to remain there until her death. The nuns of the Convent of Santa Paula seem to have provided the environment she was looking for since they allowed her to carry on with her writing and self-education and even to use her own books. Sor Juana had her own collection, one of the finest libraries in Mexico at the time, that she amassed throughout her life (she sold them all before her death, perhaps under pressure from high officials of the Church openly opposed to secular education for women).

The rules of the Hieronymite order similarly presented no impediment to Sor Juana's social life. Although required to participate in the community's religious ceremonies and perform a communal service (in her case, keeping the convent's financial records), she could remain in her cell most of the time. But this cell was no dank monastic chamber with a cot and crucifix. It was in fact a private apartment with various rooms where she could study, take her meals, and receive visitors. Sor Juana even had a maid living in her cell, a slave girl given to her when she left home to live with her grandfather. In her rooms, she often entertained high-ranking visitors, such as the viceroy and vicereine of Mexico, the official representatives of the king in the so-called viceroyalty of New Spain, a vast colonial domain with its capital in Mexico City. She also presided over animated *tertulias*—literary salons which would often include famous intellectuals and prominent figures of the local society. This seems to support Octavio Paz's conjecture[13] that, from Sor Juana's perspective, joining the nuns had little to do with religious devotion and more with pursuing her intellectual talents by the only means available to her in the circumstances.

Her friendship with some Spanish dignitaries in Mexico, especially the wives of two consecutive viceroys, seems to have contributed to the publication of some of her works in Spain. These consisted mostly of poetry and two plays, well received by the critics, that were written according to the baroque style of the day. As a result, she became a celebrated author among the educated of the Hispanic world. To this day she is sometimes regarded as "the Tenth Muse" and "the Phoenix of Mexico."[14]

Her talents brought her also the recognition of local educated men, some of whom were Spaniards and others *criollos*—native-born people of Spanish ancestry. She thus established a circle of acquaintances in Mexico that included, among others, an influential prelate, Manuel Fernández de Santa Cruz, the Bishop of Puebla, probably best known today for his role in Sor Juana's downfall. His publication of a letter[15] that sealed her tragic end had been preceded by his own admonition of the nun's intellectual practices. In fact, it is possible that he had encouraged her to write it since he undoubtedly harbored animosity toward the person who was the real target of that letter. Furthermore, Sor Juana's writing skills were well known to the bishop. What, then, was in that letter?

The Perils of a Certain Scholastic Dispute

Published under the title "Carta Antenagórica" ("Missive Worthy of Athena"), the letter takes issue with some ideas put forward by a Portuguese philosopher, the Jesuit Antonio de Vieyra, in a sermon that he had presented some forty years earlier. That Vieyra's ideas were still considered current (and *correct*) by some ecclesiastic authorities can be seen from the great storm that erupted after the letter's publication. The "Missive" was the object of numerous criticisms, causing what may, without exaggeration, be called a scandal. In 1691, Sor Juana decided to reply to one of her critics, her friend, the Bishop of Puebla himself, who under the pseudonym Sor Philotea de la Cruz had issued an admonishment against her. Her short essay, "La Respuesta" ("Reply to Sor Philotea"), was to become a classic statement of the rights of women to education and secular knowledge.[16] Publication of the "Missive" appears to have exacerbated existing feelings of distrust among Church officials who disapproved of Sor Juana's intellectual activities, leading them to increase their repressive measures against her. Ultimately, they succeeded as Sor Juana finally submitted to the discipline of her superiors and abandoned altogether her practices of self-education and writing. This may also account for her sudden decision to sell her books. By the end of her life, she passed her days in quiet seclusion completely devoted to the religious and communal practices of her convent. When an epidemic of plague struck, Sor Juana, by then in poor health, helped to nurse the sick but contracted the disease that had decimated her sisters, and she died at the age of forty-four.

What, then, was the content of the missive that triggered such a sad chain of events? The letter appears to have been part of a Scholastic dispute into which Sor Juana entered willingly in order to provoke a recently appointed Archbishop of Mexico, Francisco Aguiar y Seijas. She had some reasons to resent him. First, it was common knowledge at the time that this man avoided any contact with women, disliked them strongly, and disapproved of their being involved in intellectual practices. Furthermore, he also opposed the literary genre of drama. He had undoubtedly heard of Sor Juana and must have disliked her on all these counts, for not only was she a prominent intellectual, but she had written two plays, *The Truth of a Household* and *The Greater Labyrinth Is Love*. Moreover, Sor Juana's circle of friends appear to have harbored resentment against Aguiar y Seijas too since a prominent member of her circle, the Bishop of Puebla, probably had aspired, without success, to the post of Archbishop of Mexico. Being close to Sor Juana and knowing her talents, the bishop may well have asked her to write the fatal letter since it was in fact directed against Aguiar y Seijas, the person actually appointed to the post sought by the bishop.

Thus, reasons of her own, together with the encouragement of her friends, may have convinced Sor Juana to write the "Missive." As mentioned earlier, in this letter she offered some arguments against a sermon of the Portuguese Jesuit Antonio de Vieyra. Since it was then common knowledge that Archbishop Aguiar y Seijas sympathized with Vieyra's Scholastic views in philosophy and theology, it was the archbishop that Sor Juana set out to criticize indirectly by offering some arguments against Vieyra. The sermon in question concerned how to interpret Christ's advice to the apostles that they should love one another as he had loved them. Against Vieyra's beliefs, Sor Juana held that Christ's greatest *fineza* (proof of love, or benefaction) had been to refrain from interfering with human volition, so individuals might exercise their free will.

To us this may appear to be so much quibbling about minutiae—a tempest in a teapot. And, certainly, the best philosophers of the time would scarcely have taken notice. In the late seventeenth century, such a topic was largely passé and could have attracted the attention only of intellectuals operating within a Scholastic paradigm. Furthermore, any objection to Vieyra at that time would have been outdated in the eyes of many philosophers since he had given his sermon forty years earlier and had by now left Portugal for Brazil, where he would probably never learn of Sor Juana's arguments.

Once such circumstances are taken into consideration, the question arises: Why did Sor Juana care about writing the "Missive" at all? A plausible answer is one suggested by Octavio Paz, which we may call the plot theory.[17] According to this theory, for the reasons given above, the new Archbishop of Mexico had made enemies of Sor Juana and her friend, the Bishop of Puebla. Although Sor Juana may have agreed to the bishop's proposal that she write the letter, it is still surprising that, when published, the "Missive" was preceded by the bishop's own admonition of Sor Juana's intellectual activities. In the same publication, that is, while covering his identity under the pseudonym of Sor Philotea de la Cruz, he also included a letter of his own in which he reprimanded Sor Juana for being a woman who had the arrogance to address secular subjects in her work.

To the eyes of contemporary readers, an intrigue of this sort hardly makes sense at all. Was the Bishop of Puebla betraying Sor Juana by publishing her "Missive" without her consent? Or, as suggested by Paz, might they both have staged the whole episode to humiliate the archbishop? Although we shall probably never know the answers to these questions, there is evidence that Sor Juana did not give in to the bishop's criticisms preceding her "Missive," for in her famous "Reply to Sor Philotea," which she sent to him some time later, her defense of a woman's right to secular knowledge is unwavering.

Was Sor Juana a Radical Feminist?

Bishop Fernández had insisted in his admonition that women restrict themselves to the study of religious topics. Sor Juana's least persuasive argument against this statement was that he had assumed women's general ability to understand such topics, yet she objected that that was unreasonable. After all, Sor Juana herself may be among those unable to comprehend the mysteries of revealed religion. But in the context of the general tone of the "Reply," her response here is clearly false modesty. In any case, her most notable reasons against the bishop are those that show a pioneering feminist outlook. Sor Juana held that, as with any other rational beings, women have the right to education because they are capable of acquiring knowledge, both in classical literature and the sciences, whether these be the formal sciences of mathematics and logic or the natural ones that provide knowledge of the world. She seems to have conceived of logic in the conventional, Aristotelian way, as an instrument to improve understanding in other disciplines, including religion. But, contrary to the Scholastic prejudices of her time, she also valued empirical knowledge, which she sought not only through the study of the natural sciences but also by reasoning about her own sensory experiences—for instance, while cooking. Even during a period when doctors recommended that she avoid reading books, nothing could stop her intellectual curiosity aroused by the experience of nature itself. Applying reason to the sensory data acquired by observation, she then managed nonetheless to learn about nature without the aid of books.

For a nun of colonial Mexico, it was certainly unusual to argue that classical literature and the natural sciences were appropriate studies for women. But Sor Juana thought that such subjects had objective merit that could be proved. Furthermore, she could refute decisively, by her own experience, the claim that women had neither interest in nor aptitude to learn about them. She showed, by invoking numerous episodes in her own life, that it was in her nature to be curious about almost any discipline, and that this consuming hunger for knowledge was something she had been unable to avoid since childhood. Thus, despite the bishop's reprimand, she seemed determined to continue with her study of secular subjects.

The bishop's opposition, of course, was not to the study of such subjects but only to their being studied by women. In his view, that would be evidence of arrogance on their part. But Sor Juana held fast to her defense of the right of women to secular education, offering a long list of female intellectuals who had been outstanding scholars in various subjects since antiquity, many in secular fields. Unfortunately, the cost of the "Reply" was considerable: nothing less than her career. The pressure from high officials of the Church seems to have been too much, for as a result of the "Missive," she was not only admonished by the Bishop of Puebla but also abandoned by her friends, including her own confessor, Antonio Núñez of the Society of Jesus, to whom she wrote,

> My studies have not been to the harm or detriment of any person, having been so extremely private that I have not even enjoyed the direction of a teacher, but have learned only from myself and my work, for I am not unaware that to study publicly in schools is not seemly for a woman's honor. . . . [B]ut private and individual study, who has forbidden that to women? Like men, do they not have a rational soul? Why then shall they not enjoy the privilege of the enlightenment of letters?[18]

For writing her pioneering manifesto of women rights to education, her penalty was to be denounced by her allies. Sor Juana, her spirit crushed, retired into the seclusion of a religious life.

Beyond doubt, her attitude toward knowledge and women's rights must have been perceived as a menace by practitioners of the Scholastic paradigm, who dominated the intellectual life of Mexico during the colonial period. But it could hardly have been otherwise, given her devotion to empiricist principles. Like Acosta, she seems to have held that beliefs about the world must be grounded in the natural sciences and in one's own sensory experience, rather than the usual appeal to authorities and to philosophical argument so dear to the Scholastics. Sor Juana had addressed this topic—a major theme of the "Reply"—before in her long poem *Primero Sueño (First Dream)*, a work quite subversive at the time and probably one of the pieces the bishop had in mind when he condemned her treatment of secular subjects.

In spite of colonial Mexico's Scholastic strictures, Sor Juana managed to develop a modern mind. But could she be considered a feminist? Yes, and her feminism was quite radical in her time. On the other hand, if we were to categorize her by contemporary standards, we would have to conclude that her feminism was actually a more moderate form, for it made demands that some feminists today would probably consider uninteresting or even wrongheaded. This is because even though Sor Juana clearly rejected sexism and androcentrism, she also seems to have advocated the equality of people. When the issue was knowledge, for example, she held that *all* humans have similar rights to it, whether they be women or men. Some contemporary feminists, however, adopt what we may call the radical position, combining these two theses:[19]

1. There is *no* objective truth to be known by anyone, *and,*
2. Women and men may acquire knowledge in ways that are relevantly different.

Note that although the second claim concerns a possibility, radical feminists now often hold that there is in fact a distinctive way women acquire knowledge—which differs from, and even conflicts with, that of men. Given the first thesis, such rival ways could equally lead to truth. That women and men acquire knowledge in ways necessarily different (where the necessity derives from the laws of biology and is thus nomological) is a claim that needs the support of empirical evidence. Moreover, the whole view rests on the complex assumption that since there is no objective truth, therefore knowledge cannot be objective—which also is in need of supporting reasons. And if there is no objective truth, then, since knowledge implies truth, questions arise as to whether any group of cognizers could achieve objective knowledge at all. How are we supposed to know that the above theses are true? Furthermore, by sincerely asserting these theses, are we not claiming that they *are* objectively true? Thus construed, contemporary radical feminism appears to boil down to an inconsistent form of epistemic relativism.

In any case, Sor Juana's arguments are not vulnerable to objection on that score. Her writings provide sufficient evidence that her views need not be identified with a relativism of that sort. She championed instead more modest feminist demands, which were nonetheless very progressive for her time and are surprisingly similar to those made later by the feminist movement of the early twentieth century. The "Reply" and other documents such as the letter to her confessor clearly show that Sor Juana did not advocate any version of contemporary radical feminism as construed above. Rather, she insisted that women are rational beings and must be granted the same intellectual rights as men. Since she also championed the primacy of empirical knowledge, we may conclude that aside from her feminist demands, her writings and her tragic life were significantly progressive in the context of her culture. They clearly called for a modern revolution to rid colonial Mexico of the old Scholastic paradigm.

Modern science and philosophy offer numerous examples of dissident intellectuals like Sor Juana, whose ideas were altogether rejected because they conflicted with the ruling paradigms accepted by mainstream thinkers in their societies. Copernicus and Galileo, among others, faced tough opposition within the medieval universities dominated by the Church. They nonetheless managed to prevail in the end and helped to make the modern revolution that overthrew the Scholastic paradigm in Europe. Their cases, however, differed from those of subversive Hispanic Americans, for the latter seem mostly to have been either ignored (José de Acosta) or persecuted and crushed (Sor Juana), so that the Scholastic order in Latin America remained undisturbed. Thus their cases generate a puzzle for us: How was it possible that a paradigm already obsolete in Europe, which had been rejected by local intellectuals such as Acosta, Sor Juana, and some others, retained its grip in the colonies for more than three centuries?[20]

Colonial Scholasticism in Context

The grip of Scholasticism on Hispanic America, however, has an explanation, for during the colonial era, it was the reigning philosophical method in Spain and Portugal and thus was imposed on the New World for the whole period of their domination. In that way, an altogether stagnant paradigm came to prevail in the colonies for centuries, with only a few modifications and additions introduced as they became accepted in Iberian universities. Moreover, the introduction of Scholasticism in the colonies seems to have gone hand in hand with the elimination of the indigenous peoples' autochthonous worldviews, leading to a further impoverishment of the colonial culture. It also brought about the isolation of Hispanic Americans from the rest of the world since they were thus exposed only to ideas already passé in the continent of origin. Knowledge of modern ideas commonly found in the cities of Europe was simply not an option for the colonies for several centuries.

Although some such ideas managed to circulate underground, most of them were hardly known in the colonies. Iberian representatives and their Creole acolytes typically determined which theories could enter that part of the world, taking whatever measures were needed to keep completely out of reach those ideas deemed unacceptable. Church officials played a role in this conspiracy, as did the vast bureaucracies of the local government and the recently established universities. Because of the success of Iberian censorship, neither changes in the existing philosophical and scientific dogmas nor rival views of any kind could take root within official institutions during the golden age of Iberian colonialism. The formidable achievement of preserving a paradigm that had already fallen in major centers of Europe was the work of Iberian political authorities and their colonial minions, who were able to secure the cooperation of the Church in punishing harshly anyone whose ideas were perceived as a threat to Scholasticism. Octavio Paz describes their success in the New World as a Pyrrhic victory:

> The Church in Europe became stationary and defensive. Scholasticism, its main defense, was as ineffective as the ponderous Spanish ships that were defeated by the lighter vessels of England and the Netherlands. The decadence of European Catholicism coincided with its apogee in Spanish America: it spread out over new lands at the very moment it had ceased to be creative. It offered a set philosophy and petrified faith, so that the originality of the new believers found no way of expressing itself. . . . Catholicism offered a refuge to the descendants of those who had seen the extermination of their ruling classes, the destruction of their temples and manuscripts, and the suppression of the superior forms of their culture; but for the same reason that it was decadent in Europe, it denied them any chance of expressing their singularity.[21]

Simón Bolívar: Independence Leads to Puzzles

By the end of the eighteenth century, however, Latin American intellectuals were aware of the existence of new philosophical movements that had swept Europe: rationalism, empiricism, modern liberal theories, and other alternatives to Scholasticism. That awareness, together with political and economic reasons, contributed to their resolution to free themselves from colonial rule. The year 1810 marks the beginning of political movements to take up arms in that cause since it was in that year that Argentina and Colombia declared their independence from Spain. Iberian powers were soon to realize that these would not be isolated episodes, for similar declarations followed suit throughout their colonies. But liberation from colonial rule was not to be achieved easily. With the exception of Brazil, which obtained its independence from Portugal through peaceful negotiation in 1889, Latin American nations struggled fiercely to free themselves from allegiance to the Spanish crown.

Needless to say, questions concerning sovereignty had high currency on the agendas of Latin American thinkers during the nineteenth century and through the end of the wars of independence shortly after 1824 (with the exception of Cuba, which achieved independence only after the uprising of 1895). More than three centuries of colonial rule had made Latin Americans eager for liberation, and the revolutions of the nineteenth century generated optimistic expectations among them that they could finally be politically independent and could choose their own forms of organization. Yet achieving this goal proved to be difficult since most original ideas were not indigenous, and most indigenous ideas were not original. By and large, Latin American intellectuals simply accepted uncritically the models adopted in the United States, Great Britain, and other Western countries.

One of the leaders of the independence movement, Simón Bolívar (1783–1830), was an exception, for he seems to have held that forms of political and social organization must be contingent upon the needs of each nation. Born in Venezuela, Bolívar grew up in a Creole family of landowners. He was educated partly in Europe and served as the commander of a Latin American army that fought against the Spaniards from 1811 to 1826. His role in that war earned him the title of *Libertador* ("Liberator"), for his leadership was crucial to the emancipation of many countries from Peru to Central America. But unlike General José de San Martín of Argentina (1778–1850), who is credited with the liberation of the southern part of the continent,[22] Bolívar had political aspirations aside from his military career. He wrote a constitution for Bolivia and served as president of Greater Colombia (present-day Colombia, Venezuela, Ecuador, and Panama) after his forces defeated the Spanish army at Boyaca (on August 7, 1819). While in that post, he also organized the government of Peru and authorized the partition that created Bolivia. In 1826 he called for a conference of the newly emancipated countries, and thus he is now usually credited with having initiated Pan-Americanism. Declaring himself dictator of Greater Colombia in 1828, he managed to remain in power only until 1830, when ill health and disillusionment led him to resign shortly before his death.

Bolívar's place in history, however, is not only as a general and a political leader. In connection with these achievements, he offered certain ideas that are of interest to us, which can be found in his letters, proclamations, and public addresses.[23] In his view, there is no universally valid form of political and social organization, for each group of people should be able to choose an arrangement that best fits its own cultural traditions and social conventions as well as the physical contingencies of its environment. These, of course, will be different for different ethnic groups and nationalities. In the case of his own group, which he sometimes referred to as the "Latin American nation," he believed that political arrangements must acknowledge the *mestizo* character of its people, who were of a mixed history, race, and ethnicity. "We are not Europeans; we are not Indians," he wrote;

> we are but a mixed species of aborigines and Spaniards. Americans by birth and Europeans by law, we find ourselves engaged in a dual conflict: we are disputing with the natives for titles of ownership, and at the same time we are struggling to maintain ourselves in the country that gave birth against the opposition of the invaders [the Spaniards].[24]

According to Bolívar, that mixed makeup of Latin Americans should count as a relevant factor in any deliberation about the form of government (or social organization) their nations should adopt. The distinctive features of Latin American geography and the physical characteristics of the land should, he thought, also play a role in the deliberation. The notion that different peoples in different places with different cultural traditions may require different kinds of political systems is an idea whose time had *not* come in Bolívar's day, and apparently has not come yet. Today it is widely assumed that there is one form of political organization, liberal democracy, that is the *only* kind of arrangement that all people should have. Every society is said to be better off if ruled in that way. We may define liberal democracy as follows:

> A society is organized as a liberal democracy if and only if its members *periodically* have a say in deciding (a) common policies, and (b) who their leaders and representatives in the government will be.

After the revolutions of 1689 in Britain, 1776 in the United States, and 1789 in France, many political thinkers became persuaded that liberal democracy is universally valid. Furthermore, as is clear from the arguments of Locke, Montesquieu, Jefferson, and many others, a strong case can be made that all human beings have the equal right to live in a society organized in that way. Given this view, humans may be clearly entitled to liberal democracy, which seems to amount to nothing less than a human right. Yet such an entitlement has sometimes been challenged. The Marxist critique of liberal democracy based on capitalism represents perhaps the best-known set of objections. More recently, some political thinkers have also argued that liberal democracy may not suit the local needs of every nation, citing in particular the circumstances in Asian societies—an objection that has originated a controversy known as "the Asian-value debate" of the 1990s.[25]

This seems, however, only a revisiting of some ideas proposed long before by Bolívar. In the mid-nineteenth century, he questioned whether people should always have the *right* to periodically elect their leaders and representatives in the government—in other words, clause (b) above. But that position plainly amounts to questioning the very idea of liberal democracy, of which that clause is a necessary element. According to him, ethnic, cultural, and environmental differences among groups of people may make it impossible for *all* societies to adopt that model. Bolívar was not opposed to democracy, but the more he admired "the excellence" of such a form of government, the more he was "convinced of the impossibility of its application" to all Latin American nations.[26] In 1819, he wrote,

> [R]egardless of the effectiveness of this form of government with
> respect to North America, I must say that it has never for a mo-
> ment entered my mind to compare the position and character of
> two states as dissimilar as the English-American and the Spanish-
> American. Would it not be most difficult to apply to Spain the En-
> glish system of political, civil, and religious liberty?. . . [L]aws
> must take into account the physical conditions of the country, cli-
> mate, character of the land, location, size, and mode of living of
> the people.[27]

   Yet if people in a certain society do not have the right to elect their
leaders and their representatives in the government periodically,
then that society is not a liberal democracy as we have defined it.
Bolívar seems clearly to have rejected the view that there was any
such universal right—as is plain, both from his writings and from
his own political career, since he did assume the post of dictator of
Venezuela and New Granada for a short period of time, until overthrown by the opposition.
   Bolívar's position on liberal democracy, however, was far from rejecting it outright. On the contrary, he held that some Latin American
countries would indeed benefit from such a polity. Thus he could
maintain, without contradiction, that, for example, Chile and Mexico would make good democratic republics, a possibility about which
he speculated in a somewhat oracular tone: "The Kingdom of Chile
is destined, by the nature of its location, by the simple and virtuous
character of its people, and by the example of its neighbors, the
proud republicans of Arauco, to enjoy the blessings that flow from
the just and gentle laws of a republic." And "by nature of their geographic location, wealth, population, and character, I expect that the
Mexicans, at the outset, intend to establish a representative republic
in which the executive will have great power."[28] But unless more empirical evidence is offered to show why liberal democracy is suitable
(or even possible) in these cases but impossible in others, remarks
such as these must be taken as merely expressing Bolívar's own intuitions. Other Latin American thinkers provided well-developed arguments defending democracy as a form of political organization for

particular countries. For example, Juan Bautista Alberdi (Argentinian, 1810–1884), offered extensive arguments to that effect for Argentinian democracy in his *Bases y Puntos de Partida para la Organizacion Nacional* (1852), a work that served as the basis of Argentina's constitution, adopted in 1853.[29]

Must Political Systems Accommodate Ethnic Diversity?

Bolívar's intuitions about the optimal forms of political organization for Latin American societies are of great interest since they reveal his originality compared to other thinkers of his time. Although those thinkers were aware of the emerging nations' ethnic diversity and distinctive character, they sought to emulate Western countries as the means to their nations' development. This led them to study Western liberal democratic models of political organization and simply assume that they could be adapted to Latin American nations.

But Bolívar seems to have realized that it is difficult to fit in a borrowed dress. His clear sense of political realities may have made him more aware of the diversity of the region and more willing to respect it than most of his contemporaries were. Beyond doubt, he understood that Latin America was a vast region of mixed ethnic, racial, and historical backgrounds. For example, he wrote,

> We must keep in mind that our people are neither European nor North American; rather, they are a mixture of African and the Americans who originated in Europe. Even Spain herself has ceased to be European because of her African blood, her institutions, and her character. It is impossible to determine with any degree of accuracy where we belong in the human family. The greater portion of the native Indians have been annihilated; Spaniards have mixed with Americans and Africans, and Africans with Indians and Spaniards. While we have all been born of the same mother, our fathers, different in origins and in blood, are foreigners, and all differ visibly as to the color of their

skin: a dissimilarity which places upon us an obligation of the greatest importance.[30]

Let us call "Bolivarism" the notion that different forms of political and social organization will be appropriate for different groups of people, depending on their historical and ethnic backgrounds and the realities of their physical environment. It is a matter of dispute how Bolívar himself understood the relation between those variable factors and a determinate judgment about the best form of political and social organization for any group of people—Bolivarism can be construed in more than one way. Yet there is no doubt about how thinkers of the next generation interpreted Bolívar's principle: It was clearly understood to imply determinism. To those thinkers, any nation's optimal form of political organization is contingent, in a strong sense, upon the background of its people.

Sarmiento's Dilemma: Whose Civilization Is Preferable to Barbarism?

Among the champions of the determinist view was an Argentinian social thinker, man of letters, and politician, Domingo Faustino Sarmiento (1811–1888). According to his own autobiographical account in *Recuerdos de Provincia (Memories from the Province)*, Sarmiento's experiences in the provinces of Argentina contributed to his belief that ethnic and environmental factors must determine a society's political and social organization. This view, moreover, soon became popular among other intellectuals and prepared the ground for a more rigorous determinism that accompanied the rise of positivism in Latin America during the second half of the nineteenth century.

Sarmiento grew up in San Juan, a small town too far away from any educational institution to allow him to attend school. Nevertheless, as his autobiography reveals, his childhood was filled with intellectual curiosity. He managed to acquire completely on his own the necessary knowledge of history, politics, and foreign languages to learn about the major social and political theories then being discussed in Europe and North America. Like many other Latin American thinkers of the nineteenth century, Sarmiento took an interest in the political and social controversies of his newly independent country and immersed himself in its political life. While still a young man of the provinces, he openly opposed the rule of the dictator of Argentina, Juan Manuel de Rosas (1793–1877). For reasons we shall consider below, Sarmiento believed that Rosas represented *el espíritu de las pampas* (the spirit of the Pampas)—in effect a symbol of barbarity. The Pampas, a vast prairie then controlled partly by Rosas and partly by native Indians, Sarmiento perceived as an impediment to the organization of Argentina; and Rosas, as its defender, he regarded as a retrograde influence that must be defeated. Although Sarmiento's early efforts were crushed, he did not lose heart. Forced by the dictator into involuntary exile, he campaigned indefatigably in Chile for Rosas's overthrow. Sarmiento also opposed the *gauchos*, the nomad people of the Pampas, whose *caudillos* (or chieftains) rose to positions of power during Rosas's regime. One of them, Facundo Quiroga (1790–1835), was popular among the *gauchos* of La Rioja, a province similar in isolation to Sarmiento's own native region, and Sarmiento held this local despot in especially low regard. He referred to Quiroga as *el tigre de los llanos* (the tiger of the plains), often scorning his leadership as demagogic and ruthless, a small-potatoes imitation of Rosas himself.

After Rosas was finally brought down, Sarmiento returned to Argentina and joined the forces working to establish a liberal democracy. From then until his death, he was active in Argentine politics, serving in various official capacities, including president of the Republic, an office he held from 1868 to 1874. Sarmiento had an abiding interest in the culture and political institutions of North America and took the United States as a model for the development of Argentina. Because education figured prominently among his concerns, much of his time in government service was devoted to improving the educational system of his country following the U.S. model. Thus, he brought American teachers to Argentina and established numerous new schools where the latest pedagogical methods from the United States were applied.

Sarmiento also sought to improve his country through other forms of social planning. Because he saw the isolation of those living in the vast Argentinian plains as a threat to liberal democracy, he encouraged European immigration to populate these areas. At the same time, he perceived some ethnic groups as essentially idle and prone to violence, and these he sought to replace. In his day, however, Sarmiento was not alone in encouraging European immigration, for many mainstream intellectuals of the time were aware of the perils of vast uninhabited distances in Latin America and upheld Alberdi's slogan that to govern is to populate. For Sarmiento, the slogan would be better recast as "to govern is to populate *and* educate" since he saw access to education (and *improved* education) as the cornerstone of any program of national development. Furthermore, unlike Bolívar, Sarmiento seems to have taken liberal democracy to be the only polity appropriate for "civilized" (or industrious and progressive) nations. Of course in his preferred model, the United States, liberal democracy had acquired the status of a universal right at least since its independence from Great Britain. But in Sarmiento's thinking, there were clearly also more sinister motives at work, for he held that some ethnic groups (especially among nonwhites) were not amenable to a similar form of political organization and should be replaced with immigrants of European origins.

Is There a Connection Between Race and Character? *Facundo*'s Ethnic Stereotypes

Sarmiento's inclinations to liberal democracy may account for his numerous writings against Rosas, Quiroga, and other partisans of autocratic leadership. In those writings, however, Sarmiento consistently campaigned against *caudillos* not only on these counts but also because of some instincts or psychological traits they allegedly had that in his view predisposed them to be enemies of civilization. Although invectives against political leaders along such lines can be found in many of Sarmiento's writings, they figure prominently in *Facundo, or Civilization and Barbarism* (1845). In addition to powerful narratives against Quiroga and Rosas, written mostly to undermine these leaders in the eyes of European and North American readers, *Facundo* also contains numerous passages expressing Sarmiento's own account of what was wrong with Argentina.

That he endorsed a determinist position on the relation between an environment and the social behavior of the people who live in it is clear from *Facundo*'s opening pages. The first chapter is subtitled, "Physical Aspects of the Argentine Republic, and the Forms of Character, Habits, and Ideas *Induced* by It,"[31] and its contents, like other parts of the book, betray a determinist understanding of what we have called Bolivarism. Thus, in describing the vast and desolate territory of the country, Sarmiento implies that this physical geography causes bad character traits, amounting to "the evil from which the Argentine Republic suffers."[32] It is true that in his day, life in the Pampas entailed a bleak solitude and numerous perils for white settlers. Most of that region was inhabited by Indians, especially the fierce Tehuelches or Patagones, whose attacks on white settlements were not uncommon. Although these peoples had been forced out of their own lands during the Iberian Conquest, Sarmiento and many of his countrymen considered invalid their claim to vast territories in the Pampas. "The Argentine Republic ends at the Arroyo del Medio," Sarmiento observed resentfully, for it was well known that, beyond Arroyo del Medio (a stream of water in the southern part of the province of Buenos Aires), the rest of Argentina was predominantly Indian territory.[33]

To the perils generated by the presence of these "savages," Sarmiento thought, must be added those caused by the crude and antisocial behavior of the nomadic *gauchos*, the other typical inhabitants of the Pampas. These were a *mestizo* people of Spanish, Creole, and Indian ancestry. "This constant insecurity of life outside towns . . . stamps upon the Argentine character a certain stoical resignation to death by violence. . . . Perhaps this is the reason why they inflict death or submit to it with so much indifference, and why such events make no deep or lasting impression upon the survivors."[34]

Thus Sarmiento seems to have held a strong social determinist thesis along these lines:

> SD Not only *what* a group of people thinks but also *how* it thinks and acts depends on the physical environment where the people live in such a way that, if the environment were

relevantly different, what they think and how they think and act would be different.

But this claim would make his position inconsistent—since, as we have seen, he also encouraged European immigration to settle the Pampas. If *SD* is true, then Europeans who immigrated and lived there long enough would come to have the degenerate traits of character that Sarmiento thought he perceived in *gauchos* and Indians. To avoid such blatant inconsistency, his position may be reconstrued charitably as holding instead that it is the environment together with some features essential to a certain ethnic group (perhaps some characteristic psychological traits) that determine the thoughts and behavior of that group and thus make it fitted for one form of political and social organization rather than another.

A reading of Sarmiento along these lines can accommodate his social stereotypes since to him people in Argentina belonged to one or the other of two kinds. Each person was inherently amenable either to civilization or to barbarism. Among the former, he placed non-Spanish Western Europeans,[35] North Americans, Porteños (inhabitants of Buenos Aires, the capital of Argentina), and also other white Creole people from major cities such as Cordoba. But he also appears to have included *mulatos* (dark-skinned people of mixed Spaniard, Creole, and African ancestry) among this group. Of them he wrote, "This race mostly inhabiting cities, has a tendency to become civilized, and possesses talent and the finest instincts of progress."[36]

On the other hand, there were those groups Sarmiento considered prone to barbarism and thus inherently unfit for civilization. Among these, he included the Creole people living in isolated parts of the Pampas (white settlers of Spanish ancestry), *gauchos*, and of course the Indians. The last he took to be "characterized by love of idleness and incapacity for industry." But Pampas-dwelling Creoles of Spanish heritage were no better: He found that their "race has not shown itself more energetic than the aborigines, when it has been left to its instincts in the wilds of America."[37]

In this analysis, each Argentinian fell within either the civilized groups or the barbaric ones. "The people composing these two distinct forms of society," Sarmiento pontificated, "do not seem to belong to the same nation."[38] He probably meant this dichotomy to apply to other nations of the Americas as well since the references to barbaric practices in *Facundo* reach even the North American Indians when Sarmiento compares the *gaucho*'s skills and habits to those of the main Indian character in James Fenimore Cooper's *Last of the Mohicans*. Of course, that dichotomy also served Sarmiento's political purpose of attacking adversaries such as Quiroga and Rosas, for in this analysis they turn up within the irredeemable ethnic groups beyond all hope of civilization—the "tiger of the plains," the "spirit of the Pampas."

To us, these efforts at determinist sociology seem far-fetched. What could Sarmiento have possibly had in mind here? Perhaps he thought of the "instincts of a race" as salient psychological traits observable in the members of a certain ethnic group, which he obviously considered part of each individual's (genetic) heritage. If he was right, then such traits, together with certain features of their physical environment, completely determine the group's capacity for political and social organization. In support of this determinist view, Sarmiento appealed to authorities: "Many philosophers have also thought that plains prepare the way for despotism, just as mountains furnish strongholds for the struggles of liberty."[39] And the United States, he thought, was determined to be a confederacy simply because of its breadth—extending from ocean to ocean—while Argentina, with its borders, was bound to be one "indivisible" republic.

Although *Facundo* clearly aimed at undermining Rosas's dictatorship through a lengthy (and probably exaggerated) description of atrocities allegedly committed by his supporter, Quiroga, the main interest of the book today is in its account of the diverse Argentinian society of the time and Sarmiento's own reaction to it. Sarmiento may also have wanted to offer foreign readers a look at certain "exotic" social types since he compared the *gauchos*' way of life to that of bedouins in the Sahara, remarking on the similarity of their nomadic existence. Yet he held the *gauchos* inferior to the bedouins since among the latter association was possible, and among the *gauchos* it was not. The Arabs of the desert, after all, shared within their tribes religious beliefs, traditions, laws, moral codes, and the like. Even so, neither group could really achieve progress because of their nomadic lifestyles. The Argentinian *gauchos*, however, were in fact worse off, for they could achieve neither progress nor association.

Beyond doubt, this amounts to a harsh judgment on the *gauchos*, and why should we think it was true? In *Facundo*, the reasoning appears to be as follows:

1. Idleness and impossibility of progress are inherent tendencies in certain groups of people.
2. If those groups of people live in isolation, such features develop.
3. *Criollos, gauchos,* and Indians have those inherent tendencies.
4. Some *criollos* live in isolation and so do the *gauchos* and the Indians.

Therefore,

5. Those *criollos, gauchos,* and Indians are by nature idle and can never achieve any progress.

This argument is a possible reconstruction of how Sarmiento understood and applied the determinist principle. For reasons discussed above, his position surely assumed that social behavior was the product of more than geographic factors. But, however construed, the determinist principle is itself an empirical claim that must be supported by evidence from observation in controlled experiments of the social sciences. Likewise, the premises of this argument express empirical beliefs. Yet apart from (4), which rests on facts well known in his time, all the other premises in Sarmiento's argument are utterly lacking in the support of serious observational data. There is simply no reason to think that either (1), (2), or (3) is true.

Moreover, Sarmiento's remarks on race,[40] though sometimes obscure, do suggest that he held that Latin American Indians, together with those *criollos* and *gauchos* who lived in isolation, were—because of their race—destined to develop characteristics of backwardness and indolence. Yet this clearly presupposes hasty generalizations about entire groups of people, and we have seen that such generalizations often rest on nothing more than ethnocentric prejudice. Furthermore, how shall we determine whether the practices of a certain group demonstrate, for example, their idleness? Apart from superficial observations of what he takes to have been the actual ways of life of these peoples, Sarmiento provides no support for his stronger conclusion that they could never be industrious, cultivate habits of education and restraint, and live peaceably in a civilized society. Since Sarmiento's premises do nothing to support the severe judgment of his conclusion, the argument must be rejected. It would, however, be a mistake to dismiss Sarmiento's views, so full of bias, as unimportant. Indeed, his ideas were among the most influential of any Latin American thinker of his time. What shall we make of this unsettling conclusion? Perhaps only that popular approbation rewards wisdom less often than folly.

Discussion Questions

1. Evaluate the following claim: By the turn of the sixteenth century, Scholasticism was an obsolete paradigm.
2. How did the method used by Scholastics in the natural sciences differ from that used by modern scientists? Could they be compatible?
3. Define the notion of paradigm and list the theories or movements considered building blocks of the modern paradigm in the text.
4. In which sense did José de Acosta's views amount to a challenge to the Scholastic paradigm?
5. In their colonial expansion, Spain and Portugal contributed to the modern revolution in cosmography by promoting explorations overseas. What were the common misconceptions that those explorations help to correct?
6. Acosta argued against some of the Scholastics' authorities by using the method of counterexample. Describe the method and illustrate with some of Acosta's arguments.
7. Edmundo O'Gorman held that America was not discovered but was invented. State some common reasons for that claim and assess the resulting argument.
8. Which of the following contemporary categories would be more congenial to Sor Juana's view in her "Reply to Sor Philotea": contemporary radical feminism, moderate feminism, or antifeminism? Which of these seems more acceptable to you? Could her feminism be considered radical in her time? Explain.

9. In some construals of contemporary feminism, *truth* is taken to be relative to gender. What could be meant by this? Could this claim be supported? If so, how? If not, why not?

10. Provide an argument to defend women's right to knowledge. Evaluate that argument.

11. In the "Reply," Sor Juana holds that women are better than men at imparting knowledge—for example, as teachers. How could that claim be supported? If Sor Juana is right, must the difference between men and women in this respect be biologically based?

12. According to Simón Bolívar, Chile and Mexico were destined to be liberal democratic republics because of their locations and the character of their peoples. Is this claim compatible with denying the universality of liberal democracy? Discuss.

13. Why did Bolívar think that Latin Americans were neither Europeans nor Indians? Would that view hold today?

14. State the principle of "Bolivarism." How could the principle be read within a strong determinist construal?

15. In which sense was Argentina's geography relevant to Domingo Sarmiento's political and social thought?

16. According to Sarmiento, Argentina had certain social types, which created a dilemma. What was that dilemma? Would it, in Sarmiento's view, have arisen in other Latin American countries in the nineteenth century?

17. What did Sarmiento have in mind when he declared that the Argentine Republic ended at the Arroyo del Medio?

18. Sarmiento considered *gaucho*s, Indians, and some *criollos* as being inherently uncivilized. What did that mean for him? Did he offer any reason to support that claim?

19. In *Facundo*, Sarmiento draws an analogy between the *gauchos* and some tribal people of Asian and African countries. In Sarmiento's view, what did these groups have in common? Do you agree?

20. Why would Sarmiento's position be nonsensical or even inconsistent if his determinism held that social behavior was entirely the product of environmental factors?

Suggestions for Further Reading

Acosta, José de. 1604. *The Natural & Moral History of the Indies*, vols. 1 & 2. London: Hakluyt Society.

Alberdi, Juan Bautista. 1886–1887. *Obras completas.* Buenos Aires: Tribuna Nacional.

Bolívar, Simón. 1951. *Selected Writings of Bolivar.* Harold A. Bierck Jr., ed. New York: Colonial Press.

———. 1970. *The Libertador, Simón Bolívar: Man and Image.* D. Bushnell, ed. New York: Alfred A. Knopf.

Castro-Klarén, Sara, Sylvia Molloy, and Beatriz Sarlo, eds. 1991. *Women's Writing in Latin America: An Anthology.* Boulder: Westview Press.

de la Cruz, Juana Inés. 1988a. "Reply to Sor Philothea." In Octavio Paz, ed., *A Sor Juana Anthology.* Cambridge, Mass.: Harvard University Press, pp. 166–243.

———. 1988b. "Sor Juana: Witness for the Prosecution." Reprinted in Octavio Paz, *Sor Juana, or the Traps of Faith.* Cambridge, Mass.: Harvard University Press, pp. 491–502.

———. 1998. *Autodefensa Espiritual: Letter of Sor Juana Inés de la Cruz to Her Confessor.* San Antonio, Tex.: Galvart Press.

Dussel, Enrique D. 1976. "Colonial Christendom in Latin America." In *History and the Theology of Liberation: A Latin American Perspective.* Maryknoll, N.Y.: Orbis.

———. 1978. "Feminism and Women's Liberation" and "Scholasticism and the Modern Period." In *Ethics and the Theology of Liberation.* Maryknoll, N.Y.: Orbis.

O'Gorman, Edmundo. 1961. *The Invention of America: An Inquiry into the Historical Nature of the New World and the Meaning of Its History.* Bloomington, Ind.: Indiana University Press.

Paz, Octavio. 1961. *The Labyrinth of Solitude: Life and Thought in Mexico.* New York: Grove Press.

———. 1988. *Sor Juana, or the Traps of Faith.* Cambridge, Mass.: Harvard University Press.

Reyes, Alfonso. 1950. "The Tenth Muse." In *The Position of America.* New York: Alfred A. Knopf.

Sarmiento, Domingo F. 1998. *Facundo, or Civilization and Barbarism.* New York: Penguin.

Notes

1. See Thomas Kuhn, *The Structure of Scientific Revolutions* (Chicago: University of Chicago Press, 1962).

2. Our distinction between science and philosophy is a modern invention traceable to the early modern period and the rise of empirical science.

Up to that time, scholars would not have seen them as sharply distinguished.

3. José de Acosta, *The Natural & Moral History of the Indies* (London: Hakluyt Society, 1604). Citations correspond to this translation, here rendered into modern English.

4. See Acosta, *Natural & Moral History*, vol. 1, chapters 2, 4, 5, 7, 9, and 12, and vol. 2, chapter 6.

5. Acosta, *Natural & Moral History*, vol. 1, p. 20.

6. Acosta, *Natural & Moral History*, vol. 1, p. 4.

7. Acosta, *Natural & Moral History*, vol. 1, p. 25.

8. Acosta, *Natural & Moral History*, pp. 28–29.

9. Acosta, *Natural & Moral History*, vol. 1, p. 2. Emphasis mine.

10. Acosta, *Natural & Moral History*, p. 3.

11. Edmundo O'Gorman, *The Invention of America* (Bloomington, Ind.: Indiana University Press, 1961).

12. Juana Inés de la Cruz, "Reply to Sor Philothea," in Octavio Paz, ed., *A Sor Juana Anthology* (Cambridge, Mass.: Harvard University Press, 1988a) p. 210.

13. Octavio Paz, *Sor Juana, or The Traps of Faith* (Cambridge, Mass.: Harvard University Press, 1988).

14. Alfonso Reyes, *The Position of America* (New York: Alfred A. Knopf, 1950).

15. For a detailed discussion of that letter, see Paz, *Traps of Faith*, pp. 389–410.

16. Although Sor Juana's "Reply" may be considered an early feminist manifesto, it was not available in English until 1982.

17. See Paz, *Traps of Faith*, part 6.

18. Paz, "The Letter," in *Traps of Faith*, p. 498.

19. To Lorraine Code, for instance, mainstream epistemology has "a mask of objectivity and value-neutrality," but there is in fact a "complex power structure of vested interest, dominance, and subjugation" behind that mask. See "The Impact of Feminism in Epistemology" in *APA Newsletter on Feminism and Philosophy*, reprinted in M. Griffiths and M. Whitford, eds., *Feminist Perspectives in Philosophy* (Bloomington, Ind.: Indiana University Press, 1988), pp. 188ff.

20. The Scholastic mentality persisted in Latin American universities until the advent of positivism in the late nineteenth century. In "Contemporary Argentine Philosophy," Risieri Frondizi describes the unfortunate situation of Father Juan Crisóstomo Lafinur, who in 1819 was expelled from the philosophy faculty of the Colegio de la Union del Sur for advocating

the new ideas of French philosophy, was tried, and was sent into exile. But the seeds of subversion were planted, for in 1822 Father Juan Manuel Fernández de Agüero, the first to teach philosophy at the Universidad de Buenos Aires, followed Lafinur's views (*Philosophy and Phenomenological Research* 4 [1943], pp. 180–187).

21. Octavio Paz, *The Labyrinth of Solitude: Life and Thought in Mexico* (New York: Grove Press, 1961), p.105.

22. A *locus classicus* in the study of the wars of independence is Bartolomé Mitre, *The Emancipation of South America* (trans. 1893, repr. New York: Cooper Square Publishers, 1969).

23. Bolívar's political philosophy seems to have been inspired by Jean-Jacques Rousseau through his own readings and through the teachings of a Venezuelan pedagogue, Simón Rodríguez. See Mariano Picón-Salas, "Rousseau in Venezuela," *Philosophy and Phenomenological Research* 4 (1943), pp. 201–208.

24. Simón Bolívar, "The Angostura Address," in Harold A. Bierck Jr., ed., *Selected Writings of Bolívar* (New York: Colonial Press, 1951), pp. 175–176.

25. In *Can Asians Think?* Kishore Mahbubani has recently defended a position that challenges the universalist view of liberal democracy (Singapore: Times Books International, 1998).

26. Bolívar, "The Angostura Address," p. 179.

27. Bolívar, "The Angostura Address," pp. 179–180.

28. Bolívar, "Jamaica Letter," in *Selected Writings*, pp. 117 and 119.

29. Juan Bautista Alberdi, *Obras completas* (Buenos Aires: Tribuna Nacional, 1886–1887).

30. Bolívar, "The Angostura Address," p. 181.

31. Domingo F. Sarmiento, *Facundo, or Civilization and Barbarism* (New York: Penguin, 1998), p. 9. Emphasis mine.

32. Sarmiento, *Facundo*, p. 9.

33. Sarmiento, *Facundo*, p. 12.

34. Sarmiento, *Facundo*, p. 10.

35. In the century of wars of independence, Latin American thinkers were undecided as to whether or not Spaniards should be counted as Europeans. See, for instance, the last citation from Bolívar's letters above. Sarmiento himself appears quite ambivalent about the matter in *Facundo*, especially on p. 19.

36. Sarmiento, *Facundo*, p. 16.

37. Sarmiento, *Facundo*, p. 17.

38. Sarmiento, *Facundo*, p. 19.

39. Sarmiento, *Facundo*, p. 14. Unfortunately, he does not tell us who these philosophers are (and, perhaps as a result of his self-education, when Sarmiento does provide a citation or a reference, it is often in error). See Ilan Stavans's introduction to *Facundo*.

40. Sarmiento, *Facundo*, especially p. 17.

7

LATIN AMERICANS, NORTH AMERICANS, AND THE REST OF THE WORLD

*While Ibero-Americanism finds support in emotions and tradi-
tions, Pan-Americanism finds support in interests and com-
merce. . . . The Yankee model, the Yankee style, is being propa-
gated throughout Indo-Iberian America, while the Spanish
heritage is being destroyed and lost. The hacendado, the
banker, and the rentier of Spanish America look much more at-
tentively toward New York than Madrid. The dollar's rate of
exchange interests them a thousand times more than the
thoughts of Unamuno or Ortega y Gasset's* Review of the West.
*To these people who govern the economy, and therefore the
politics, of Central and South America, the Ibero-American
ideal has little import.*

José Carlos Mariátegui,
"Ibero-Americanism and Pan-Americanism"

From the late nineteenth century to the present, a topic of perennial concern to Latin Americans has been their collective identity. Questions about their nations' sovereignty—in cultural and

economic matters as well as political matters—became important with the final defeat of Spain as a colonial ruler in 1898 and the emergence of a new foreign threat, the United States. Latin Americans at the time, however, also wondered how their own worldviews and practical achievements compared with those of Western powers. In this chapter, we shall examine some ideas Latin Americans developed in their attempt to answer these questions, mindful that the problem of identity remains very much at issue today and seems to arise whenever Latin Americans reflect upon their own position in the context of world cultures.

Autochthonous Positivists

Between 1880 and 1900, a cluster of philosophical doctrines prevalent at the time in Western Europe and known as "positivism" rapidly spread throughout Latin America. Its chief proponents were Auguste Comte (French, 1798–1857)—whose work shows the influence of his teacher Saint-Simon (French, 1760–1825) and other utopian socialists of an earlier generation—and the utilitarians Jeremy Bentham (English, 1748–1832) and John Stuart Mill (English, 1806–1873).[1] By and large, these philosophers embraced "social positivism," a theoretical framework at odds with the received tradition in philosophy—like that of many nineteenth-century natural scientists—because it held that important changes in the empirical world could be explained by appealing only to natural causes. According to those scientists, the universe itself and all living creatures in it should be regarded as the products of evolutionary processes that, in accordance with the laws of nature, had determined the development of all things from simple forms to more complex ones over time. In geology, for example, the complex superorganic world was believed to have developed from an original, simple cosmic nebula. Similarly, the work of several notable biologists popularized the view that species have evolved according to natural selection, random shifts, and other mechanisms that explain the passage from simple organic forms to better adapted systems more fit for survival and reproductive success.[2]

These theories were rapidly accepted in Latin America due in part to their compatibility with views made familiar by local social thinkers who reasoned in ways consistent with social positivism and evolutionary science at a time when these were still unknown on that side of the Atlantic. The "autochthonous positivism"[3] of the mid-1800s can be seen, for example, in the work of Domingo Sarmiento. His *Facundo* clearly displays a positivist concern with human progress, together with deterministic explanations of social phenomena in Argentina, which he thought faced the stark choice of either civilization or barbarism. In his view, each ethnic group in Argentina had actually elected one or the other of these options merely by supporting or opposing what he perceived as social progress. And in his proposed remedies for barbarism, as we saw earlier, Sarmiento appealed to natural causes in his attempt to explain the sociopathic behavior of certain ethnic groups. Although *Facundo* was written before European positivism had spread to Latin America, already it manifests a faith in human progress and a tendency to provide deterministic accounts of social phenomena that are plainly positivist in spirit. In his later work, Sarmiento's endorsement of positivism is patent.[4]

Compare the view of the Italian positivist school of penal law founded by Cesare Lombroso, whose "criminal anthropology" became popular at the end of the nineteenth century.[5] According to that school, criminal behavior is the result of some hereditary organic traits that have affected the psychology of the individuals who engage in it. Clearly, such a view is consistent with Sarmiento's theses in *Facundo*, even though the latter does not invoke the organic constitution of individuals as a factor determining criminal behavior but takes instead hereditary ethnic traits, triggered by the geography of Argentina, to be responsible for the indolent and bellicose character of entire groups. In the same period, the positivist founder of experimental psychology, Wilhelm Wundt,[6] popularized the idea that evolutionary processes condition the customs, languages, and other social behavior of peoples, which is of course also compatible with Sarmiento's views.

That positivism's influence in Latin American countries was pervasive by the end of the nineteenth century has often been noted by scholars, who point out that it affected academic institutions in ways comparable only to those of colonial Scholasticism.[7] But positivism did not last: During the first decades of the twentieth century, thinkers of different, sometimes conflicting, traditions reacted against the generation who had introduced it in the 1880s. Some criticized them for their inability to accommodate values essential to Latin culture. Others found in their doctrines insurmountable obstacles to the development of good philosophy. After all, positivists had concerned themselves mostly with problems of applied social and political thought, which they hoped to solve by emulating the methods of the empirical sciences. Furthermore, they disdained the traditional problems of certain fundamental areas of philosophy, such as metaphysics and epistemology. On the other hand, some critics found positivism unacceptable on moral grounds since positivist-inspired policies were clearly complicit with some notorious instances of social injustice in Latin America. The failure of positivist projects that led to the notorious dictatorships of Porfirio Díaz (1830–1915) in Mexico and Juan V. Gómez (1857–1935) in Venezuela and to genocidal campaigns against the Indians, such as those undertaken by Julio A. Roca (1843–1914) in Argentina, provided formidable reasons for objection on moral grounds. And since the good effects of positivism were evident only in Brazil, it was clear to early-twentieth-century critics that its shortcomings in the subcontinent as a whole far outweighed its merits.

But how are we, today, to judge the role of positivism in Latin America more than a hundred years after its heyday? The movement comprised different doctrines that have been absorbed by Latin Americans in many different ways, some laudable, others disastrous. Arturo Ardao, a contemporary scholar who has investigated those differences at the University of Uruguay, takes this to show both the lack of communication among Latin American nations at the end of the nineteenth century and some idiosyncratic features that developed after independence.[8] Be that as it may, it is clear that, in view of such differences, generalization must be avoided. We shall therefore examine two paradigm cases, Brazil and Mexico, and these will be seen to generate a puzzle, for they appear to support conflicting evaluations of positivism in Latin America.

But first, let us be sure we are clear on just what that position was. In both Europe and Latin America, nineteenth-century positivists agreed that

P 1. All that exists is the natural world.
2. Any adequate explanation of real phenomena in the world must invoke natural causes.
3. The only legitimate methods of inquiry are those of the empirical sciences.
4. Progress, understood as evolution, is inevitable and takes place according to the laws of nature and society.

At the time, theses of this sort amounted to a *naturalistic turn:* a radical departure from the ways Western philosophers and scientists had thought about reality and knowledge since antiquity. For if *P1* is true, then since the only real phenomena would be those of the *natural* world, it follows that there are no *supernatural* beings. Therefore such terms as "angel" and "God" do not name any entities that actually exist: They would be similar to "Santa Claus" or "Superman" in that they are merely names of fictional entities. *P2* entails that it makes no sense to invoke supernatural causes to explain natural phenomena such as the origin of the universe or living creatures. *P3* is a tenet of *scientism*, the view that all disciplines that wish to be taken seriously, including those traditionally considered normative or evaluative, such as ethics, aesthetics, and epistemology, must use the methods of the natural sciences and aim exclusively at scientific explanations. To positivists, the only legitimate ways of learning reduced to those of the natural sciences, so all methods of study then boiled down to scientific ones. Finally, *P4* expresses faith in progress, which went hand in hand with the positivists' support of science and sometimes appeared in their mottoes vindicating order and progress.

Positivism in Brazil

During the second half of the nineteenth century, theses along these lines, together with some other characteristic tenets of Comtism, were embraced by scientists and thinkers at Brazil's Military Academy. In fact, Comtean positivism seems to have had more practical consequences in Brazil than in France.[9] Among the leaders of Brazilian Comtism were Miguel Lemos, Raimundo Teixeira Mendes, Demetrio Ribeiro, and Benjamin Constant Botelho de Magalhaes. In 1881, Lemos and Teixeira Mendes organized the Positivist Church of Brazil, which preached the *anti*religious "Religion of Humanity" envisioned by Comte and led to the creation in 1897 of the Temple of Humanity, another organization to expound their atheistic creed.

In addition, many positivists were active in politics. Benjamin Constant, for example, was prominent among those who participated in the events leading to the proclamation of a republic in November 1889.[10] Under his influence, local scientists and philosophers founded a positivist society in Rio de Janeiro, the *Sociedade Positivista* (1871), a group often associated with the triumph of republicanism over the old, colonial regime.[11]

These Brazilians' devotion to Comte, at least at the outset, was beyond dispute, as the motto on the Brazilian flag, "Order and Progress," makes clear. According to Joâo Cruz Costa, a contemporary historian of Brazilian thought, the influence of orthodox Comtism in Brazil can be traced to 1868, when Tobias Barreto introduced it. He was soon followed by Luís Pereira Barreto (1840–1923), who in 1874 published the first volume of his influential *As Três Filosofias (The Three Philosophies)*. The unopposed dominance of Comtism in Brazil is a distinctive feature of Brazilian positivism since in other parts of Latin America the movement was forced to coexist (and sometimes to merge) with utilitarianism and certain evolutionist theories.[12]

Brazilian Comtism inherited social concerns that had been emphasized by Comte himself in his discussions of the distribution of wealth in mature societies that have reached the final stage of progress. Those concerns gave a distinct character to their movement, yet it is worth asking whether this was in fact due entirely to Comte's influence. Social concerns, after all, were not found solely among Comtean positivists; the British utilitarians clearly had them too, as did the utopian socialists. But then the distinctiveness of Brazilian intellectuals in this respect may be due not to their Comtism, but to their charitable reading of nineteenth-century positivists.

After independence, Brazilian positivists strove to bring about social progress by organizing a sociocracy—which they conceived as a dictatorship of intellectuals. Although this type of polity had been recommended by Comte, the idea that intellectuals should either advise or control their governments was already familiar to the utopian socialists of a previous generation. Brazil never realized such a sociocracy at a national level, even though Julio de Castilhos appears to have established something similar locally in Rio Grande do Sul.[13] In any case, Brazilian Comteans were devoted to the idea of a sociocracy because they believed Comte's general thesis that social progress was not only inevitable but must follow a certain sequence. Such progress, Comte thought, obeys a necessary law of human history that regulates the evolution of humanity itself, as well as that of each person in particular, and determines three stages for any society: theological, metaphysical, and positive. A society that reaches the third stage will be ruled by positivist philosophers and characterized by industry and the prevalence of scientifically formed beliefs that provide real knowledge of facts. It was precisely that final stage that some positivists thought Brazil could enter after its liberation.

However unrealistic their political ideas may have been on the grand scale, Brazilian positivists did have other, more down-to-earth projects for their country that showed their characteristic concern with social issues. In 1880, to help overcome the malignant legacy of colonialism, they advocated the immediate abolition of slavery and corporal punishment, the legal establishment of monogamy as the only form of marriage, some improvements in public education, and important social reforms aiming at better conditions of labor and wages for workers.[14] Their devotion to such reforms distinguished them from their peers in Mexico and other parts of Latin America.

But Brazilian positivists shared with other positivists of the time a general antipathy toward religion—at any rate, toward *theistic* religion. Given the tenets of positivism (see *P* above), it follows that there are no supernatural beings, and that since God does not exist, he cannot be invoked in explanations of any phenomena in the natural world. Because the positivists were atheists, their odd habit of referring to their creed as a *Religion* of Humanity is of course a misnomer. But they were eager to devise a popularly acceptable ideology to compete with Christianity since they were convinced that the latter amounted to nothing more than a pernicious superstition that had a powerful grip on the people's imagination. The Positivist Church of Brazil was therefore created with the intention of undermining the practice of Christianity in that country, a step they believed essential to enlightened social progress. In this, positivists achieved only partial success, for although they gained many converts (and still have some to this day), Roman Catholicism had been enforced for too long to be quickly displaced by positivist doctrines. Some insight into the well-intentioned but unrealistic zeal of these reformers can be gained from Pereira Barreto's *Three Philosophies*, which enthusiastically promoted the positivists' creed as well as the total suppression of Catholicism and any other form of organized, traditional theology. And as Cruz Costa has pointed out, although Pereira Barreto's views on this matter cannot be called authentically Brazilian or even original, they "are to some extent surprising, since Pereira Barreto was well aware of the nature of the environment in which he lived and knew that they would not easily be accepted. . . . Contrary to what he believed, theology still had [after independence] the strength to muster the same influence on which it had counted in the past."[15]

In fact, the influence of the Catholic Church and its philosophy, Scholasticism, had been pervasive in Latin America, not only during the three hundred years of colonial rule, but long after independence. Thus, establishing a beachhead for empiricist skepticism— and even for atheism—in the new nations that may bring about a general change of view proved to be difficult. In that context, the positivist movement of the turn of the century amounted to an intellectual revolution. Among its practical results in Latin America, often acknowledged even by its critics, were the separation of state and religion and the end of the Scholastic domination of academia. Risieri Frondizi (1910–1983), an Argentinian philosopher who has criticized positivists and other Latin Americans thinkers of the nineteenth century for their neglect of theoretical philosophy, nonetheless notes:

> It is unfair to judge the positivists' contribution to philosophy in terms of their written work or in terms of the new ideas developed. Positivistic theories arose as a protest against Scholasticism; their job was to free philosophical issues from the monopoly of the Catholic Church. And they did it very well. Since positivism, a free examination of any philosophical question is possible in Latin America, and even those who later on repudiated positivism took advantage of this definite and fundamental contribution of the positivists.[16]

Brazilian Comteans, in particular, certainly deserve credit for having promoted the natural sciences, hardly cultivated at all in Latin America during the centuries of dogmatic Scholasticism. Ardao considers this "the greatest contribution of positivism in the field of education," noting that "Latin American positivism anticipated and precipitated scientific culture," instead of resulting from scientific thought as in Europe.[17] But all positivists, Latin American as well as European, invariably agreed that philosophy must go hand in hand with science, and this endorsement encouraged many young intellectuals to study the natural sciences. That, in turn, led to a significant enrichment of university curricula and a new freedom of scholarly inquiry.[18] In ridding the region's intellectual life of the iron grip of Scholasticism, positivists no doubt deserve substantial credit for contributing to the advancement of philosophy and science in Latin America.

Latin American Positivists and "First Philosophy"

Like the utopian socialists of the previous generation, Latin American positivists showed interest in a philosophy of the sort predicted by Juan Bautista Alberdi in his *Posthumous Works* (1841), who held that in the newly independent nations, pressed by social, political, religious, and moral problems, thinkers would devote themselves to applied philosophy. In a context where an urgent need of practical solutions was the rule, there was a turning away from the core areas of philosophy—like that of European positivists at the turn of the nineteenth century—and this clearly suited the needs of Latin American thinkers. At the time, they recognized that they faced immediate, large-scale problems in creating a stable and coherent social order and therefore welcomed the practical ideas of positivism, which they believed could shed light on how to go about solving them.

Unfortunately, the long-term effect of this approach, together with the kind of problem it attempted to solve, made positivist philosophers vulnerable to the critique that, having "nonphilosophical interests," they failed to practice philosophy as such. In twentieth-century Latin America, philosophy became a discipline practiced by specially trained professionals interested in strictly theoretical questions. When these later philosophers reflected on the history of the discipline in their countries, they sometimes disparaged the positivists of the 1880s, whose concerns seem predominantly *non*philosophical. To Risieri Frondizi, for example, the positivists cared only about nonphilosophical "aspects of our life," thus failing to produce "a real philosopher in all of Ibero-America." And to Coriolano Alberini, positivism "neglects the fundamental problems of philosophy, and . . . repudiates—at least in theory—all metaphysical preoccupations, professing instead a vague spirit of agnosticism."[19]

These philosophers, however, seem to assume that philosophy must always be theoretical and concerned with the most abstract questions of metaphysics and epistemology. That assumption, common in the West since Plato's day, is sometimes conveyed by referring to these areas of philosophy as "first philosophy," or the most fundamental part of the subject. Yet it is difficult to find a non-question-begging reason for this view, and the current revival of applied philosophy no doubt argues against it. Nineteenth-century positivism in Latin America was, in any case, bound to have some nonphilosophical consequences, as illustrated by the much discussed cases of the political emancipation of Brazil and the efforts at educational reform in Mexico. But that is simply because positivism in Latin America was never only a philosophers' movement but was endorsed by many leaders who had a say in their countries' politics and social organization.

We have seen that positivism entails some philosophical theses, *P1–P4* above. These equally inform the views of Mexican positivists, to whom we turn next, thinkers who put forward views of their own about social progress, race, identity, technology, and other issues that have fueled philosophical debates continuing to this day. Of course, since the basic tenets of positivism were proposed with an eye to solving some urgent social and political problems, a fair assessment of positivist thought in Mexico, as elsewhere, must ask how the movement performed in those practical domains.

Positivism in Mexico

When Latin Americans adopted positivism at the end of the nineteenth century, they believed that this modern way of thinking, with its respect for science, would lead to enlightened social progress. But with the exception of Brazil, most of their attempts to apply positivism were, all things considered, disastrous. Under the influence of positivism, for example, many local ethnic groups were considered unfit for social progress and were excluded from society. This was the fate of the Chilean *roto* and the Argentinian *gaucho*. And entire Indian populations, also thought unsuitable for "civilization," suffered campaigns of economic oppression and outright elimination under the policies of Roca in Argentina and Díaz in Mexico.[20]

The cruel excesses of the Díaz regime are often cited as a paradigm of positivism's notorious consequences in Latin America.[21] Twice the president of Mexico (1878–1880 and 1884–1911), Díaz enjoyed not only the support of local positivists but their active participation in his government. For instance, as minister of finance, he appointed José Ives Limantour (1854–1935), a publicly declared positivist, admirer of Comte and Herbert Spencer, and a leader of the Mexican positivist group dubbed "*los científicos*" by their opponents. These positivists, founders of the political party *Unión liberal* (1892), had been influential since the 1880s, when Pablo Macedo, Rosendo Pineda, Francisco Bulnes, and Justo Sierra (whose accomplishments in education seem to have distinguished him from the rest)[22] served in the chamber of deputies.

Díaz and his positivist advisers paid lip service to ideals of social progress, but only the true advancement under their rule was for international capital and the local landowners. And Limantour instituted an abusive system of common land, the *ejido*, which was not (as might be thought) similar to the Aztecan communal ownership of the land but resembled instead the colonial *encomiendas* introduced by Spain and Portugal to enslave the Indians. Such policies, together with Díaz's dictatorial style, contributed to the inevitable collapse of his regime, best remembered to this day for its fraud, economic inequality, and despotic contempt for human rights.

Leopoldo Zea, a contemporary Mexican philosopher, has proposed the term "Porfirism" to refer to the positivist ideology of the Díaz regime, from the military uprising that led him to power in 1878 to its downfall in 1911.[23] But positivism in Mexico antedates Porfirism, having first appeared there in the work of Gabino Barreda (1818–1881), a lawyer and medical doctor who had learned Comtean theory in France. When Barreda returned to Mexico in 1867, he began campaigning for a positivist reform of Mexico's institutions, especially in education.[24] Through his efforts, Comtism was adopted by the first generation of Mexican positivists, who thought of themselves as "liberal conservatives" since they were persuaded that social progress could be achieved only through conservative means—that is, by evolution rather than revolution.

Mexican positivists later became more attracted to utilitarianism and evolutionary theory (especially in the works of Mill and Spencer), though they never entirely abandoned Comtism.[25] With this eclectic theoretical framework, sometimes considered their most original contribution, they were inclined toward a skeptical empiricism and so recoiled from traditional Mexican attitudes and beliefs rooted in religion and folkish customs. These, the positivists thought, were remnants of a colonial worldview that had only retarded their development as a nation. Needless to say, the positivists sought to replace these retrograde beliefs with ways of thinking grounded in science that could bring about modernization and prosperity. According to Zea, traditional Mexican beliefs generated a certain inferiority complex among Mexicans and other Latin Americans with respect to powerful nations of the West. "To South Americans," he writes, "their own race appeared romantic, idealistic, given to utopias and to sacrificing reality to dreams. . . . Nations founded by this race . . . could not but be inferior to those with a practical sense, such as England and the United States."[26]

Not surprisingly, the positivists preached the value of practical politics as an essential element in their project of reform. They were out to effect a change of worldview among the Mexicans, and for this they would of course need control of key offices in the government. Once in control of education, they took their mission to be one "of emancipation: the riddance of superstitions. This task . . . is the responsibility of science, of the schools, of the teacher."[27] But they also realized that a modern country required economic development and that this could not be achieved without political stability. They therefore became convinced that order should be brought to their country by whatever means available. To some, an "honest dictator" could bring order (and therefore progress) to Mexico,[28] provided that he ruled under the guidance of positivist advisers. Of course, Díaz believed that he was himself the personification of that role and thus counted on the positivists' support. This they obligingly provided, not only joining his government but praising his policies in the pages of their newspaper, *La Libertad*, where they also proclaimed the eclectic ideals of liberty, order, and progress.

But are not the values of order and liberty at odds? In fact, Mexican positivists had both together since the time of Barreda. To resolve this apparent tension, they declared order to be a condition for liberty, so in cases of conflict, the former would be regarded as the more essential.[29] Furthermore, Barreda himself held that "true freedom recognizes that a man is limited by his social environment, from which he receives his laws. His liberty consists in his acting in accordance with these laws."[30] Clearly, if liberty is understood in this qualified way, no conflict arises with order.

But Porfirists maintained that most Mexicans were so benighted in their worldview as to be unsuited for even a restricted liberty of that sort. These people required a proper education first; only then would they be ready for liberty. Although Porfirists allegedly aimed at converting Mexico into one of the modern industrialized nations of the West, they made sure, by force of restrictive laws, that their compatriots could neither freely elect their representatives in the government nor have the rights usually respected in democracies. When it came to economic policies, however, the liberty of entrepreneurs was inviolable. To them, Porfirists happily granted absolute liberties so that foreign capitalists and local landowners and industrialists could obtain high returns on their investments. (Here the Mexican positivists had departed again from Comte's doctrine, which held that the leaders of mature societies should have a say in the distribution of wealth among its members.)

Needless to say, social and economic inequalities among Mexicans grew as a result of such policies. By 1910, the fall of Porfirism was inevitable. Zea has described Mexico's situation as follows:

> The government continued to be the principal source of privileges; and the material progress that might have engendered a powerful bourgeoisie was not achieved. Despite all positive education middle-class mentality remained the same as in colonial times. The principal source of wealth remained the same: the exploitation of the rural worker. The social structure set up by Spain remained the same.[31]

In 1911, the dictatorial regime was finally overthrown in a revolution that was as much antipositivist as it was anti-Díaz. But by then, antipositivist movements had already spread in various parts of Latin America. The reaction against positivism was part of a larger international trend of collapse and realignment of power among nations, and these affected the subcontinent deeply. The European crisis that would precipitate World War I had already begun to dash positivist expectations of uninterrupted, universal progress. The earlier defeat of Spain as a colonial power, together with the rise of the United States as an influence in Latin America, considerably affected intellectuals in the region. For better or for worse, these events encouraged a reassessment of the role of positivists, as well as of the place of their young nations in the world.

Rodó on Hispanic Identity: A True Latin Americanist?

In *Ariel,* a short narrative essay that was to assume the status of a manifesto in Latin America during the first decades of the twentieth century, the Uruguayan José Enrique Rodó (1872–1917) offered some novel ideas about the cultural identity of the region, comparing the values that he took to be prevalent in each of the Americas. Although it is clear that his works adopted some evolutionist views on social progress, they were in fact an altogether different sort of view and inspired a great wave of antipositivist demonstrations among university students and young intellectuals of the subcontinent. As we shall see, *Ariel* offers arguments against social positivism that suggest Rodó was well versed in the political and ideological issues of his day.

During his lifetime, Rodó participated actively in the institutional life of Uruguay, but his achievements also included his own considerable erudition—having learned, mostly on his own, literature, philosophy, and the history of Western culture. The evidence of his political and cultural activities is abundant: He founded *La revista nacional de literatura y ciencias sociales* in 1895, served twice as a member of the chamber of deputies, and was appointed director of Uruguay's national library in 1900. To create a narrative as ambitious as *Ariel*, which concerns issues of social and political philosophy and the history of world cultures, Rodó needed some knowledge of those disciplines as well, and in this his efforts were only partly successful. Even so, his achievement here should not be minimized, for the book contains original views that are crucial to understanding how Latin Americans think about themselves in the context of Western culture.

Ariel appeared in 1900 and was immediately taken to convey an important message to the youth of the subcontinent. Carlos Fuentes, a contemporary Mexican thinker and literary figure, has summarized some relevant historical events surrounding the publication of this book as follows:

> Spain, our old empire, was defeated and dismantled by the United States, our new empire, in 1898; the Philippines and Puerto Rico became North American colonies, Cuba a subject state. Our sympathies shifted to the defeated empire: the United States desatanized Spain while satanizing itself. Walker's takeover in Nicaragua, the mutilation of Colombia so that the Panama Canal could be held independently of Latin America, the intervention in Mexico in 1914 and again in 1917, Marines in Haiti, Honduras, Nicaragua, and the Dominican Republic. In the center of the period . . . Rodó's *Ariel* appears as the emotional and intellectual response of Latin American thought and Latin American spirituality to growing North American imperial arrogance, gunboat diplomacy, and big stick policies.[32]

In this context, *Ariel* was remarkable as a vindication of the thought and culture of Latin America in contrast with those prevalent in the United States. Rodó's views expressed there, like those of his positivist predecessors, had practical consequences, for they led directly to the creation of the Mexican antipositivist *Ateneo de la Juventud* (Athenaeum of Youth, 1907), the uprising of Argentinian students in support of the University Reform Movement (1918), and even some criticisms of positivism offered by Justo Sierra, a major Mexican positivist. What, then, was the message of *Ariel* that could have ignited such a diverse series of reactions?

The book was inspired directly by *Caliban*, a literary work by the French historian and author Ernest Renan (1864–1910), and indirectly by William Shakespeare's *The Tempest*. Through the voice of *Ariel*'s main character, Próspero, Rodó champions the uniqueness and commonality of Latin American nations, pointing to their youth and their common heritage of Mediterranean culture derived ultimately from ancient Greece and Rome. Like Sarmiento, Rodó aims at promoting civilization in Latin America, but in contrast he contends that the United States could *not* be the model for it. To Rodó, North America is the paradigm of barbarism, just as the ancient Mediterranean nations are of civilization. In *Ariel*, we find Sarmiento's dilemma recast and symbolized by the narrative's two major characters, Ariel and Caliban, who represent the "higher values" of older cultures and the "mediocrity" of the United States. The dilemma then represents that of civilization versus barbarism as faced by societies. But Ariel versus Caliban is also the opposition between good character traits and bad ones that arises inside every person when intellect clashes with instinct.

In social terms, Caliban represents, among other things, the appetites of the masses, U.S. popular culture, and utilitarianism (which, as we have seen, comprises the versions of social positivism developed by Bentham and Mill).[33] To Rodó, these all amounted to new forms of barbarism because they could not accommodate high ideals or aesthetic, moral, and social values such as beauty, rationality, and charity.[34] On the other hand, Ariel stands for civilization, the leadership of the intellectual elite, and the subordination of material needs to such values.[35]

When such a dichotomy is applied to the populace itself, the uneducated masses would of course fall within barbarism while the intellectual elite would be considered civilized. Like Sarmiento's *Facundo*, Rodó's *Ariel* responds to a political agenda, but the contents of these agendas are different. The former is devoted to vindicating the modern, capitalist standards of the United States whereas the latter rejects such a model, defending instead values that he considers essential to Latin Americans: roughly, those they have allegedly inherited from ancient Greek and Christian Roman cultures. But what could Latin Americans possibly have inherited from cultures as remote as those of ancient Greece and Rome? In Rodó's view, nothing less than civilization itself. Although both ancient Greece, with its ideal of beauty, and Christianity, with its ideal of charity, have created civilization, he thinks it is chiefly because of their Greek heritage that the young Latin American nations may have a chance to become civilized. For, according to Rodó, that culture's ideal of beauty is a superior moral concept, in some ways connected to rationality.

Such judgments require supporting reasons, however, and these are nowhere to be found in *Ariel*. Rodó takes the truth of his claims for granted and repeatedly urges Latin Americans to retain their Mediterranean heritage and avoid wasting their lives in the ignoble pursuit of material well-being. Of course, it was precisely the unflagging pursuit of material gain that was held praiseworthy in the United States in Rodó's time (as now). In the 1920s, when *Ariel* was still popular in Latin America, U.S. President Calvin Coolidge proudly proclaimed that "the business of America is business"—a slogan that would seem to many to be perfectly up to date. To anyone sharing Rodó's ideals of civilization, however, manifestations of that sort could only have counted as confirmation that the United States was hopelessly devoid of civilized values and an example of what happens to people who pursue pedestrian goals. In other words, they are doomed to mediocrity and, as result, are unable to make any contribution to world culture.

Yet, as we have seen in previous chapters, judgments about a culture other than one's own may sometimes be ethnocentric. In Rodó's case, that bias takes the form of an elitist Eurocentrism since he held that only certain ideals of European elites are universally desirable. In the absence of a good justification for that claim, it is difficult to see how it could avoid the ethnocentrism objection. Moreover, many of Rodó's assumptions in *Ariel* seem vulnerable to similar criticisms. Consider, for example, the following:

1. Latin Americans' cultural ties with ancient Greece and Rome are essential to their being who they are; it is part of their identity to have such an ancient Mediterranean background.
2. Because of its Mediterranean heritage and its youth, Latin America has a glorious destiny, provided that its nations

adopt elitist meritocracies. Then, equal opportunity would allow the best people to rise to positions of leadership and to guide the region to peace and prosperity.

3. Natural selection will encourage the development of a superior type of human being, always able to overcome instinctive impulses and act according to good motives.

Views of this sort are implausible since they are belied by well-established facts about the cultural diversity of Latin American societies and by acceptable construals of the relation between evolution and morality. As we have seen earlier, it is far from true that all Latin Americans can be said to have "Mediterranean heritage." It is not obvious why we should think either that meritocracies will inevitably lead to social flourishing or that evolution will favor the survival of individuals of good character. Given the vulnerability of Rodó's views here to the ethnocentrism objection, and since his central claims are both dubious and unsupported, it seems that we have no choice but to reject them. Even if Rodó aimed at the Bolivarian idea that all Latin American peoples share a common identity and fate, he failed to find a convincing way to defend this historically popular belief.

Ariel Vindicated: The Latin American Critique of the United States

Some may think, however, that our dismissal of Rodó's views has been altogether too hasty. It is worth asking, therefore, whether *Ariel*'s message to Latin American youth could perhaps be saved by a charitable reconstrual. Suppose we take him to be making the following claims:

1. U.S. mass culture cannot stand comparison with popular Latin culture in terms of their respective aesthetic, moral, and social values.

2. Moral theories such as utilitarianism and ethical egoism would sometimes fail to accommodate such values.

3. Utilitarianism and ethical egoism are prevalent theories in the United States.

It is not uncommon to find people of Latin origins who would be in agreement with something like (1).[36] Are they being cultural chauvinists? First, let us understand "Latin culture" in a broad sense, as referring to any contemporary culture that, having been historically influenced by ancient Greek and Roman civilizations, retains to this day some definitive traits of that relation (in a way to be determined) no matter how remote historically or geographically. In this sense, European countries such as France, Italy, and Spain belong to that culture, but so, as well, do Latin American ones such as Brazil, Ecuador, and Guatemala.

We may recast Rodó's argument as beginning with the question of how U.S. mass culture fares when compared with popular culture in any Latin country. What, for instance, are the activities or products that are held valuable within the former? Rodó now seems to have his teeth in an interesting problem. Mass culture in the United States promotes, among other things, fast-food restaurants, video games, radio and television talk shows, films and other artistic products that encourage sexist and violent behavior, and gigantic shopping malls where personal interaction is minimal as well as online shopping where it is altogether absent. And, of course, there is recreational shopping, where one spends money on items one may not even need. Now surely this is consumerism run amok. Is it not precisely this consumerist mentality that, in the United States, has led to the violent crimes sometimes reported in the newspapers, where young people commit murder in the pursuit of a pair of sun glasses, sneakers, or some other trivial but newly advertised items? Another issue is the capacity for aesthetic discrimination—or rather, the lack of it—in U.S. popular culture. The keen aesthetic sense that Rodó takes to characterize Latin cultures seems to be altogether absent in most of the practices encouraged by mass culture in the United States. Clearly, that way of life places little value on leisure time, where people may devote themselves to human interaction and to the pleasures of ordinary life—including carefully prepared meals, visits to museums, and evening strolls.

What about moral and social values? Charity, for example, which in Rodó's scheme of things is one of the highest virtues and an essential element of Latin culture, seems to fare rather badly in the individualistic society of the United States, especially when construed as requiring sympathy toward the plights of our fellow human beings. In a notorious crime committed in 1964, Kitty Genovese was murdered in her own neighborhood of Kew Gardens, Queens, New York. She was first stalked, then beaten and stabbed in three separate attacks on the street near her home over a period of more than half an hour as 138 of her neighbors watched from behind their windows and did nothing. Finally, a seventy-year-old woman called the police. When they arrived two minutes later, it was too late. Ms. Genovese was dead. Only one of her neighbors was willing to testify to what she had seen. Some of the witnesses later spoke up about it—when asked why they did not do anything, one said, "I don't know"; another, "I was tired"; and another said, "Frankly, we were afraid."[37]

Since Rodó assumed that values are objectively grounded and constitute guiding ideals relevant to the shaping of a nation, we can imagine that any society whose values led to behavior of this sort would, to him, be utterly beyond the pale of civilization. If one agrees with his assumptions, one may feel inclined to say, after all, that U.S. mass culture is inferior in some respects with that of Latin nations. On the other hand, one may reject the assumption that values are objective and argue, for instance, that different cultures hold different things to be praiseworthy; thus both the values of U.S. popular culture and those of Latin nations are equally acceptable. This line of response, however, seems unsatisfactory since it entails a strong form of relativism; moreover, if successful, it shows at most that such conflicting values may be acceptable. That is, it falls short of proving that they *are* equally acceptable, which appears to be the only way of avoiding the implications of Rodó's strident critique of the United States as reconstructed here. Yet we still need to consider the other criticisms Rodó seems to have had in mind—namely, that moral theories such as utilitarianism and ethical egoism would sometimes fail to accommodate "high values," such as beauty, rationality, and charity, and that utilitarianism and ethical egoism are in fact the moral theories prevalent in the United States.

Of course, the second of these assertions is not a matter for philosophical dispute at all, but rather a putatively factual claim whose truth-value must be assessed by empirical means (and may in fact have been false in Rodó's time). The more interesting claim here is the other, for it amounts to an objection commonly raised against what we would today call "ethical egoism" and "act-utilitarianism." Although Rodó fails to distinguish between these theories, he offers a critique that equally applies to each of them. These are *consequentialist* theories because they take the rightness or wrongness of actions to depend on their results. Standardly construed, ethical egoism is the view that one should do whatever maximizes one's own good, or well-being, in the long run. Clearly, maximizing one's own good may sometimes come into conflict with maximizing what is good for the community—or it may come into conflict with other values that are intrinsically desirable.

For example, imagine that I am stranded by a shipwreck and know that I shall never be able to return to society. I can nevertheless remain alive by keeping the available food supplies for myself, but doing so will cause some other survivors to die. It seems that, in this situation, ethical egoism sanctions that my action would be morally justified, even though it would clearly fail to maximize what is good for my community. Certainly it is easy to imagine other thought experiments showing that maximizing one's own good might in some situations conflict with maximizing values such as beauty or charity.

On the other hand, act-utilitarianism suggests that the right thing to do in any moral dilemma is to take the action that maximizes good results for most persons involved. Now Rodó again seems right, for if a society follows that principle, there will be cases where a certain value must be sacrificed in order to benefit most of the parties affected. For example, we may end up justifying slavery in a situation where the deprivation of freedom for a few is beneficial in the long run for most of the people involved.

Of course, the controversy about whether consequentialists of either sort can accommodate other important values is complex and well beyond the scope of our discussion here. But it is significant that

Bentham famously disparaged the notion of universal human rights. This, together with the argument sketched above, suggests that (in the absence of countervailing reasons) act-utilitarians are vulnerable to Rodó's criticism.[38] It now appears that even though *Ariel*—the product of little more than elitist prejudices and ethnocentrism—offered a wrongheaded picture of Latin American identity, when properly reconstrued, its message is nonetheless insightful regarding the moral impoverishment of U.S. mass culture and the weaknesses of moral theories such as ethical egoism and act-utilitarianism.

Martí on Social Justice and the Americas

Looking to ancient Greece and Rome for Latin America's cultural roots seems in the end as misguided a project as that of the positivists who tried to make their people think like the French or the British—for it clearly ignores the reality of the region. It is diversity, rather than uniformity, that characterizes the culture, ethnicity, and history of Latin Americans. An alternative way of thinking about this *mestizo* identity could be found in the tradition of Simón Bolívar, examined briefly in Chapter 6. At the end of the nineteenth century, that tradition acquired renewed interest in part because of the work of a poet and social thinker, José Martí (Cuban, 1853–1895), who consciously reclaimed[39] and developed Bolívar's tradition in numerous letters, speeches, and newspaper articles. An active Cuban patriot, Martí helped to prepare the ground for the arrival of two European-born social theories, Marxism and socialism, that were to be influential in Latin America.

Partly as a result of his own experience growing up in Cuba, Martí resented the inequalities—political, social, and economic—prevalent in Latin America. That sentiment, which was to become pervasive among Marxists and socialists of subsequent generations, may have begun in early childhood because of the influence of his teacher Rafael María Mendive (1821–1886), an educator and reformer well known in the island at the time for his opposition to the colonial regime. Perhaps because of his relationship with Mendive, Martí came to know the sting of colonial oppression firsthand when he was arrested and condemned to hard labor at age sixteen. His letters from prison testify to his suffering there, as do those he sent later to family and friends from Spain, to which he was deported in 1871.

While in Spain, however, he pursued further studies, earning a degree in law from the University of Zaragoza in 1874 and publishing, among other essays, the famous pamphlet *El presidio político de Cuba* in 1871.[40] Martí traveled in France, Mexico, and Guatemala before returning to Cuba in 1878. But troubles with the local authorities arose again, and the following year he left for Spain. In a nomadic existence that led him again to France and then to New York City, he landed finally in Venezuela in 1881, but his welcome there was less than cordial. The dictator, Antonio Guzmán Blanco (1829–1899), was suspicious of those he perceived as potential subversives and had no wish to share his country with a free-thinking social democrat like Martí. When the authorities censored the *Revista venezolana*, a journal edited by Martí, he was forced to return to New York. With a few exceptions, he remained there until the year of his death, when he joined a group of patriots in an invasion of Cuba to fight for its independence. He was killed in combat before the island was finally liberated in 1898.

Martí was both a poet of recognized merit and a journalist whose numerous newspaper articles and speeches place him squarely within Bolívar's Latin Americanist tradition. Like the latter, Martí emphasized the importance of developing forms of political organization that would fit the nature of the people and their unique situation in each Latin American country. Martí held that Latin America is a diverse group of nations, where each should have the right to govern itself. Thus he campaigned vigorously for Cuban independence while condemning the United States' plan to occupy the island.[41] Martí's devotion to the liberation of Cuba was a natural outgrowth of his Bolivarism and his more global concerns regarding social and economic justice, as may be seen from his many articles. He argued, for example, against racism, especially the sort prevalent in the United States, which he knew from firsthand experience. Against any form of racial or ethnic discrimination, Martí maintains that all races are equal and must be treated accordingly. If an unfair discrimination against one race or ethnic group were permitted, he thought, then we should have to permit it as well against *all* such groups, including our own, which no one would accept.[42]

Of course, issues concerning Latin America were Martí's great passion. In his efforts to encourage emerging populist sentiments in those young nations, he came to believe that the failure of most governments of the time was due to their ignorance: They had simply failed to achieve a proper understanding of either the history of Latin America or the diversity of its people.[43] This conviction was related to Martí's view regarding how Latin Americans should think about themselves, in which he disagreed sharply with the positivists. To him, all Latin American nations shared a common nature and fate, which (as Bolívar saw) was determined by the region's history and its ethnic diversity. A clear understanding of this idea, Martí believed, was essential for anyone who would be a leader of Latin Americans:

> Knowing is what counts. To know one's country and govern it with that knowledge is the only way to free it from tyranny. . . . The history of [Latin] America, from the Incas to the present, must be taught in clear detail and to the letter, even if the archons of Greece are overlooked. Our Greece must take priority over the Greece which is not ours. We need it more. Nationalist state men must replace state men.[44]

In contrast to the received tradition, he took the real dilemma to be between false erudition on the one hand and an understanding of the true nature of Latin America on the other. Intellectuals like Sarmiento and Rodó would exemplify the first, whereas Bolívar and some other leaders of the independence movement who had understood the local people would illustrate the second.[45] Since, according to Martí, understanding a nation's unique nature was a condition for good government, he campaigned against the ambitions of some foreign powers that appeared to have designs on Latin America. In his eyes, the United States and Spain (and other European nations) posed serious threats to Latin American sovereignty, even though they could not possibly understand the region or its people. "Neither the European nor the Yankee," he insisted, "could provide the key to the Spanish American riddle."[46]

But Martí's attitude here rests also on his conviction that Latin American countries, like other nations, required governments committed to political, economic, and social justice. The individualism he experienced during his North American exile appears to have reinforced his belief that no real happiness could exist in a society marked by social inequality—whether or not it had achieved material well-being, as in the case of the United States. Though not strictly a philosopher, Martí was an important, original thinker who not only took up the Latin Americanist tradition of Bolívar but developed it further, incorporating his own concerns about economic and social justice. Yet Martí was not to remain alone for long in his campaign against the economic exploitation of the poor and working class. His ideological successors in Latin American thought soon appeared, embracing philosophical traditions sympathetic to Martí's pioneering concerns—viz., Marxism and socialism, to which we now turn.[47]

Indians, Land, and Race

In the early part of the twentieth century, a Peruvian thinker, José Carlos Mariátegui (1895–1930), came to believe that only if every Latin American received her fair share of her society's wealth could there be social and economic justice in the subcontinent. Mariátegui shared with Marxists and socialists[48] of the time the conviction that justice was not possible within capitalism, the socioeconomic system prevalent in the West, including Latin America. In his view, capitalism always produces social and economic inequalities because some own the means of production and others only their ability to work, which they must then sell in a free market at whatever price the owners of those means find appropriate to pay.

After the industrial revolution of the early nineteenth century, the labor force in that market became increasingly abundant, and this of course led to lower wages. The few rich became richer, and the poor, who were many, became poorer. Since capitalism in this period seemed to lead inevitably to large disparities in the distribution of resources, Marxists and socialists held it to be incompatible with any more egalitarian model of social and economic justice. In their view, the workers of capitalist nations must eventually take up arms to claim what they deserve—and this they would do by organizing revolutions that first eliminate private property and then socialize the means of production, so that these can then be given to the workers and managed by their representatives in the new governments.

Such a state-controlled economy, together with a social arrangement that would abolish class distinctions, could solve the problem of inequality caused by capitalism, Marxists think, because in a socialist society of that sort, each person may aspire to receive a retribution (or deserved share of the wealth) proportionate to what she can produce. Here Marxists part company with socialists, for according to the former, history will culminate in a final, communist stage where all members of society will have achieved a degree of solidarity and organization among themselves so that the state will cease to be necessary. The state will then disappear, and every worker will be in a position to obtain a retribution proportionate to her needs.

That every capitalist society must eventually undergo a socialist and a communist phase is, according to Marxists, "a law scientifically established" on the basis of empirical evidence—hence the name "scientific socialism" often used to refer to Marxism. The evidence stems from studies of the various forms of socioeconomic organization adopted in human history, which purport to show that socioeconomic systems are retained only insofar as they maximize material well-being. Capitalism was initially progressive in that respect, but after the industrial revolution, Marxists believe, it became unable to maximize material well-being. Since capitalism always fails to distribute wealth evenly, giving to each person what he deserves, Marxists and socialists hold that it must inevitably be replaced by socialism, a system that performs better at production and distribution of wealth.

In 1923, Mariátegui predicted the death of capitalism and its ideologues: "I share the opinion of those who believe that humanity is
living through a revolutionary period. And I am convinced of the
imminent collapse of all social-democratic, reformist, evolutionist
theses."[49] These Marxist views, first acquired in Peru, he defended
throughout his life. After some years of study in Italy (1919–1923)
during which he made the acquaintance of prominent Marxists and
socialists of the time (such as Henri Barbusse, Antonio Gramsci, and
Maxim Gorky), he returned to Latin America to become active in
Peru's politics. He first supported a popular revolutionary front, the
Alianza Popular Revolucionaria Americana, but later organized a
party more congenial to his own convictions, the Communist Party,
in 1928. He also took an interest in progressive aesthetic ideas,
which he developed in the pages of *Amauta*, a journal he founded in
1926 to expound current political and social thought and avant-
garde literature.

Mariátegui argued for his Marxist ideals in numerous articles and
speeches that aimed at bringing social justice to the oppressed of
Latin America and at denouncing the imperialist menace of the
United States. He was also outspoken in condemning the totalitar-
ian doctrines advanced by Italian fascists and German National Socialists, then increasingly popular in Europe. In 1925, he urged
Latin American intellectuals to rally together against those forms of
totalitarianism in his pioneering essay "La escena contemporánea."
Such political views clearly distinguished him from some of his contemporaries, such as the Mexican philosopher José Vasconcelos,
who gained notoriety as an admirer of Adolf Hitler.[50]

Latin American Marxists and socialists are sometimes justly criticized for excessive vigilance toward the evils of regimes in faraway
countries while neglecting those prevalent at home. Mariátegui,
however, would not be vulnerable to that charge because—although
he did have an internationalist agenda—he was careful to adapt his
general strategy to local needs, especially to the problems of social
and economic justice in Peru.[51]

North American politicians were never held in high esteem by
Mariátegui, but we may imagine that he would have heartily endorsed Thomas P. O'Neill's famous dictum that "all politics is lo-

cal"—for he saw clearly the central problem facing Peru. Whether in Mariátegui's time or today, any serious reflection upon Peruvian society must first consider the situation of the Indians. It could be said without exaggeration that the indigenous peoples of the former Inca Empire never recovered from the degraded and subservient way of life forced upon them during the Conquest. Mariátegui suggested that this be referred to as the "indigenous question," pointing out that its origins were in the unfair, feudal system of distribution of the land imposed upon Hispanic America by Spain during the period of colonial domination.[52] No one seriously committed to the cause of social justice in Peru, Mariátegui thought, could afford to avoid this question. Moreover, he argued that the problem could not be resolved without liquidating the feudal system, for it still prevailed in many areas of Latin America in his own time.[53]

If Mariátegui is correct here, then the "indigenous question" boils down to the "question of the land," the problem of the massively unequal distribution of rural property and wealth that has systematically disadvantaged the native peoples of Peru. Mariátegui thus differed from other Marxists and socialists in that, rather than invoking some general flaws of capitalism to account for the destitution of the Indians, he considered the problem in its Peruvian context, identifying it as part of the legacy of colonialism. Both the "indigenous question" and the "question of the land" were, he then perceived, related to a third, the "race question." Racism was also introduced by the Spaniards in order to increase their profit in the Latin American colonies by taking advantage of racial prejudice among the major ethnic groups that met there during the Conquest: the local Indians, Africans, and Iberians.

Mariátegui's view on racism was thus consistent with his Marxist outlook since it found an economic motive at work in the exploitation of the masses by the dominant class. But his view was also informed by an understanding of the history of his country: The racial prejudice endured by the Indians was a specifically Peruvian form of racism, the product of Peruvian historical factors. Mariátegui argued that, with the defeat of the Spaniards in the nineteenth century, patterns of racial prejudice shifted and came to favor the *criollos*, who therefore did nothing to eliminate them during the period after independence. Peruvian *criollos* (and even the *cholos*, mestizo people of Indian and Spanish ancestry) were in the end no less to blame than the Spaniards for having inflicted on the indigenous peoples a debasing oppression grounded partly on racial prejudice.

To Mariátegui, of course, the "Indian is in no way inferior to the mestizo in his abilities to assimilate progressive techniques of modern production."[54] Racism against them (or against any other ethnic group) can only rest on the false belief that certain races are inferior, a belief easily refutable by counterexample. Unlike Sarmiento and many others, he thought that *no* character traits could be proved essential or inherent to any race. "If such were the case," he argued, "[then that trait] would have expressed itself in the same way in all the periods of history." Yet there is no empirical evidence for this; therefore, "[t]he obvious inference is that the 'nature' of races is constantly changing with the conditions of their existence. But these conditions are determined by nothing more nor less than the relation between society and nature, i.e., the condition of the productive forces."[55]

Mariátegui, however, equally rejected any sentimental view of the Indians. He opposed any attempt to romanticize them, or any other group of oppressed peoples, as somehow racially or culturally superior.[56] In his own view, the right attitude toward the Indians was instead that of assisting their economic progress by overturning the feudal Peruvian system of distribution of the land. To him, the "possibilities that the Indians will raise themselves materially and intellectually depend on a change in their socioeconomic conditions."[57] And to achieve that, he thought, a socialist revolution would be necessary. But it seems that Mariátegui himself may have fallen into a romantic view of the psychology of the oppressed—for, as we shall now see, the Indians of South America have shown no interest in political militancy of that sort.

The Actual Needs of the Oppressed

To Mariátegui's mind, nothing short of a socialist revolution could bring socioeconomic progress to the Peruvian Indians and allow them to overcome the grinding poverty born of racial prejudice and postcolonialist exploitation. Such a revolution, he believed, was not far in the future; thus he predicted that a socialist economic and political system "will *soon* root itself among the indigenous masses"[58] as result of the propaganda disseminated by the most enlightened within their group. When the Indians engage in ordinary manual work among themselves, Mariátegui noted confidently, they employ a socialist form of communal ownership of the means of production that is one of the native folkways traceable back to the customs of the ancient Incas. "The Indian," he wrote, "has an established habit of cooperation. Even when communal property becomes individual property (and not only in the sierra, but also on the coast, where a greater degree of cultural amalgamation weighs against indigenous customs), cooperation is still maintained and heavy labor is carried out in common."[59]

But did the existence of such communal practices among the Peruvian Indians really give Mariátegui good reason to believe that they could be easily won over by socialism? In fact, optimistic predictions of this sort have historically been common among Marxists (who, after all, want very much to believe that they are right, just as anyone else does) ever since the rise of dialectical materialist thought as an important political ideology more than a century ago. But it is also true that such predictions may be confounded by the facts. Clearly, the actual behavior of the people whose conversion is predicted is relevant to confirm or refute the prediction; in fact, they have sometimes failed to behave in the way predicted by Marxism. But that seems to count against the theory, suggesting, for instance, that it may involve a false picture of the psychology of the oppressed.[60]

When we consider the actual behavior of the Peruvian Indians when offered the opportunity to become socialists, Mariátegui's optimism seems vulnerable to this very objection. For his prediction that the Indians would join the socialist cause once they had learned about it ultimately proved false. Guerrilla movements operating in rural areas of Peru and Bolivia (both former Inca territories still inhabited by Indians of Inca descent) have persistently failed at advancing the socialist cause among the population, as may be seen by the case of the *Sendero Luminoso*. But other guerrilla groups aiming at a socialist conversion of oppressed people in Latin America have not obtained better results. Uruguay and Argentina in the 1970s offer a vivid illustration of this. The group *Tupac Amaru*, named for the Inca prince ceremoniously put to death by the Spaniards, operated in the former, while the *Montoneros*, named for the *gaucho* troops led by Facundo Quiroga (among others), were active in the latter. Although both groups carried out actions that did attract public attention to socialist ideas, neither succeeded in winning substantial support among the oppressed of those countries. And members of those organizations detained by the police almost invariably turned out to be educated *criollos* of European descent.

Furthermore, in the late 1960s there was the much publicized case of a Cuban guerrilla group led by Ernesto "Che" Guevara (Argentinian, 1928–1967), who hoped to persuade Bolivian Indian peasants to join their socialist cause. Some evidence suggests, however, that it was precisely those Indians who informed the Bolivian army[61] of the whereabouts of Guevara and his group, and this led to a predictable result. Guevara and his men were captured and summarily shot. By and large, such *guerrilleros* were pursuing ideals of social and economic justice on behalf of the Indians in just the way envisioned by Mariátegui, for the destitution of the indigenous peoples and the related questions of land and race were every bit as pressing in Bolivia as in Peru.

Yet another counterexample can be seen in the general indifference of the indigenous peoples of Latin America to the wars of independence in the nineteenth century. That the Indians of that period seemed to care little about the success of the independence movement is difficult to explain; the war was fought partly in pursuit of socioeconomic changes that would have materially improved their conditions of life. Among the chief aims of the independence struggle was the abolition of the *encomienda* system as well as all other forms of slavery. And since it was mostly the Indians who were exploited in these forms of involuntary servitude, it is a puzzle why they remained so indifferent. Moreover, some leaders of the independence movement, such as Bolívar, had expressed their support of las

Casas's idea that the rights of the Indians must be held inviolable. Others even suggested replacing the Spanish colonial administration with parliamentary monarchies headed by Indian kings. Unfortunately, as Mariátegui acknowledged in 1924, the wars of independence were a movement of *criollos*, with no Indian support.[62]

Clearly, the "indigenous question" was more complex than Mariátegui imagined. He assumed that the Peruvian Indians valued progress and integration in Latin American societies, but why should they? After all, progress and integration are Western goals, held valuable by descendants of the very Europeans who had been responsible for the destruction of Indian cultures. Furthermore, as we have already seen, Mariátegui's solution to the "indigenous question" appears to presuppose a false picture of the relation between the material conditions of a certain group and their psychology. Those who are oppressed, it seems, are not always interested in revolution, even when they stand to gain by a radical reordering of social and economic relations.

The Oppressed Against Mariátegui

Could Mariátegui meet this objection? It seems not, for, on the one hand, if he held on to his views in the face of the evidence offered above, that would be simply dogmatic. Yet, on the other hand, could he really save his position if he undertook to accommodate such counterexamples by adding further assumptions to his own view? He might reply, for instance, that in any of the cases described above, the oppressed had "false consciousness"—that is, a distorted view of what is truly best according to their own interest. Marxist theory, after all, sometimes appeals to the notion that the oppressed may be misled into adopting the perspective of their oppressors. I believe, however, that such an appeal to false consciousness cannot succeed. We can scarcely doubt that Mariátegui was a devoted Marxist, and a corollary of that fact is that he held Marxism to be a theory that is scientific. It is a well-known principle of scientific method that, when a theory has been clearly refuted by the evidence, if its proponents attempt to save it by adding further assumptions so that the theory is thereby made invulnerable to counterexamples, then they have at the same time made that theory nonscientific. If Mariátegui were to attempt such a move by resorting to the false consciousness assumption as above, his theory would then have the same status of astrology or palm reading.

Why do people sometimes remain loyal to social systems that are clearly unjust and unfavorable to them? This is a complex question that belongs to the social sciences. In any case, the counterexamples offered above make it plain that Mariátegui's confidence in the prompt conversion of the Indians to socialism, like that which led Guevara to such a tragic end, rested less on reality than on a praiseworthy but ultimately romanticized view of the psychology of the oppressed.

Discussion Questions

1. Domingo Sarmiento's *Facundo* may be taken to express an autochthonous positivism. Support this claim.
2. Evaluate this argument: Sarmiento held that the behavior of *gauchos* and Indians was completely determined by their race and physical environment. If such determinism is correct, then those people had no choice but to act as they did. But then they were neither responsible for their behavior nor blameworthy.
3. Sarmiento thought that the dilemma facing Latin America was that of "civilization versus barbarism." But subsequent thinkers, such as José Rodó and José Martí, rejected that dichotomy, proposing some of their own. Select two such dilemmas and compare them.
4. At the end of the nineteenth century, the Latin American positivists' faith in social progress was shaken by certain important events. Which events? (Provide some examples.)
5. Which nineteenth-century economic and social phenomena may have contributed to the positivists' faith in progress?
6. Positivists held that the natural world is everything that exists and that it could be explained by the sciences. If this is true, what would follow for belief in God and other supernatural entities? And what about appealing to entities of that sort in our explanations of natural phenomena? Would that be legitimate?
7. According to positivism, the method of the sciences must also be the method of philosophy. But could this claim be demonstrable by science? If not, what kind of claim would it be?

8. Define *scientism* and explain how positivism is related to it.

9. Explain why positivism may be taken to have caused a "naturalistic turn" in Western philosophy.

10. In what sense may positivism in Latin America be comparable to Scholasticism?

11. When was positivism prevalent in Latin America? And was it a uniform position?

12. In 1881, Lemos and Teixeira Mendes founded the Positivist Church of Brazil, yet that organization cannot count as a true church in the usual sense of this term. Explain.

13. The Brazilian flag bears a positivist-inspired motto. What is that motto? And how is it related to positivism?

14. After the Portuguese domination, some Brazilian Comteans thought that their country was ready to become a sociocracy. What kind of political organization is that? And was Brazil actually ready to have it? In your view, what would be the pros and cons of having such a form of organization in your country?

15. List some social concerns of Brazilian Comteans. At the time, were such concerns held exclusively by Comtean positivists? And did the Mexican positivists have similar concerns?

16. How is the term "Porfirism" used in this chapter? If you were a Mexican living at the turn of the nineteenth century, would you be a Porfirist? If so, why? If not, why not?

17. Mexican positivists promoted the eclectic ideals of liberty, order, and progress. But can we not imagine some cases where any two of these may be in conflict? Describe some such cases.

18. According to Gabino Barreda, the only acceptable liberty is that which remains subject to the laws of society. Do you agree? If so, explain why. If not, explain why not.

19. Porfirists may be said to have had a double standard in their policies about freedom. Explain.

20. At the end of the nineteenth century, Porfirists granted Mexico freedom of trade. Since Mexico was then an underdeveloped country, it is not difficult to imagine reasons that would have been offered against that policy. What are some of these? And today, should such countries have free trade?

21. In what sense, if any, could Rodó's *Ariel* be considered an antipositivist book? Explain.

22. Rodó's *Ariel* may be taken to offer a wrongheaded picture of Latin American identity. Why?

23. This chapter argues that Rodó's message to Latin American youth, when properly construed, is insightful with regard to the shortcomings of U.S. mass culture and some moral theories such as ethical egoism and act-utilitarianism. Select one of these claims and justify it.

24. Although Rodó held that the nations of Latin America share a certain nature, he fails to qualify as a Bolivarian Latin Americanist. Why?

25. Martí may be taken to have revived Bolivarian Latin Americanism. Why? And did he add anything to that tradition?

26. In which of Martí's concerns must he be said to have prepared the ground for the arrival of Marxism and socialism in Latin America?

27. Marxists hold that racism can be understood only in the context of social and economic inequalities. In what sense could José Mariátegui be said to have avoided a dogmatic application of this view? Evaluate his treatment of the "race question" in Peru.

28. How did Mariátegui and Vasconcelos differ in their attitudes toward national socialism?

29. Outline Mariátegui's three major questions about Peru.

30. How did Mariátegui propose to solve the "indigenous question"? In this chapter, an objection was raised against his proposal. How could Mariátegui reply to it? (If you think he could not, why not?)

Suggestions for Further Reading

Alberini, Coriolano. 1927. "Contemporary Philosophic Tendencies in South America." *The Monist* 37:328–334.

Ardao, Arturo. 1963. "Assimilation and Transformation of Positivism in Latin America." *Journal of the History of Ideas* 24:515–522.

Bar-Lewaw, M. Itzhak. 1971. *La revista "Timón" y José Vasconcelos.* Mexico City, Mexico: Casa Edimex.

Cappelletti, Angel J. 1991. *Filosofía Argentina del siglo XX.* Rosario, Argentina: Universidad Nacional de Rosario.

Coutinho, Afranio. 1943. "Some Considerations on the Problem of Philosophy in Brazil." *Philosophy and Phenomenological Research* 4:186–193.

Cruz Costa, Joâo. 1964. *A History of Ideas in Brazil: The Development of Philosophy in Brazil and the Evolution of National History.* Berkeley: University of California Press.

Frey, R. G., ed. 1984. *Utility and Rights*. Minneapolis, Minn.: University of Minnesota Press.

Frondizi, Risieri. 1943a. "Tendencies in Contemporary Latin-American Philosophy." In *Inter-American Intellectual Interchange*. Austin, Tex.: Institute of Latin American Studies, University of Texas.

————. 1943b. "Contemporary Argentine Philosophy." *Philosophy and Phenomenological Research* 4:180–187.

Jaksić, Iván. 1988–1989. "The Sources of Latin America Philosophy." *Philosophical Forum* 20:141–157.

Lyons, David. 1994. *Rights, Welfare, and Mill's Moral Theory*. Oxford: Oxford University Press.

Mariátegui, José C. 1971. *Seven Interpretive Essays on Peruvian Reality*. Austin, Tex.: University of Texas Press.

————. 1996. *The Heroic and Creative Meaning of Socialism: Selected Essays of José Carlos Mariátegui*. M. Pearlman, ed. Atlantic Highlands, N.J.: Humanities Press.

Martí, José. 1999. *José Martí Reader: Writings on the Americas*. D. Shnookal and M. Muñiz, eds. Hoboken, N.J.: Ocean Press.

Miliani, Domingo. 1963. "Utopian Socialism, Transitional Thread from Romanticism to Positivism in Spanish America." *Journal of the History of Ideas* 24:523–538.

Rodó, José E. 1988. *Ariel*. Austin, Tex.: University of Texas Press.

Romanell, Patrick. 1952. *Making of the Mexican Mind: A Study in Recent Mexican Thought*. Freeport, N.Y.: Books for Libraries Press.

Santayana, George. 1989. "The Poetry of Barbarism." In *Interpretations of Poetry and Religion*. Cambridge, Mass.: MIT Press.

Sierra, Justo. 1969. *The Political Evolution of the Mexican People*. Austin, Tex.: University of Texas Press.

Zea, Leopoldo. 1949. "Positivism and Porfirism in Latin American." In F. S. C. Northrop, ed., *Ideological Differences and World Order: Studies in the Philosophy and Science of the World's Cultures*. New Haven: Yale University Press.

————. 1974. *Positivism in Mexico*. Austin, Tex.: University of Texas Press.

Notes

1. Auguste Comte's doctrine may be found in his *Cours de philosophie positive*, a series of volumes he published between 1833 and 1842. He developed his own view while studying with Saint-Simon, whose pioneering *Nouveau Christianisme* (1825) expounded some ideas about the reorganization

of mature societies that had influenced Comte's own work. Utilitarianism in moral and political philosophy was founded by Jeremy Bentham in his *Introduction to the Principles of Morals and Legislation* (1789) and developed further by his disciple John Stuart Mill, best remembered for his *Utilitarianism* (1861).

2. Theories along these lines appeared in *Elements of Geology* (1838) by Charles Lyell (English, 1797–1875), *Origin of the Species* (1859) by Charles Darwin (English, 1809–1882), *The Principles of Biology* (1864–1867) by Herbert Spencer (English, 1820–1903), *The Evolution of Man* (1874) by Ernst H. Haeckel (German, 1834–1919), and *Evolution and Ethics* (1893) by T. H. Huxley (English, 1825–1895).

3. The existence of an autochthonous positivism in Latin America has been suggested in Angel J. Cappelletti, *Filosofía Argentina del siglo XX* (Rosario, Argentina: Universidad Nacional de Rosario, 1991) and Domingo Miliani, "Utopian Socialism, Transitional Thread from Romanticism to Positivism in Spanish America," in *Journal of the History of Ideas* 24 (1963), pp. 523–538. Miliani, a contemporary scholar of Latin America philosophy at the University of Venezuela, holds that "Comte in his early years coincides with the ethical thought of European socialists, but more clearly with the Spanish-Americans who saw themselves compelled to adopt methods and procedures in greater objective agreement with those fixed by positivist sociology" (pp. 537–538).

4. Domingo F. Sarmiento's *Conflictos y armonias de las razas en America* shows a clear assimilation of European positivism. See Miliani, "Utopian Socialism."

5. Cesare Lombroso (1835–1909), whose *L'uomo delinquente (Criminal Man)* is often credited with having turned criminologists' attention from legal aspects of crime to the scientific study of those who commit it, considers atavism as the main factor involved in criminal actions. Lombroso's positivist determinism was compatible with a humane treatment of criminals, which he in fact advocated.

6. In *Elements of Folk Psychology* and *Introduction to Psychology*, Wilhelm Wundt (German, 1832–1920), who founded the first laboratory for experimental psychology, promoted the scientific study of psychology, especially by means of introspection.

7. See, for instance, Risieri Frondizi, "Contemporary Argentine Philosophy," in *Philosophy and Phenomenological Research* 4 (1943b), pp. 180–187, and Coriolano Alberini, "Contemporary Philosophic Tendencies in South America," in *The Monist* 37 (1927), pp. 328–334.

8. Arturo Ardao, "Assimilation and Transformation of Positivism in Latin America," in *Journal of the History of Ideas* 24 (1963), pp. 515–522.

9. See Afranio Coutinho, "Some Considerations on the Problem of Philosophy in Brazil," in *Philosophy and Phenomenological Research* 4 (1943), especially pp. 187–188.

10. See Coutinho, "Some Considerations on the Problem of Philosophy in Brazil" and João Cruz Costa, *A History of Ideas in Brazil* (Berkeley: University of California Press, 1964).

11. In "Some Considerations on the Problem of Philosophy in Brazil," Coutinho states that positivism played a major role in the events of November 1889. But in *A History of Ideas in Brazil*, Cruz Costa disputes that view, arguing that Benjamin Constant was the only positivist actually involved in the creation of the republic. If Cruz Costa is correct, then the importance of positivism in bringing about the fall of the colonial regime has been exaggerated, sometimes by positivists themselves.

12. Apart from the Brazilians, there were also orthodox Comteans in Chile, led by the brothers Lagarrigue. Yet in Uruguay and Argentina, for example, positivists favored Mill and some evolutionary theorists such as Spencer and Haeckel. And in Mexico, although positivists were initially Comteans, they later came to favor Mill and Spencer. See Ardao, "Assimilation and Transformation."

13. See Cruz Costa, *A History of Ideas in Brazil.*

14. See Cruz Costa, *A History of Ideas in Brazil*, p. 106.

15. Cruz Costa, *A History of Ideas in Brazil*, p. 92.

16. Frondizi, "Contemporary Argentine Philosophy."

17. Ardao, "Assimilation and Transformation," p. 517. See also Iván Jaksić, "The Sources of Latin America Philosophy," in *Philosophical Forum* 20 (1988–1989), pp. 141–157.

18. Some Latin Americans went further and embraced scientism, thus making themselves vulnerable to criticism of the sort presented by subsequent generations. And many positivists seem to have had a bias against evaluative and normative disciplines such as epistemology and aesthetics, as well as against traditional metaphysics. In this, they showed their own dogmatism, becoming easily vulnerable to the critiques of thinkers of other persuasions.

19. See Alberini, "Contemporary Philosophic Tendencies," p. 329, and Frondizi, "Is There an Ibero-American Philosophy?" in *Philosophy and Phenomenological Research* (1949), especially pp. 329 and 349.

20. Latin American literature is perhaps what best shows the social and economic inequalities that affected local people at the time. A critique of discriminatory policies against the *gauchos* is vividly presented in an epic poem, *Martín Fierro,* by José Hernández (Argentinian, 1834–1886). *Rebellion in the Backlands,* by Euclides da Cunha (Brazilian, 1866–1909), is among the best works attempting to show the struggles of the rural poor in Brazil. And *Raza de bronce,* an Indianist novel by Alcides Arguedas (Bolivian, 1879–1946), attempts to offer the Indians' view in their struggle against the *criollos.*

21. A good summary of this period in Mexico's intellectual history is Leopoldo Zea's "Positivism and Porfirism in Latin American," in F. S. C. Northrop, ed., *Ideological Differences and World Order* (New Haven: Yale University Press, 1949). But see also Zea's *Positivism in Mexico* (Austin, Tex.: University of Texas Press, 1974) and Patrick Romanell's *Making of the Mexican Mind* (Freeport, N.Y.: Books for Libraries Press, 1952).

22. A philosopher, educator, and historian, Justo Sierra (1848–1912) served as Díaz's minister of education, a post in which he appears to have excelled. Although his positivism was unquestionable, he also famously challenged some tenets of that movement. Under the influence of Spencer, Sierra believed that the only way Mexicans could survive in the struggle of life was by effecting a change of worldview through education. See, for instance, his *The Political Evolution of the Mexican People* (Austin, Tex.: University of Texas Press, 1969).

23. In Mexico at the turn of the nineteenth century, "[m]ental order was based on positivism, social order on Porfirism." See Zea, "Positivism and Porfirism," p. 171.

24. On this occasion, Gabino Barreda delivered a speech that was to have profound impact on the first generation of Mexican positivists, the "Civic Prayer." He applied Comte's law of three stages to the history of Mexico, holding that the country had passed through a colonial stage, the wars of independence, and, finally, the era that he was witnessing.

25. Among those who introduced other versions of positivism was José María Luis Mora (1794–1850), whose utilitarian concerns showed clearly in his campaigns to change the Mexicans' worldview.

26. Zea, "Positivism and Porfirism," p. 169.

27. Sierra, *Political Evolution of the Mexican People,* p. 88.

28. Francisco G. Cósmes notoriously declared: "Since we have gone on granting rights over rights which have produced nothing but misery and

malaise, we will now try a little honest tyranny." (Cited by Zea, "Positivism and Porfirism," p. 174.)

29. Romanell, a contemporary scholar of Mexican thought, takes the inclusion of liberty, a Millean ideal, with the more Comtean ideals of order and progress to be an original contribution of local positivists. See his *Making of the Mexican Mind.*

30. Barreda, cited in Zea, "Positivism and Porfirism," p. 180.

31. Zea, "Positivism and Porfirism," pp. 189–190.

32. Carlos Fuentes, prologue to José E. Rodó, *Ariel* (Austin, Tex.: University of Texas Press, 1988), p. 16.

33. See Bentham's *Principles of Morals and Legislation,* in *The Utilitarians* (Garden City, N.J.: Doubleday, 1961) and Mill's *Utilitarianism* (Indianapolis, Ind.: Hackett, 1978). For introductions to utilitarianism, see William Frankena, *Ethics* (Englewood Cliffs, N.J.: Prentice-Hall, 1963) and James Rachels, *Elements of Moral Philosophy* (New York: McGraw-Hill, 1999).

34. See Rodó's critique of Caliban in *Ariel,* p. 57.

35. See Rodó, *Ariel,* p. 31.

36. Cf. George Santayana, "The Poetry of Barbarism," in *Interpretations of Poetry and Religion* (Cambridge, Mass.: MIT Press, 1989).

37. Martin Gansberg, "138 Who Saw Murder Didn't Call Police," *The New York Times,* March 27, 1964.

38. For the compatibility of utilitarianism with universal human rights, see R. G. Frey, ed., *Utility and Rights* (Minneapolis, Minn.: University of Minnesota Press, 1984) and David Lyons, *Rights, Welfare, and Mill's Moral Theory* (Oxford: Oxford University Press, 1994).

39. See, for instance, José Martí, "Simón Bolívar" (1893), in D. Shnookal and M. Muñiz, eds., *José Martí Reader: Writings on the Americas* (Hoboken, N.J.: Ocean Press, 1999), pp. 163–171.

40. See Martí, "Political Prison in Cuba," in Shnookal and Muñiz, *José Martí Reader,* pp. 25–31.

41. See Martí's letter to the *New York Herald* (1895) in Shnookal and Muñiz, *José Martí Reader,* p. 232. Martí also made his views on the Americas clear in, for instance, "Mother America" (1889), "Emerson" (1882), "Whitman" (1887), "Our America" (1891), and "The Truth About the United States" (1894).

42. Martí, "My Race" (1893), in Shnookal and Muñiz, *José Martí Reader,* p. 119. See also his "Indians in the United States" (1885), pp. 51–58.

43. See Martí, "Our America," in Shnookal and Muñiz, *José Martí Reader,* pp. 111–120.

44. Martí, "Our America," p. 114.

45. Martí, "Our America," p. 113.

46. Martí, "Our America," p. 117.

47. Martí was of course familiar with these traditions. See, for instance, his "Memorial Meeting in Honor of Karl Marx" (1883), in Shnookal and Muñiz, *José Martí Reader,* pp. 43–45.

48. The one point on which both socialists and Marxists generally agree is that the means of production should be publicly owned (rather than privately, as in capitalism). However, socialist theories, whether these be the early versions offered by the utopian socialists or the views of other leaders are often attacked by communists, who see their own perspective as more radical. Karl Marx (German, 1818–1883) is the founder of communism. Best remembered for his *Communist Manifesto* (1848), written in collaboration with Friedrich Engels (German, 1820–1895), Marx notably questioned the inequalities of capitalism in *The Economic and Philosophical Manuscripts of 1844.* The *Manifesto,* however, sets the principles of "scientific socialism" and argues for the inevitability of revolution in capitalist societies, leading first to socialism and then to communism. Marxists usually refer to their theory as "historical materialism" or "dialectical materialism."

49. See José C. Mariátegui, "The World Crisis and the Peruvian Working Class," in M. Pearlman, ed., *The Heroic and Creative Meaning of Socialism* (Atlantic Highlands, N.J.: Humanities Press, 1996), p. 7.

50. See, for instance, M. Itzhak Bar-Lewaw, ed., *La revista "Timón" y José Vasconcelos* (Mexico City, Mexico: Casa Edimex, 1971).

51. Mariátegui's *Siete ensayos de interpretación de la realidad peruana,* written in 1928, clearly illustrates such efforts (in *Seven Interpretive Essays on Peruvian Reality* [Austin, Tex.: University of Texas Press, 1971]). But see also Mariátegui's essays in Pearlman, *Heroic and Creative Meaning of Socialism.*

52. Mariátegui, "The Indigenous Question," in *Meaning of Socialism.*

53. Mariátegui, "The Indigenous Question." This problem, it may be argued, has never been fully resolved in Latin America.

54. Mariátegui, "The Indigenous Question," p. 98.

55. Mariátegui, "The Indigenous Question," pp. 98–99.

56. Mariátegui, "The Indigenous Question," p. 99, especially the last paragraph.

57. Mariátegui, "The Indigenous Question," p. 99.

58. Mariátegui, "The Indigenous Question," pp. 101, 104–105, and part 3. Emphasis mine.

59. Mariátegui, "The Indigenous Question," p. 107.

60. That Marxism and socialism may presuppose a false psychology has been argued by Stephen Nathanson in his *Economic Justice* (Upper Saddle River, N.J.: Prentice-Hall, 1998), among others.

61. Soldiers of the Bolivian army were apparently trained and equipped by the U.S. government and acted in that instance with at least the approval (and very likely on a direct order) of the CIA.

62. See Mariátegui, "The Unity of Indo-Hispanic America," in *Meaning of Socialism.*

8

LATIN AMERICAN IDENTITY: ETHNICITY, NAME, AND THOUGHT

[Latin American] Nations stand up and greet one another. "What are we?" is the mutual question, and little by little they furnish answers. When a problem arises in Cojímar, they do not seek its solutions in Danzig. The frock coats are still French, but thought begins to be [Latin] American. The youth of [Latin] America are rolling up their sleeves, digging their hands in the dough, and making it rise with the sweat of their brows. They realize that there is too much imitation. . . .

José Martí, Our America

What are the defining elements of Latin American identity? What characteristic features, if any, distinguish Latin Americans from other peoples and cultures of the world? These are questions that have often preoccupied Latin American thinkers, but in the course of answering them, they have sometimes conflated problems that are better treated separately. It is one thing to be concerned with the cultural, ethnic, and political identity of a people and quite another to ask about the originality of their philosophy and ways of reasoning. The former question involves issues of collective identity that can be found in the writings of thinkers as dissimilar as Simón Bolívar, José Rodó, José Martí, José Vasconcelos, and José Mariátegui. The latter concerns the very different question of whether there is or could be a distinctively Hispanic American philosophy, a matter that has been taken up by thinkers of various periods and traditions—from Juan Bautista Alberdi to Augusto Salazar Bondy, Leopoldo Zea, Risieri Frondizi, and Jorge Gracia— who have offered a great variety of answers. Here we shall look more closely at all of these issues, together with the related problem of what name, if any, is the correct one to use in referring to Latin Americans and their descendants in other parts of the world.

The Collective Identity of Latin Americans: A Puzzle

In a series of articles written during the 1920s, José Mariátegui[1] argued that all "Indo-Hispanic Americans" have something in common and that *that* constitutes their characteristic collective identity. But what sort of commonality could there be among people who are so diverse? Even during the period when Iberian rulers adopted policies of unification, it was diversity rather than unity that characterized these people. Consider for instance the Irish Chilean patriot Bernardo O'Higgins, a leader of the independence movement and later dictator of Chile, and the half-Inca Peruvian historian Garcilaso de la Vega, best remembered for his *Royal Commentaries*. From the wars of independence to the present, although it has always been common to find local people of Iberian descent *(criollos)*, there are of course also those who have no Iberian background at all. The list would include, for example, some former presidents, such as Benito Juárez (Mexico), Alfredo Stroessner (Paraguay), Carlos Menem (Argentina), and Alberto Fujimori (Peru)—Latin Americans of Indian, German, Syrian, and Japanese heritage, respectively.

These are by no means isolated cases; thus they may indeed be taken to show that, although some Latin Americans have European background (which may or may not be Iberian), others are of Indian, African, Middle Eastern, or East Asian descent. Some speak European languages, mainly but not uniquely Spanish and Portuguese; others Indian ones such as Quechua and Guaraní. Some have dark skin, others light; some listen to classical music, others to salsa, tango, or *chamamé*. Clearly, they are a very diverse group.

Yet Latin American thinkers have often noted that, in spite of their diversity, these people share a common past marked by the world-changing encounter of 1492. To Mariátegui, the unity of these people stems precisely from that history, with the Conquest seen as a process that "standardized the ethnic, political, and moral physiognomy of Hispanic America."[2] Above all, the colonial regime encouraged solidarity among those who had endured it for more than three hundred years. By the time of the wars of independence, there had already been widespread intermarriage among peoples, which created various *mestizo* social groups such as the Peruvian *cholo*, the Chilean *roto*, the Venezuelan *llanero*, and Argentinean *gaucho*. But a common religion, Roman Catholicism, was imposed with unifying intolerance, and a single economic system, based on slave labor and feudal distribution of the land, reigned throughout colonial Ibero-America.

This was of course very different from the experience in the British colonies of North America. While the Iberian peninsula was still in the grip of feudalism, these English-speaking colonies had, from their very beginnings, developed a market economy similar to that which was already well established in Great Britain. Moreover, the British did not generally intermarry with the native peoples, and so *mestizos* never reached a substantial number that would have enabled them to form a cohesive ethnic group in North America like those so typical in the south. Also, white North America grew out of a Protestant religious tradition that not only spread in ways quite different from those implemented by Iberian Catholics during the Conquest but also may have fostered an ideology more congenial to the growth of capitalism.[3] This was certainly Mariátegui's view. He writes, "upon their arrival . . . the Anglo-Saxon colonizers laid the foundations of the capitalist order. . . . The Civil War also constituted a necessary assertion of capitalism, liberating the Yankee economy from the sole snake-in-the-grass of its infancy—slavery. . . . The Jew . . . joined the Puritan in the business of building the most powerful industrial state."[4] Be that as it may, the Inquisition operating in the Spanish and Portuguese colonies had made it certain that neither Jews nor Protestants would be welcome there, and the absolute dominance of Roman Catholicism did much to unify its inhabitants in spite of their diverse cultural background or ethnicity.

But the sentiment of commonality among Latin Americans did not end with the wars of independence, in part because leaders such as San Martín and Bolívar, lacking nationalist goals, instead promoted Latin Americanist ideals. Mariátegui seems correct when he submits that "there could not be nationalism where there were not yet nationalities."[5] But independence was followed by a period of national organization during which political and socioeconomic differences arose among the new nations as their internal policies began to be dictated more and more by the interests of Britain and the United States. In this way, the early spirit of political and economic unity that had prevailed in Latin America came to be lost.

In the twentieth century, however, Latin Americans began to rediscover their common identity, and traces of this can be found in their artistic and intellectual works today. "The same ideas," observed Mariátegui, "the same emotions travel through all of Indo-Hispanic America. All powerful intellectual personalities have an influence on the continental culture. Sarmiento, Martí, and Montalvo do not belong exclusively to their respective countries; they belong to Hispanic America."[6] But then differences among Latin Americans at a national level would be more of shade than of color. Latin Americans of different nationalities sometimes do feel a sense of being from the same nation when they meet in foreign lands, a sentiment that would scarcely arise among, say, English speakers from the United States and Australia in similar circumstances.[7]

But to say that there is a sense of unity among the diverse peoples of Latin America that is rooted in their history is to make a descriptive claim about their social behavior, whose truth can be determined only by the methods of the social sciences. On the other hand, it is a philosophical matter to assess the plausibility of the evaluative conclusions about Latin Americans that have appealed to such claims for support. We shall now examine some of these.

Describing Versus Evaluating Ethnic Groups

In the history of Western culture, some groups of people have imagined themselves to be superior to other groups (or others inferior to them) on the basis of their natural properties, such as their racial, national, or historical backgrounds or the environment in which they live. These have included, for example, being white, black, American, German; being historically connected to certain ancient civilizations; and living in regions with a certain climate.[8] Yet how could such properties (even if truly predicated) support evaluative conclusions when they seem plainly to sustain only descriptive judgments about ethnic groups?

A descriptive judgment differs from an evaluative one in that the former makes an empirical claim whose truth or falsity, in this context, would depend on whether or not the people to whom those properties were ascribed actually had them. But judgments concerning the supposed superiority of an ethnic group amount to appraisals that cannot be justified by appealing to properties of that kind. To determine whether its members actually have those properties is one thing; to judge that they are therefore superior is quite another. For the former, ordinary observation of some natural properties, perhaps supplemented with scientific research, will be sufficient, but any appeal to observation and science would fail to justify the latter.[9]

That is why we earlier took Mariátegui's view of the collective identity of Latin Americans to fall beyond philosophy. That is, he was making a descriptive claim about their unity in a certain respect. But the truth or falsity of that judgment can be established only by the methods of the social sciences, and it appears that Mariátegui himself was well aware that from such a premise no evaluative claim involving the superiority of Latin Americans could be deduced.

On the other hand, if such an evaluative claim followed nondeductively from certain descriptions of people's natural properties, then philosophers might be in a position to assess the cogency of that argument. In fact, some twentieth-century Latin American thinkers did offer arguments of this sort. As we saw in Chapter 7, after the fall of positivism, there was an increasing interest among Latin American thinkers to compare their own culture with those of Europe and North America. Unlike the positivists, thinkers of diverse (and sometimes incompatible) persuasions who were their successors appealed to observable, natural characteristics of peoples in arguing that Latin Americans were in a certain sense superior to other groups. Should such arguments be taken seriously? We shall next consider some paradigm arguments of this kind and try to determine whether any could succeed. It is important to bear in mind that since the conclusion of any such argument amounts to an evaluation of an *entire* group of people, the burden of proof in each case is on the arguer. After all, twentieth-century anthropologists and other social scientists have shown that evaluations of level of achievement among ethnic groups tend to rest on nothing more than "cultural chauvinism."[10]

A Latin American Race?

Some Latin American thinkers of the early twentieth century appear to have had no hesitation about inferring evaluative conclusions from statements of facts. In nationalist and racialist arguments of various forms, they offered either explicit or implicit evaluative judgments about their own culture and those of others, on the basis of premises that were entirely descriptive. Not only politicians but also social thinkers and even philosophers of the time often invoked natural properties of a group to support evaluative claims about them—in the style of, for instance, Adolf Hitler's ideologues in Germany or Benito Mussolini's in Italy. Yet, as we shall see here, in Latin America it was possible to find representatives of this way of thinking on both the right and left wings of the political spectrum.

Consider, for example, the views of the Latin American socialist leader Alfredo L. Palacios (Argentinian, 1880–1965). In a speech delivered to university students in 1925, Palacios offered a comparative evaluation of the fate of Europe and Latin America as he foresaw it.[11] Recall that at the beginning of the twentieth century, positivism had lost favor in Latin America in part because of certain values and attitudes held by its followers, and that among these had been the positivists' admiration for the highly industrialized societies of the West. Palacios's speech amounted to an endorsement of the views of the students themselves (who had been a central force in the reaction against positivism), for he held that there was no point in emulating the nations of the West since they were already in a natural process of decline that would lead to their eventual collapse. In this, of course, Palacios had largely adapted the views of Oswald Spengler (1880–1936), the German historian, philosopher, and scientist whose *Decline of the West* argues that cultures are subject to cycles of life and death similar to those of biological beings and that European culture of the time was undergoing its inevitable decline. To Palacios, the European crisis after World War I was confirmation of Spengler's theses and heralded the incipient rise of Latin America. "Our America," Palacios observed, "has, until now, had Europe as its guide. Its culture has been nurtured and oriented there. But the last war has made evident what had already been prophesied—that at the heart of this culture were the seeds of its own dissolution."[12] Latin Americans, Palacios insisted, should think of themselves as "nascent peoples, free of ties and atavisms, with immense possibilities and vast horizons before us. The intermingling of races has given us a new soul. Humanity is encamped inside our borders. We and our children are the synthesis of races."[13]

The idea of a Latin American synthesis of races was popular among thinkers of the time, but not all perceived it, as Palacios did, as certain to speed the arrival of socialism. The philosopher José Vasconcelos, his contemporary who led the reaction against positivism in Mexico, similarly hailed the rise of a Latin American culture based on a fusion of races, even though he rejected altogether Palacios's socialist ideology. Vasconcelos opposed the positivism of his teachers chiefly through criticizing their empiricism, for he aligned himself with idealistic traditions in philosophy and defended belief in Christianity. But he was also an ardent advocate of capitalism, as can be seen from his numerous essays on political topics. Some of these were popularized by the Mexican magazine *Timón*, in whose pages Vasconcelos later expressed his enthusiasm for anti-Semitic ideas emerging then in Germany.

Like the militant German nationalists galvanized by the magnetic personality of Hitler, Vasconcelos was deeply drawn to a certain romantic ideal of race as a driving force in world history. But where the Nazis developed a cult of Teutonic racial purity, Vasconcelos held fast to Palacios's ideal of a synthesis of races. In his *Raza cósmica (The Cosmic Race)*, Vasconcelos maintained that Latin Americans, because of their mixed racial background, were to originate a new ethnic group that would have a great destiny. Such a "cosmic race" would arise in the Amazon through the synthesis of different races of the world[14] and would embody a universalist spirit representing the values and historic mission of Latin America. Eventually, Vasconcelos predicted, the cosmic race would defeat the egoism and individualism of the Anglo-Saxons (especially North Americans), who he believed were a menace to the world.

Yet what evidence is there to support the view that Latin Americans, many of whom do already have a mixed racial background, are going to go further to produce the grand synthesis of races envisioned by Palacios and Vasconcelos? So far, the available record of historical, geographic, social, and economic factors in Latin America provides no evidence at all to suggest that such a synthesis will occur. Well-established demographic facts indicate that the percentages of Indian population are high in some regions of Central America and South America but not in others because of specific policies of genocide conducted in some countries, first by Iberians and then by the *criollos*. On the other hand, European immigration of non-Iberian descent is ostensible, for example, in Uruguay and Argentina but not in Peru, Bolivia, and Guatemala. Similarly, although people of African heritage were brought by Portuguese slave traders to Brazil in large numbers, the Spaniards brought them only to selected areas of their domains—usually to replace languishing Indians in mining and other heavy-duty tasks—so that African presence in Hispanic America today varies greatly from region to region.

Even so, suppose we assume that Palacios and Vasconcelos are correct and that a synthesis of races of the sort they imagined will in fact occur in Latin America. What, if anything, would follow from that? The assumption amounts to a descriptive claim, which would fail to support any evaluative judgment concerning the superiority of the emerging race. To Mariátegui, indeed, Palacios's reasoning was pernicious. "Should we," he asked rhetorically, "see this optimism as a sign and testimony to the affirmative spirit and creative will of the new Hispanic-American generation? I believe it should first be recognized as characteristic of our America's old and incurable verbal *self-aggrandizement.*"[15] Although Mariátegui acknowledged that the West was in deep crisis after World War I, he held, contra Palacios, that "there is no indication that it is about to definitively collapse."[16] History has of course proved Mariátegui right on this count: The decline of the West has not happened yet. But was he also right in rejecting the claim that Latin Americans were inherently superior, destined eventually to make up a new race, the synthesis of existing races? Such a prediction (so far highly disconfirmed by the evidence) suggests that Palacios and Vasconcelos indeed suffered from what we may call an ethnic group superiority complex. They offered no good reason to believe that Latin Americans are in any sense superior. As we have seen previously, such ungrounded evaluations are usually nothing more than ethnic chauvinism run amok.

Collective Identity: A Resolution

Although evaluative judgments of the sort offered by Palacios and Vasconcelos are of no help at all in determining the collective identity of Latin Americans, Mariátegui's appeal to a historically based unity could be, for it is a starting point toward a more full-fledged response to the question of whether Latin Americans and their descendants in various geographic locations do in fact have anything in common. Note, however, that if historically based unity is one thing these peoples have in common, then, on a broad construal of that, Iberians may be part of the ethnic group too, a view not without supporters.[17] In any case, assuming that all of these peoples constitute a single group, how should the historic unity account be spelled out?

Historical and demographic facts mentioned earlier suggested that there is no single characteristic common to all Iberians, Latin Americans, and their descendants abroad that would distinguish them sharply as one group. If we focus chiefly on their diverse racial backgrounds and complex cultural heritage, that is what we should expect to find. Yet since Latin Americans and their descendants abroad, together with the Iberians, have been fundamentally related in some periods of history, this makes it plausible to say that they do share a common past, marked for example by the development of Indian civilizations and their fateful encounter with Europeans, the physical destruction of native cultures and people, Iberian colonialism, wars of independence, and foreign (especially North American) economic and political interference—including occasional military interventions.

I submit that the property of sharing a past marked in this way is the clue to the collective identity of Latin Americans and their descendants in other parts of the world. If I am right, then there is a hope that social scientists could at some point determine (a) a broader set of properties possessed, in different combinations, by members of that group, and (b) the number of those properties that would be sufficient for membership in the group. Even if we can agree on all that, however, that would still leave a vast problem yet to be resolved: the whole vexing question of what to call them. Accordingly, we shall now examine the question of their name.

Should Latin Americans Have No Name at All?

A major question that arises in discussions of collective identity is What name, if any, is the correct one to use to refer to a given ethnic group? Within a descriptivist view of ethnic group names, it would be one whose descriptive content is true of all the members and only the members of that group. But what could serve as the descriptive content for "Hispanics," "Latinos," and "Iberoamericans"? Consider, respectively,

(a) Being people related in some fundamental ways to Hispania, a former Roman territory in what is now Spain and Portugal,

(b) Being people related in some fundamental ways to Latin countries, and

(c) Being people related in some fundamental ways to the Americas and the Iberian peninsula.

The property associated with "Hispanics," however, clearly fails to fit all members of the group. For example, it excludes the Indians as well as several generations of Latin Americans who have no fundamental relation with Hispania. Furthermore, when the term is used in the United States, the associated description is often precisely that of having some Latin American Indian background. In addition, "Hispanics" would designate people from the Philippines. "Latino," the name preferred by some minorities in the United States, is no better off. If its descriptive content is (b), would it not end up picking out also Romanians, Italians, and the French? (Winston Churchill had Huguenot ancestry through his American-born mother; does he then fall within the reference of "Latino"?) Similarly, "Latin Americans" would designate the peoples of the French colonies in America and their descendants while failing to denote indigenous peoples and Latin Americans of non-Latin origins. What name, then, could pick out Carlos Menem, Alberto Fujimori, and Bernardo O'Higgins?

If the descriptivist view is adopted, it appears that there could never be any ground for preferring one of these ethnic group names. The argument is as follows:

1. Iberians, Latin Americans, and their descendants abroad constitute an ethnically and culturally diverse group of people.

2. An ethnic group name can secure its referent only in virtue of a certain descriptive property (or cluster of them) that is true of all members of the referent group.

3. Given (1), there is no single property (or cluster of them) that could be truly predicated of all Iberians, Latin Americans, and their descendants abroad.

Therefore,

4. No ethnic group name *could* succeed in picking out that group of people.

5. Furthermore, some available names have ethnocentric connotations, so their use would be questionable on ethical grounds.

Therefore,

6. It is reasonable to conclude that the adoption of a term to name Iberians, Latin Americans, and their descendants abroad would always be unjustified and even ethically wrong.

Let us call the conclusion of this argument "nihilism." If the premises of this argument are true, then nihilism about ethnic group names would be unavoidable. Premise (1) seems grounded on sound empirical evidence. Premise (2) assumes that the descriptivist view is correct. To support (3), the nihilist may remind us that no adequate single term has so far been found to name Iberians, Latin Americans, and their descendants in other parts of the world. As we have seen, ethnic group names proposed to pick out all and only members of that group do so through descriptive properties that do not in fact apply to all its members. It appears, then, that descriptivists are committed to (4). And (5) is a premise that few would want to dispute. It is well known that, in the United States, names such as "Latino," "Hispanic," "Chicano," and "Tejano" are sometimes used as epithets of contempt associated with imagined bad character traits and with the low social or economic status of the members of the group.

Latin Americans themselves often resent being identified by these names, and with good reason. First, some of the names connect them with Spain and Portugal; why should the victims of colonialism accept ethnic group names that remind them of (and even glorify) their former oppressors? Second, these terms—and even worse names we can think of—may have questionable connotations of a different sort often used to convey prejudiced views of the group as, for example, impoverished, lazy, shiftless, and ignorant. All of these considerations taken together provide a formidable argument against the use of any ethnic group names at all since they appear to undermine the justification for any such use. In the absence of better reasons to the contrary, the nihilist can then conclude that the adoption of any term to refer to those peoples would be unjustified and even ethically wrong.

Is There a Reason to Name Groups of People?

It has been argued, however, that the adoption of an ethnic group name could sometimes have desirable consequences for those identified by it.[18] The availability of an adequate group name may, for example, contribute to empowerment, pride, and even actual liberation from oppressive relations of dependence and exploitation. That would count as a pragmatic consideration to be taken into account in assessments of the adequacy of ethnic group names. Yet that is still not enough to defeat the "name nihilist" argument. Although that consideration undermines the assumption that it is practically wrong to use such names, it leaves untouched the larger claim that, on a descriptivist account of the semantics of those names, their use is always unjustified. A fundamental problem remains for any defender of that account, for if that claim is true, then ordinary scenarios involving ethnic group names must remain a mystery. How could names whose content fails to be true of their referents nonetheless succeed in regularly picking out those referents? After all, under normal circumstances there is no failure of reference when any such name occurs in our thought or discourse.

Yet opponents of the descriptive account have problems of their own. The attempt to raise pragmatic objections against name nihilism rests on the assumption that adopting an ethnic group name could sometimes have beneficial consequences. But that is an empirical claim that would need to be confirmed by evidence. Are we really justified in believing that the adoption of some such names does in fact produce desirable social outcomes? May it not as easily produce the reverse result? For has not the practice of naming groups of people also been an essential tool in the most notorious instances of ethnic discrimination and racism? There are good grounds for skepticism here; it is truly difficult to say with confidence whether naming ethnic groups really helps those groups or hurts them. Resolution of this question, however, can come only through empirical methods and so is not really a matter for philosophers at all but rather for social scientists. It appears, then, that the "pragmatic" reply is not really sufficient in itself to refute the descriptive account; therefore nihilism about ethnic group names may be indefeasible.

"Hispanics" Versus "Latinos"

The problem of finding grounds for correctly applying ethnic group names—especially those that might be used to name Iberians, Latin Americans, and their descendants—does have a solution. The problem arises only if such names are taken to pick out their referents in virtue of their descriptive contents. If we suppose instead that the referents of those terms are secured directly, without the mediation of any descriptive content at all, then it is a simple matter to see how a name of that sort could after all succeed in picking out a group of people, even when its descriptive contents are not true of that group. Each of the cases discussed earlier—all of which proved so embarrassing to a descriptivist approach—counts in fact as evidence supporting a direct theory of reference for ethnic group names. In this view, a referential term of that sort picks out its referent, whether or not the descriptive property (or cluster of properties) conventionally associated with it could be truly predicated of the referent group at all. It is clear, for instance, that people in the United States regularly succeed in using such terms as "Hispanics" and "Latinos" to refer to a certain group of people, even when they have in mind different, and sometimes false, descriptions that they associate with the bearers of these names.

To support this view, let us consider some cases involving terms of other types that also appear to be directly referential. Consider, first, natural kind terms such as "water," "whale," or "bat." Although the scientific practice of associating the property of being H_2O with "water" is fairly recent, that obviously did not undermine successful reference by means of that term previous to the discovery of such an essential property. Not only were whales and porpoises once considered fish, but the marsupial mouse was mistakenly grouped with ordinary mice instead of with kangaroos and opossums, now considered their kindred species. Similarly, although a bat is not a flying mouse, German speakers appear to have assumed at some point that it was, hence the term "Fledermaus."

Misconceptions about the essential properties of such natural kinds, though widespread among members of certain linguistic communities, surely did not undermine their success in using conventionally available terms to pick out whales, porpoises, marsupial mice, and bats. To fix the reference of terms of that sort, it is enough that some of the speakers have been in contact with those kinds— whether or not discriminatory knowledge of the underlying structure of the items of reference is available. Both causal interaction with the source and social cooperation in preserving the referential links between terms and items in the world may account for the speakers' success in using them referentially in cases where the community lacks knowledge of the complete application conditions of those terms (e.g., primitive uses of "water" and "fish"), and also where information conventionally associated with any of these terms is false of the items of reference (e.g., primitive uses of "whale," "porpoise," and "marsupial mouse").

If ethnic group names are in this way analogous to natural kind terms, then it becomes unremarkable that referential success does not depend on the accuracy of the descriptions conventionally associated with a term. At the same time, we need not deny that there are descriptive properties associated with ethnic group names that may sometimes play a role in fixing the reference of these names during initial transactions with ethnic groups. For in-

stance, that seems to be the case with "Eskimos," a term now rejected by the Inuits on the ground that those who dubbed them
that way associated "people who eat raw meat" with the term,
based on nothing more than ethnocentric prejudices. And history
has it that some Spaniards exploring South America dubbed the
Tehuelches "Patagones" ("big feet") after discovering their gigantic footprints.

But once a description has contributed to securing the extension
of a name, that referential link may then take hold in a linguistic
community so that even if the description is later discredited (or if it
is no longer true of the individuals to whom it was applied), the link
may nonetheless stick. This appears to have happened with "Eskimos" since a proposed new term, "Inuits," has caught on only
among groups in Canada and Greenland. It clearly happened with
"Patagones," which to this day designates a group of people who
have feet of average size (what the Spaniards really saw were footprints of feet wrapped in fur). These cases can be accommodated
within the view we are proposing here. We take the reference of ethnic group names, like that of natural kind terms, to be secured in
dubbing transaction, by means of ostentatious sometimes accompanied with descriptions. The referential links thus established do not
depend on the accuracy of those descriptions since certain names
may catch on in a linguistic community even when their associated
descriptions fail to fit the referents.

At the same time, ethnic group names are in this sense analogous
to proper names and nicknames, for in the case of the latter, speakers also often associate false descriptions yet succeed in using those
names to designate a certain individual or thing. For example, in the
United States, a town near a polluted stream or lake may be called
"Clearwater," and a South American river believed to lead to a trea-
sure of silver was named "Rio de la Plata" even though there was
never any silver to be found there. Associated descriptions may likewise have played a role in the original dubbing of certain institutions even when they clearly fail to fit the objects of reference (e.g.,
Salvation Army, Boy Scouts, Christian Science). Similarly, nicknames often have inaccurate or altogether false descriptive contents.

Gangster "Fat Tony" Salerno would probably have to live with that nickname even if he were to become thin.

As in the case of these names, the reference of ethnic group names is determined by interaction between speakers and the items of reference. Once the referent of any such term is fixed in that way, the link between name and group of people may be transmitted to others within a linguistic community through social interaction. This view accommodates everyday scenarios involving uses of ethnic group names and explains how the referential links of those that stick are initially established.[19] We can now maintain that nihilism about them must be false since those names turn out to be indispensable to thought and language. Typically, they are referential, and, as in the case of natural kind terms, their role is to enable our beliefs, desires, and other attitudes to be about plural objects. Can anyone seriously deny that we do sometimes need to make groups of people the objects of our thought and language—just as we need to refer to kinds in the world?

What, then, is the correct name to refer to Latin Americans and their descendants abroad? First, note that in the United States there is a practice of using such names as "Latinos" and "Hispanics" to refer at least to Latin Americans and their descendants abroad. Those names have caught on in that linguistic community, whereas other names such as "Indo-Ibero Americans" are only rarely used in translations of the works of Mariátegui and a few others. Given the direct view of reference adopted here, "Latinos" and "Hispanics" count as correct names to use in referring to Latin Americans of diverse background, and the reason is simply that there is a practice of using such names to refer to those peoples. Of course some individuals associate properties with these names that fail to apply to that ethnic group. But there seems to be no social practice of using those names as epithets of contempt, associating with them imagined bad character traits or social and economic status of the members of the group. If that were the case, then we should reject those names on ethical grounds—because, as we have seen above, evaluations of that sort could rest on nothing more than ethnic chauvinism or worse.

A Characteristically Latin American Philosophy?
Getting Critical

Is there characteristically Latin American thought? Mariátegui posed this question in 1925, and Hispanic thinkers ever since have often raised the issue again. Although the question may be understood in several ways, as shown by an extensive literature,[20] here we shall consider it in the form of two smaller questions. One asks whether there is a typically Latin American philosophy—and hence, it is a factual question, for any answer to it would depend on how things are and therefore be either true or false. The other involves a modal question about possibility and is better cast as asking whether there *could* be such a philosophy. Accordingly, affirmative answers to each of these would read as follows,

> *Factual Claim*: There *is* a characteristically Latin American philosophy.
> *Modal Claim*: There *could be* a characteristically Latin American philosophy.

Note, first, that these claims may concern either "thought" or "philosophy" in Latin America (throughout this book I have used these terms as if they were roughly interchangeable). Second, if the factual claim is true, then the modal one is also—but not vice versa. Naturally, a negative answer to the modal question would conflict with the factual claim and, if well supported, undermine the currently growing interest in Latin America philosophy—as well as the rationale for this book. But I intend to show that there are no good reasons to deny that claim.

Mariátegui, however, was led to deny it on the grounds that

> All the thinkers of our America have been educated in European schools. The spirit of the race is not felt in their work. The continent's intellectual production lacks its own characteristics. It does not have an original profile. Hispanic-American thought is generally only a rhapsody composed from the motifs and elements of

European thought. To prove this, one can merely review the work
of the highest representatives of the Indo-Iberian intellect.[21]

It is clear that this sort of criticism has force and that Mariátegui
is not entirely wrong here. It is plausible to hold that Latin America
has been (or even is) culturally dependent on Western societies as
maintained in this passage. That, then, would support a negative
answer to the factual question, even though it would have no bearing at all on the modal one. After all, cultural dependence need not
last forever. Mariátegui, like other proponents of this "critical
view,"[22] has addressed only the question of *what is*, without drawing any further conclusion about the *possibility* of a characteristically Latin American philosophy.

As we have noted, however, a negative answer to the factual question would (if sound) be sufficient to challenge the currently growing interest in Latin American philosophy and the rationale of this
book. But could that answer really be supported? The above passage takes cultural dependence to be one reason to think that it
could. And it was invoked not only by Mariátegui but also by other
critical theorists in the course of some heated debates.[23] Since the
question is factual, it can be answered only by looking closely at the
history and current status of Latin American philosophy.

Some proponents of the critical view believe, however, that that will
only reveal that this philosophy fails to be *characteristically* Latin
American, for it has produced neither major philosophical figures nor
significant local "-isms" that suggest the existence of original traditions. The Peruvian Augusto Salazar Bondy (1927–1974), for example, claims to have found intellectual bad habits among Latin American thinkers that are traceable back to the colonial period—and those
thinkers are no less imitative and universalist today than in the past,
he believes, because they still continue to welcome foreign schools
and traditions.[24] And is there not a sense of intellectual frustration
conveyed by their theories, he asks, perhaps because the proponents
realize that they lack a definitive profile and can contribute nothing
interesting to philosophy and their community?[25] Yet these shortcomings may be only inevitable results of external factors causing Latin

America's cultural dependence and underdevelopment. Salazar Bondy in fact appeals to such factors when he notes that, in the subcontinent, philosophy "was originally a thought imposed by the European conqueror in accord with the interest of the Spanish Crown and Church. It has since been a thought of the upper class or of a refined oligarchical elite, when it has not corresponded openly to waves of foreign economic and political influence. In all these cases underdevelopment and domination are influential."[26]

Salazar Bondy is, of course, not the only critical theorist who has pointed to external factors of this sort to deny the factual claim. For example, Afranio Coutinho, a twentieth-century Brazilian philosopher, has issued a similar indictment of his country's philosophy. With the exception of the positivists, he maintains, Brazil has had no original philosophers at all, for Brazilian thinkers have a "colonial mentality, which is not the ideal mentality for building a creative philosophy." And, he continues, ". . . I cannot imagine how we could have any other mentality without having complete independence—economic, and cultural—from the imperialistic powers."[27]

None of these passages, however, provides any support for the further claim that there could be no characteristically Latin American thought—for it is consistent with them that, once obstacles such as cultural dependence and underdevelopment are overcome, such a philosophy may indeed take root and flourish. But then it seems the critical theorist has drawn a rather modest conclusion. We may summarize his argument as follows: Given the available evidence of past and current philosophy in Latin America, nothing characteristically Latin American has been developed *yet*.

Even so, this conclusion is quite damaging. As noted earlier, it would appear to undermine the rationale for studying Latin America philosophy—and indeed for this book. But it is worth asking whether the critical theorist has in fact interpreted the works of Latin American thinkers in a way that is faithful to their intentions and appropriately charitable toward what is true in their writings. Salazar Bondy, for example, has clearly overstated his case, for although many thinkers at different times did accept Western paradigms, it is not the case that all of them did or that they always did so, as may be seen from the cases of Sor Juana Inés de la Cruz and José de Acosta, who notably rebelled against Iberian Scholastics. And Mariátegui is certainly wrong when he claims that "the motifs" of Latin American philosophy are European—since, after all, Bartolomé de las Casas, Francisco Vitoria, and many others did address problems that arose out of the *local* realities of the subcontinent. But does it not matter that some of these philosophers were born in the Iberian peninsula? Surely not, for insofar as they were concerned with philosophical problems generated by issues specific to Latin America, they deserve a place in its philosophy.

Furthermore, they clearly did develop original schools of thought. For example, Vitoria created a school that made original contributions to natural law theory and to the philosophy of international law and human rights. And what of the critics' charge that these thinkers fostered no "-isms"? In fact, nothing could be further from the truth. Las Casas is widely acknowledged as a precursor of Indigenism, and Latin American philosophy did flourish in Sor Juana's feminism, in an autochthonous positivism, in Bolivarism, and in Arielism. As for Salazar Bondy's indictment of Latin American thinkers for their careless and unoriginal habits of mind, it could be met by appealing to the exemplary intellectual character of thinkers of different periods and traditions such as las Casas, Sor Juana, Bolívar, Martí, and Mariátegui himself. Sarmiento and Rodó, when *Facundo* and *Ariel* are charitably interpreted, are counterexamples to Coutinho's claim that those who have a colonial mentality can never think creatively. In the absence of better reasons, we can therefore retain the factual claim.

Philosophy *in* Latin America Versus Latin American Philosophy

If we were to take the view that what is to count as philosophy must always be the same sort of thing, so that it could not vary according to where or when it is practiced, then the modal claim would be false, and this would entail the falsity of the factual claim as well. Such a universalist objection to these claims seems to rest on an analogy between philosophy and the sciences. According to a widely held view, although contextual factors matter in the process of developing a scientific theory, once it has been formulated, such factors are then irrelevant to its justification. Why should not the same be true of philosophy? After all, the problems that have traditionally been thought most typically philosophical include questions about the nature of reality (or, what is real), about how to solve skeptical challenges to knowledge—and what it means to know something—about whether belief in God can be justified, and about what it means for a statement to be true, and these problems all do appear universal. Moreover, as suggested earlier, rational argumentation seems a necessary method for any philosophers, no matter when or where they live.

On the other hand, given our reading of certain thinkers, it also seems abundantly clear that there is a characteristically Latin American philosophy. Las Casas, Sor Juana, Sarmiento, and many others not only addressed themselves to philosophical problems that arose in the subcontinent, but they attempted to solve them in novel ways. We appear to be left, then, with a paradox, for the existence of a characteristically Latin American philosophy seems incompatible with universalism about that discipline. In other words, the following theses are both inconsistent and independently plausible:

(a) There is a characteristically Latin American philosophy.
(b) The problems and methods of philosophy are universal.
(c) (a) and (b) are incompatible.

To resolve this paradox, one of these theses must be shown false, but which one? On a certain culturalist solution—defended by, among others, Leopoldo Zea—when (b) is cast in the proper way, (c) would be false. To show this, the culturalist appeals to relations philosophers bear to some culture, society, or, more generally, a circumstance, holding that these are always relevant to the framing of their philosophical theories. Although the latter may concern universal problems and proceed by universalist methods, the product of the philosophers' reflection would invariably show their characteristic cultural perspectives. In fact, in this view no philosophical thought of any kind could be perspectiveless since it is only from within a certain cultural perspective that a thought could be entertained at all.[28] In a culturalist construal, then, the universality of philosophy appears compatible with the existence of a characteristically Latin American philosophy. Zea insists that

> The abstract issues [of philosophy] will have to be seen from the Latin American man's own circumstance. Each man will see in such issues what is closest to his own circumstance. He will look at these issues from the standpoint of his own interests, and those interests will be determined by his way of life, his abilities and inabilities, in a word, by his own circumstance. In the case of Latin America, his contribution to the philosophy of such issues will be permeated by the Latin American circumstance. Hence, when we [Latin Americans] address abstract issues, we shall formulate them as issues of our own. Even though being, God, etc., are issues appropriate for every man, the solution to them will be given from a Latin American standpoint.[29]

Unfortunately, this line of argument is doomed to fail. It cannot succeed in proving the compatibility of (a) and (b) for the simple reason that it is invalid. It does not follow from the fact that a certain group belongs to a distinct culture that the philosophical theories set forth by some of them would necessarily show that culture's perspective. Compare with vision: Clearly, human eyes vary in size, shape, and color across different groups. But this does not entail that such characteristic features of people's eyes will somehow affect the visual images framed by them.

Furthermore, the culturalist must argue that distinctive cultural perspectives will be evident in the work of philosophers not only in Latin America but also in other parts of the world. To Zea, philosophy in, for example, Greece, France, or Great Britain is universal and at the same time characteristically Greek, French, and British. The idea begins to seem suspicious if we try to test it with examples from the history of philosophy. What, if anything, could possibly count as *characteristically Greek* in Aristotle's theory of the syllogism, *characteristically French* in Descartes's attempted solution to the mind-body problem, or *characteristically British* in Hume's skepticism about induction?

Is there no way, then, to resolve the paradox? In fact, a culturalist may suggest that in Latin America "even in imitation, there was creation and re-creation."[30] But does it really make sense to regard theories entirely "borrowed" from foreign sources as part of a *characteristically* Latin American philosophy? The culturalist view here seems too liberal since it would permit almost any philosophical theory proposed by a Latin American to count as "Latin American philosophy." Surely it is one thing to hold that there is Thomism *in* Latin America, and quite another that there is a characteristically Latin American Thomism. Of course, if we were to decide, in the end, that there is a *characteristically* Hispanic American thought, then it will be as result of our having found more examples of the latter sort. Given the culturalist's failure to demonstrate that there is such a thing, however, perhaps universalism must prevail after all.

How Is Latin American Philosophy Possible?

Although the triumph of universalism in this debate may seem a plausible conclusion, there is an important reason why that solution would be too hasty. Thesis (c) is false. Universalism can in fact be shown compatible with a characteristically Latin American philosophy. This becomes clear when we take a philosophy of that sort to be defined as follows:

A philosophical theory is *characteristically* Latin American if and only if
1. It offers original philosophical arguments, and
2. Its philosophical topics are in part determined by the relation its proponent bears to social and/or historical factors in Latin America.

Let (1) be "originality" and (2), a special case of "sensitivity to the environment." When the notion of a characteristically Latin American philosophy is construed in this way, we find ample evidence of its existence in the works of the Latin American thinkers discussed in this book. The writings of las Casas, Sor Juana, Sarmiento, and many others plainly score high in both originality and sensitivity to the environment.

Moreover, this view has the advantage that it can easily accommodate universalism. It can grant that some issues, such as the problem of knowledge, the mind-body problem, and whether belief in God can be justified, have a universal import grounded in the tradition of Western philosophy, but it can also acknowledge that that discipline is widely conceived as having a core of universal problems and numerous branches where elements of a general theory are analyzed more narrowly in connection with specific contexts. What, exactly, is the relation between the core and those branches? That is a complex problem of metaphilosophy that goes well beyond our concern here, but it is important to note that the existence of some standard branches and their relation to the core are ordinarily taken for granted and not often disputed among philosophers. This then raises a suspicion that a double standard may be at work when some philosophers object to the idea of a Latin American philosophy. Although universalist objections to the existence of, for example, medical ethics are rare, objections to a Latin American philosophy are not at all uncommon. Yet if there is a role for philosophical analysis in thinking about the problems that arise in the practice of medicine, then why not also in thinking about the issues that arise in the ordinary lives and experiences of Latin Americans? After all, this diverse group of peoples, related by very idiosyncratic cultural connections, have, as we saw earlier, a distinct identity rooted in their history. In the absence of reasons to the contrary, then, we may conclude that the universalist's objection to the modal claim has been met and the paradox thus resolved. It seems that the universality of philosophy is, after all, compatible with the existence of a characteristically Latin American philosophy.

Latin American Thought Versus
Latin America Philosophy

We are not done yet, however, for there is an altogether different maneuver that may still undermine our argument, and it is grounded in a distinction between two different understandings of what philosophy is: a broad conception and a more narrow one. According to Risieri Frondizi,

> It is undeniable that the works of Sarmiento, Bello, or Martí—to mention three great examples—contain philosophical ideas. But such ideas appear as a result of literary or political concerns to which they remain subordinated. *In none of them does philosophy have an independent status; none of them set forth philosophical problems motivated by philosophical interests.* We are, of course, not reproaching them for this; their work fills us with satisfaction and admiration. Nor are we trying to understand the historical causes, the cultural and political circumstances that hindered the growth of a philosophy in the strict sense. We only wish to point out what seems an undeniable fact: *that philosophy has been subordinated to non-philosophical interests.*[31]

If this is correct, then what we earlier called "the factual claim" would break down into two smaller claims, depending on whether it involves philosophy construed strictly or more broadly. It would then be one thing to grant the existence of a characteristically Latin American "philosophy" (in a broad sense), but quite another to concede that there was a Latin American *philosophy* (in the strict sense). By Frondizi's definition, most of the works discussed in this book would amount only to philosophy in the broad sense (hereafter, "thought")—for although they raise philosophical topics, these are often brought into service only for the sake of the thinker's other interests, usually political, literary, or social concerns. By "philosophy as such"—that is, *philosophy* in the strict sense—Frondizi understands something different: the pursuit of philosophical questions for their own sake (hereafter, "philosophy") that is the occupation of professional philosophers at the universities.[32]

Once these notions have been distinguished, it is possible to agree that there is a characteristically Latin American thought while denying that any of it is philosophy. Since the works las Casas, Sor Juana, Sarmiento, and others certainly meet the criteria of originality and sensitivity to the environment—defined as (1) and (2) above—there is then a characteristically Latin American thought.[33] But these works all fall short of philosophy in Frondizi's definition, for

> 3. A theory is *philosophical* (in the strict sense) if and only if it sets forth philosophical problems motivated by philosophical interests.

Note, however, that scoring high in (3) may sometimes be combined with a poor performance in criteria (1) and (2). Consider, for instance, the so-called *fundadores* (founders) of the early twentieth century, a group of Latin American philosophers who rejected the positivist emphasis on practical concerns and strove to develop a practice of philosophy in the subcontinent more like what their peers were doing at the time in major centers of the West. Through their efforts, journals, conferences, and other forms of professional interaction among philosophers were created. This, together with the new status thereby achieved for philosophy within the community, earned the founders credit for having established philosophical "normalcy" in Latin America. According to Frondizi, they were the first generation of real philosophers in the region because their theories, unlike those of previous thinkers, were independent of non-philosophical interests.[34]

All this amounts to evidence that the founders met criterion (3). But what about (1) and (2)? Heavily influenced by European philosophers of the time, they emulated in their methods and philosophical concerns the style of the continental tradition—viz., philosophy as developed on the continent of Europe under the influence of Hegel, Nietzsche, and Husserl.[35] When the *fundadores* rejected positivism in the early twentieth century, it was because of their general antipathy toward the positivists' scientific orientation and their emphasis on empirical knowledge. As an alternative to these, the *fundadores* championed metaphysics, defined somewhat obscurely as "the study of Being *qua* Being," and nonempirical knowledge based on reason alone. Metaphysics and epistemology, construed in those ways, were the hallmark of the *fundadores* and their numerous disciples.

At the beginning, the expectations about these philosophers were high. One of the leaders of the antipositivist movement, Coriolano Alberini, saw the *fundadores* as having initiated "a movement which has an authentic philosophic restlessness behind it, and which justifies many a hope for the future."[36] But their actual contribution to philosophy fell short of Alberini's expectations. Some cultivated theories and topics first conceived by German existentialists of the time and later recast in the work of José Ortega y Gasset (Spanish, 1883–1955). Others turned to idealistic trends then in vogue in France and Italy. And a few, of course, remained faithful to Thomas Aquinas by endorsing neo-Thomist currents then growing in France and other parts of Europe. But, for all of these reasons—and since a concern with issues bearing on the local realities of Latin America figured hardly at all in these philosophers' agenda—we must conclude that the *fundadores* demonstrated neither sensitivity to their environment in the choice of subjects nor originality in their arguments. Thus we cannot credit them with having developed a characteristically Latin American philosophy. On the other hand, because their works meet criterion (3), they are clearly philosophical and find a place in the local history of ideas—even though it is difficult to see what contribution, if any, they have made to philosophy.

The *fundadores*, however, are not the only strict philosophers of Latin America who may be vulnerable to a critique of this sort. Many thinkers working within other traditions have also imported methods and problems while neglecting philosophical issues that have arisen in their own backyards, in the welter of social problems and ideological controversies that characterize contemporary Latin American societies. For example, some who work in the analytic tradition (a style of philosophy, mainstream in English-speaking countries, that emphasizes conceptual analysis, logic, and empiricism) would be vulnerable to the same charge.[37] And although Latin American Marxist and socialist philosophers, including the so-called liberation philosophers of the 1970s and 1980s,[38] have often urged thinkers to be mindful of issues arising in their cultural and socioeconomic environment, they have done little to produce original philosophical arguments addressing such issues (Mariátegui is a notable exception).

If the actual practice of strict philosophers in Latin America is as described here, then when the above criteria (1), (2), and (3) are taken together, it follows that there is *no* characteristically Latin American philosophy to be found in their work.[39] Crucial to this unhappy conclusion, however, is Frondizi's notion of strict philosophy captured by (3) above. But must that definition be accepted? Note that, if applied consistently, it yields startling consequences, for then we should have to exclude the works of Thomas Hobbes, Saint-Simon, Jeremy Bentham, John Stuart Mill, Karl Marx, Jean-Paul Sartre, John Rawls, and many others from philosophy. These works, after all, contain philosophical ideas that are clearly subordinated to their authors' social, political, and literary interests—and so would not qualify as philosophy according to criterion (3). On the other hand, Latin American thinkers, such as the *fundadores*, who gave hardly any thought to philosophical issues arising locally in the reality of their own societies but devoted themselves instead to alien problems and methods, making no significant contribution to them, would count as philosophers according to (3). Now surely, something has gone wrong here.

Furthermore, that criterion invites a sharp distinction between philosophy and thought—as it explicitly distinguishes between a strict conception of philosophy and a broader one. But then nearly all the works examined in this book would fail to qualify as (strict) philosophy, as would most of what is done today in the flourishing areas of applied philosophy. Again, something has gone wrong. Given the odd consequences that seem to follow from (3), we may do better simply to abandon it. Are there, then, any good reasons at

all to retain criterion (3)? Can anything be offered in its support beyond the outdated prejudice that conceives of a "first philosophy"
as having a higher status than the rest?

First, it must be acknowledged that in Latin America, only in the
twentieth century have most thinkers concerned with philosophical
issues had access to philosophical training, for it was not until then
that the practice of philosophy there had achieved a social status
like what it enjoyed in major Western centers. Yet many Latin
American thinkers of all periods, whether formally trained or not,
have been concerned with problems of social and political philosophy, ethics, and even feminist epistemology that arose in their own
historical and social contexts, thus meeting criterion (2). And, to resolve these problems, they have devised arguments of their own—
thus meeting criterion (1). Because of this, their works have continued to be of philosophical interest, and remain so today, making up
a large body of characteristically Latin American philosophical
thought. If criterion (3) drives us to conclude that all these, too, are
devoid of philosophical content, properly construed, then it is surely
counterintuitive. The distinction between philosophical thought and
strict philosophy, therefore, seems to be an unhelpful contrivance
that is better rejected.

It does not really matter whether Sor Juana's proclamation of
women's right to knowledge, Acosta's rebellion against Aristotelian
science, Mariátegui's "indigenous question," and so on are classi-
fied as either philosophy or philosophical thought since it is difficult to see how anything of importance hinges on that distinction.
In fact, many of the major figures I have dealt with here are not by
any stretch of the imagination philosophers as these are conceived
of today. But it is clear that they had ideas that are philosophically
interesting and were often quite astute in their insights related to
these ideas even when they did not argue rigorously, as philosophers are expected to do now. Unquestionably, there is philosophy
in Latin American thought—even though it is not always philosophers who have produced it. Progress in encouraging fruitful work
in the philosophy of the subcontinent can be made only if, starting
with those thinkers' clear and provocative ideas, we ourselves en-

gage in reflecting upon issues specific to the diverse experience of Hispanic America.

Discussion Questions

1. Why might it be said that it is diversity, rather than uniformity, that characterizes Latin Americans?
2. Can you identify some defining elements in the historical constitution of Latin American identity?
3. Some defining elements in the historical constitution of North American identity have differed greatly from those of Latin American identity. Compare two of these.
4. José Mariátegui attempted to solve the puzzle of Latin American identity by appealing to the idea of a historical unity. Provide some reasons in support of that solution.
5. In philosophical discussions about value, descriptive judgments are often held to differ from evaluative ones. Discuss one way in which they might differ.
6. Evaluative claims about entire groups of people are often vulnerable to the "cultural chauvinism" objection. Explain that objection and provide some supporting examples.
7. Why might Alfredo Palacios have thought that Europe was declining in the early twentieth century? What evaluative claim, if any, would follow were Latin Americans to produce a synthesis of races?
8. Reconstruct José Vasconcelos's view about a future synthesis of races in Latin America. How might that view be undermined?
9. In which sense, if any, are Palacios's and Vasconcelos's views concerning a Latin American race similar? Would they be vulnerable to the "cultural chauvinism" objection? If so, how? If not, why not?
10. A description theory provides a certain account of ethnic group names. How would such an account run?
11. Why is the description theory said in this chapter to lead to ethnic group name nihilism? And what does that mean?
12. Are you an ethnic group name nihilist? If yes, why? If not, why not?
13. This chapter outlined a certain pragmatic strategy against ethnic group name nihilism. Reconstruct that strategy.

14. Could a pragmatic argument against ethnic group name nihilism be successful? If so, how? If not, why not?

15. In which sense, if any, might ethnic group names be similar to natural kind terms? What about proper names and nicknames? Provide some examples of each of these.

16. According to the theory proposed here, ethnic group names are directly referential. Does that entail that they do not have any meaning at all? How is the reference of those names fixed?

17. In the approach defended in this chapter, does it matter which name is chosen to name Latin Americans and their descendants abroad? Is this approach compatible with the "no name" nihilist view?

18. Discuss some problems involved in finding a name for Latin Americans and their descendants abroad.

19. What could count as an ethical reason against some ethnic group names?

20. Which name, if any, would you use to refer to Latin Americans and their descendants abroad? Why?

21. Do you think that there is a common name to designate Iberians together with Latin Americans and their descendants abroad? If so, which one? If not, what would be some obstacles to having such a name?

22. According to the critical view, is there a Latin American philosophy? What, exactly, is being asked here? Could that view be supported? If so, how? If not, why not?

23. Provide an objection against the critical view, then assess how that view would stand up in the face of your objection.

24. What is the universalist objection to a Latin American philosophy? Explain that objection and provide an argument to support it.

25. Reconstruct the principal culturalist's argument for the compatibility of a Latin American philosophy and universalism.

26. In this chapter, a semantic difference was found between the expressions "Latin American philosophy" and "philosophy in Latin America." Does that difference matter? If so, which of these two expressions would be more philosophically interesting?

27. What criteria must be met by *characteristically* Latin American thought? On the basis of the works discussed in this book, is there such a thought?

28. Formulate the criterion for a "strict philosophy." Provide one reason to support it and another against it.

29. If the criterion (3) above is accepted, what would follow for Latin American thought?

30. On which grounds was that criterion rejected in this chapter? Could the proponent of "strict philosophy" meet those objections? If so, how? If not, why not?

Suggestions for Further Reading

Cerutti-Guldberg, Horacio. 1989. "Actual Situation and Perspectives of Latin American Philosophy for Liberation." *The Philosophical Forum* 20:43–61.

Coutinho, Afranio. 1943. "Some Considerations on the Problem of Philosophy in Brazil." *Philosophy and Phenomenological Research* 4:186–193.

Diamond, Jared. 1999. *Guns, Germs, and Steel: The Fates of Human Societies*. New York: W. W. Norton.

Dussel, Enrique D. 1995. *The Invention of the Americas: Eclipse of "the Other" and the Myth of Modernity*. New York: Continuum.

Freyre, Gilberto. 1943. "A Consideration of the Problem of Brazilian Culture." *Philosophy and Phenomenological Research* 4:171–175.

Frondizi, Risieri. 1943. "Contemporary Argentine Philosophy." *Philosophy and Phenomenological Research* 4:180–187.

———. 1949. "Is There an Ibero-American Philosophy?" *Philosophy and Phenomenological Research* 9:345–355.

Gracia, Jorge J. E. 1986. *Latin American Philosophy in the Twentieth Century*. Buffalo, N.Y.: Prometheus Books.

———. 1989. "Latin American Philosophy Today." *Philosophical Forum* 20:4–32.

———. 2000. *Hispanic-Latino Identity: A Philosophical Perspective*. Oxford: Blackwell.

Gracia, Jorge, et al. 1984. *Philosophical Analysis in Latin America*. Dordrecht, Holland: Reidel.

Jaksić, Iván. 1989. "The Sources of Latin American Philosophy." *Philosophical Forum* 20:141–157.

Liss, Sheldon B. 1984. *Marxist Thought in Latin America*. Berkeley: University of California Press.

Löwy, Michael. 1992. *Marxism in Latin America from 1909 to the Present: An Anthology*. Atlantic Highlands, N.J.: Humanities Press.

Marti, Oscar R. 1983. "Is There a Latin American Philosophy?" *Metaphilosophy* 1:46–52.

Mariátegui, José C. 1996. *The Heroic and Creative Meaning of Socialism: Selected Essays of José Carlos Mariátegui*. M. Pearlman, ed. Atlantic Highlands, N.J.: Humanities Press.

Paz, Octavio. 1961. *The Labyrinth of Solitude: Life and Thought in Mexico*. New York: Grove Press.

Reyes, Alfonso. 1950. *The Position of America*. New York: Alfred A. Knopf.

Salazar Bondy, Augusto. 1967. *Historia de las ideas en el Perú contemporáneo: el proceso del pensamiento filosófico*. Lima, Peru: Francisco Moncloa Editores.

———. 1986. "Can There Be a Latin American Philosophy?" In Jorge Gracia, *Latin American Philosophy in the Twentieth Century*. Buffalo, N.Y.: Prometheus Books.

Sánchez Vázquez, A. 1989. "Marxism in Latin America." *Philosophical Forum* 20:114–128.

Schutte, Ofelia. 1993. *Cultural Identity and Social Liberation in Latin American Thought*. Albany, N.Y.: State University of New York Press.

Vasconcelos, José. 1948. *La raza cósmica*. Buenos Aires, Argentina: Espasa-Calpe.

Zea, Leopoldo. 1948. "The Actual Function of Philosophy in Latin America." In Jorge Gracia, *Latin American Philosophy in the Twentieth Century*. Buffalo, N.Y.: Prometheus Books.

———. 1963. *The Latin-American Mind*. Norman, Okla.: University of Oklahoma Press.

———. 1989. "Identity: A Latin American Philosophical Problem." *Philosophical Forum* 20:33–42.

Notes

1. See, for instance, José Mariátegui's "The Unity of Indo-Hispanic America" (1924) and "Is There Such a Thing as Hispanic-American Thought?" in *Meaning of Socialism* (1925).

2. Mariátegui, "The Unity of Indo-Hispanic America," p. 113. For a detailed examination of this process as it took place in colonial Mexico, see also Octavio Paz's *Sor Juana, or The Traps of Faith* (Cambridge, Mass.: Harvard University Press, 1988).

3. That Protestantism contributed directly to the rise of capitalism is a thesis famously defended by Max Weber in *The Protestant Ethics and the*

Spirit of Capitalism, first published in 1905 (New York: Charles Scribner's Sons, 1958), but it has been the subject of much dispute.

4. Mariátegui, "The Destiny of North America," in *Meaning of Socialism,* pp. 26–27.

5. Mariátegui, "The Unity of Indo-Hispanic America," p. 113.

6. Mariátegui, "The Unity of Indo-Hispanic America," p. 115.

7. Arguments along these lines can be found in Alfonso Reyes's *Position of Americas* (New York: Alfred A. Knopf, 1950) and Paz's *The Labyrinth of Solitude* (New York: Grove Press, 1961).

8. Jared Diamond, *Guns, Germs, and Steel* (New York: W. W. Norton, 1999).

9. In all this I am adopting the general philosophical position that facts and values are distinct. This view, once almost universally accepted, is now a matter of some dispute among moral philosophers. See, for example Geoffrey Sayre-McCord, ed., *Essays on Moral Realism* (Ithaca: Cornell University Press, 1988).

10. See, for instance, Diamond, *Guns, Germs, and Steel.*

11. Excerpts from Palacios's speech are in Mariátegui, "Is There Such a Thing as Hispanic-American Thought?"

12. See Mariátegui, "Is There Such a Thing as Hispanic-American Thought?" p. 117.

13. See Mariátegui, "Is There Such a Thing as Hispanic-American Thought?" p. 118.

14. José Vasconcelos, *La raza cósmica* (Buenos Aires: Espasa-Calpe, 1948).

15. Mariátegui, "Is There Such a Thing as Hispanic-American Thought?" p. 118.

16. Mariátegui, "Is There Such a Thing as Hispanic-American Thought?" p. 118.

17. See, for instance, Jorge Gracia, *Hispanic-Latino Identity* (Oxford: Blackwell, 2000).

18. Gracia, *Hispanic-Latino Identity.*

19. Something along these lines has been argued for terms of another sort and is often considered a new theory of reference. But it is not at all new, having been sketched by Mill in his *System of Logic* in 1843.

20. See our list of suggested readings. Gracia's *Hispanic-Latino Identity* and Oscar R. Marti's "Is There a Latin American Philosophy?" in *Metaphilosophy* 1 (1983), pp. 46–52, attempt to clarify some of the issues involved in a question of this sort.

21. Mariátegui, "Is There Such a Thing as Hispanic-American Thought?" p. 118.

22. The traditional parties in this debate have been regarded as defending either a "critical view," "universalism," or "culturalism." See Gracia, *Latin American Philosophy in the Twentieth Century* (Buffalo, N.Y.: Prometheus Books, 1986) and Iván Jaksić, "The Sources of Latin American Philosophy," in *Philosophical Forum* 20 (1989), pp. 141–157.

23. For details on these debates, see Ofelia Schutte, *Cultural Identity and Social Liberation in Latin American Thought* (Albany, N.Y.: State University of New York Press, 1993).

24. Augusto Salazar Bondy, *The Meaning and Problem of Hispanic American Thought* (1969). See reprint "Can There Be a Latin American Philosophy?" in Jorge Gracia, *Latin American Philosophy.*

25. Salazar Bondy, "Latin American Philosophy," especially pp. 233–234.

26. Salazar Bondy, "Latin American Philosophy," p. 241.

27. Afranio Coutinho, "Some Considerations on the Problem of Philosophy in Brazil," in *Philosophy and Phenomenological Research* 4 (1943), pp. 187–188.

28. Leopoldo Zea, "The Actual Function of Philosophy in Latin America," in Gracia, *Latin American Philosophy.*

29. Zea, "The Actual Function of Philosophy in Latin America," p. 226.

30. See Zea, "Identity: A Latin American Philosophical Problem," in *Philosophical Forum* 20 (1989), p. 41. In "Philosophy in Latin America" (p. 220), Zea similarly argues that "[t]he existence of Latin American philosophy depends on whether or not there is Latin American culture. However, the formulation and attempt to solve this problem apart from the affirmative or negative character of the answer, are already Latin American philosophy, since they are an attempt to answer affirmatively or negatively a Latin American question. Hence, the works of Ramos, Romero, and others on this issue, whatever their conclusions, are already Latin American philosophy."

31. Risieri Frondizi, "Is There an Ibero-American Philosophy?" in *Philosophy and Phenomenological Research* 9 (1949), p. 346. Emphasis mine.

32. Frondizi, "Is There an Ibero-American Philosophy?" p. 347.

33. Cf. Marti, "Is There a Latin American Philosophy?"

34. Founders such as Alejandro Korn (Argentinian, 1860–1936), Carlos Vaz Ferreira (Uruguayan, 1872–1958), and Antonio Caso (Mexican, 1883–1946) prepared the ground for philosophers of the generation that

followed, among whom are Vasconcelos, Romero, and Ramos—all prominent thinkers we have encountered in previous chapters. Romero held the early founders in high esteem, coining the expression *normalidad filosófica* (philosophical normalcy) to refer to the contribution of that group to philosophy in Latin America. More recently, Jaksić has suggested that perhaps the importance of that group has been overrated ("The Sources of Latin American Philosophy," p. 145).

35. G. W. F. Hegel (1770–1831) was a German idealist philosopher vastly influential in nineteenth- and twentieth-century thought; Friedrich Nietzsche (1844–1900), a German philologist and philosopher, is usually counted as one of the precursors of existentialism. Edmund Husserl (1859–1938), a German mathematician and philosopher, was the founder of the philosophical method known as phenomenology.

36. Coriolano Alberini, "Contemporary Philosophic Tendencies in South America," in *The Monist* 37 (1927), pp. 331–332.

37. The development of para-consistent logic in Brazil and deontic logic in Argentina appears to be an exception to this line of criticism against analytic philosophers in Latin America.

38. "Liberation philosophy" is the name associated with the ideas of a group of philosophers who began to be active in Argentina in the 1970s, roughly at the same time as the liberation theologians of Latin America developed their movement in connection with a conference held in Medellín. The liberation philosophers include, among others, Horacio Cerutti Guldberg, Arturo Andrés Roig, and Enrique Dussel—all of whom maintain that radical economic and social reforms are urgently needed in Latin America. Their approach to philosophy is eclectic, combining elements of continental philosophy (especially French structuralism), Marxism, and, in some cases, Christian theology. The group had a revival in the 1980s after Argentina's return to democracy. See Schutte, *Cultural Identity and Social Liberation*.

39. There may be a characteristically Latin American thought. It is not part of my purpose to deny that—but only to suggest that academic philosophers in Latin America have done little to contribute to it. In "Is There an Ibero-American Philosophy?" Frondizi in fact observes that a very small part of the philosophical work in Latin America may have any claim to originality and creativity at all.

Name Index

Subject Index

Absolutism, 95–96
Antipodes. *See* Torrid zone
Apeiron. See Anaximander
A priori knowledge, 10
Argument
  from authority, 106
  to the best explanation, 32
  ad hominen, 118
  inductive, 4, 31
  question-begging, 17
  reductio ad absurdum, 39
  sound, 16
  valid, 16. *See also* Entailment
Arielism, 243. *See also* Rodó
Aristotelian science, 143–149
Azande, 7, 22n, 33
Aztecs, 2, 56ff, 64, 71ff, 81, 94

Bedouins, 172
Belief,
  as a propositional attitude, 9
  ritual, 15, 26
Bolivarism, xx, 166–168, 243. *See also* Bolívar
Books of *Chilam Balam*
  of Chumayel, 5, 8ff,

of Maní, 5, 7ff,
of Tizimín, 5
Bridgehead view, 14ff, 25ff, 30, 37ff, 43ff

Caribs, 93ff
Caudillos, 167ff
Charity, principle of, 12ff
Chauvinism
  species 83ff
  Western, 12,
Chilam Balam, 4ff, 72
Cholos, 208, 225
Civilization versus Barbarism, 166–168, 189, 195. *See also* Sarmiento
Cognition, 41
Cognitive relevance, 60ff
Colonial period, xviii, 138–160
Comtism, 183ff
Conquest, 94–136
Contextualism, 33, 44
Cosmography, xix. *See also* Acosta
Council of the Indies, 116
Criollos, 152, 168ff, 207f, 218n, 230

265

CPSIA information can be obtained at www.ICGtesting.com
Printed in the USA
LVOW07s0818301215

468336LV00001B/36/P